THIRTY YEARS WITH G.B.S.

IN THE STUDY AT WHITEHALL COURT

THIRTY YEARS WITH G.B.S.

by

BLANCHE PATCH

LONDON
VICTOR GOLLANCZ LTD
1951

Printed in Great Britain by
The Camelot Press Ltd., London and Southampton

It is not only G.B.S.
Whom all the Quick and Dead confess—
Whose power exceeds one hundred horse,
The Drama's greatest Living Force,
The This and That and That and This
Of too emphatic emphasis
That never the renown outran
Of those two simple words Great Man.
It is not only He. I feel
That we should praise the worlds that wheel
About this comprehensive Sun
Whose light has far, yet far to run,
And of those spheres who'd dare to match
The one directed by Miss Patch?
It can't be altogether sport
To stem the tide at Whitehall Court
And to admit to S. (G.B.)
The Oligoi (that's you and me)
Not only this—but to suggest
When one can find him at his best.
Not only he who does this thing
Deserves the credit, and I sing
As our undying creditor
As much as Shaw—his editor
Miss Patch—the doyen of her age
Amanuensis to the Sage—
Tell me Miss Patch, how does one start
To Learn to drive an Apple Cart?

GEOFFREY DEARMER—*7th Oct. 1927.*

CONTENTS

CHAPTER I

WE MEET

"WILL YOU COME and be my secretary? My own has gone and got married on me." I was somewhat taken aback when, in the summer of 1920, I received this brisk summons from Mr. George Bernard Shaw.

A string of coincidences had brought us together. Looking along Fleet Street towards St. Paul's from the Griffin at Temple Bar is the head in stone of one to whom primarily I owe my thirty years' close association with G.B.S. Sir Horace Jones, designer of Tower Bridge, and the man responsible for removing Temple Bar from the Strand, was my uncle and godfather. He left me the £100 without which I could not have got myself trained as a dispenser and gone off to Radnorshire where I met the Webbs and G.B.S.

I will here confess that, when my father entrusted me with the certificate relating to this legacy, he urged me to keep it in a safe place, evidently thinking I should be satisfied with the small amount of interest it produced. But he did not know the practical turn of mind I possessed. I very soon cycled off to a bank in Rye and converted the certificate into hard cash. My first adventure with it yielded an experience which, when I came to know G.B.S., seemed to me to give me as much authority as he had to expound one of his pet theories, the training of children. He believed that satisfactory adults grew from children who had had a little discipline mingled with a lot of cuddling. Children, he thought, ought to be "tirelessly noisy, playful, grubby-handed, except at meal times, soiling and tearing such clothes as they need wear, bringing not only the joy of childhood into the house but dust and mud as well." Because, after some mild tuition from a governess, he had, at the age of ten, endured the sterner curriculum of the Wesleyan Connexional School, Dublin, Shaw would have it for ever afterwards that all children were too disciplined and that parents sent them to school just to get rid of them. He rather altered his view of parsons when I told him what we had been allowed to do when we were children. I never accepted those theories of his; I am rather inclined to agree with G. K. Chesterton who could not conceive what would happen to a child brought up on Shaw's principle. "I should think," commented G.K.C., "he would commit suicide in his bath."

I remember hearing G.B.S. holding forth at some length on the subject at a meeting on the care of children.

"Damn the man's impertinence," a charming old lady remarked as we came out, "why doesn't he go and have a few before he comes and tells us how to bring them up?" I was all with her; but G.B.S. had his answer ready for an Aberdeen woman who criticised him in the same strain. An author's children, he retorted, were his books, and his wife had "quite trouble enough nursing him through his confinements without having any of her own".

My parents gave much thought to our education, and we were fortunate to have in our village at Winchelsea a plentiful supply of ladies who were only too pleased to act as daily governesses to the Rectory family until we each went off to boarding school. My turn came at the age of eleven, when I joined my two elder sisters at a small private school near Portsmouth Harbour. Looking back on my life at school I should say that they were happy days, and, although I was not of a studious nature, I never had any difficulty in learning unless I was given a subject which bored me, and then a kind of mental inertia set in, much to the annoyance of my teachers. We had none of the advantages possessed by modern schools, such as playing fields and gymnasia, but we did have a very indifferent tennis court, which enabled us to become quite expert players in later life. In addition to our daily walks, we were drilled once a week by a sergeant from the Royal Marine Barracks, a form of exercise not exactly suited to growing girls; but we enjoyed this break in the ordinary routine, and our most popular sergeant was the one who taught us the topical songs of the day so that we could sing them as we bent and swayed in the exercises. The French mistress, who sat with us as a chaperone, could hardly have realised that "Stop the cab! Stop the cab! Whoa! Whoa! Whoa!" was not exactly a suitable song for a class of young ladies. But evidently it gave our limbs a certain elasticity, for I remember a terrific uproar when a party of day-girls arrived for morning school walking on stilts. Later in the day an old lady living in the neighbourhood wrote to the

headmistress protesting against this most unbecoming behaviour.

Well, I think I may say that when I left this school, and
settled down to a few years of country life at home, I was as
well educated as many of the present-day young women who
have many more advantages; certainly I was already more
aware how futile it was for Shaw or anyone else to generalise on
the subject of children. Moreover, I grew up among ten brothers
and sisters, and, encouraged by my mother, the first thing I did
when I cut adrift on my own account was to train as a Norland
nurse, or what is known as a nursery nurse. The Norland
Institute sent me for three months to a kindergarten where I
picked up a hobby which I still pursue, making children's toys.
On finishing my training, I went on to a boys' school in Somerset in charge of the headmaster's two children, one of whom,
as a small boy, was such a positive little fiend that I decided the
work was not for me; in fact I disliked it heartily. After a brief recuperation from dealing with this young devil I set off for Canterbury to learn hand-loom weaving, but when I had actually made
several lengths of cloth my health broke down for some months.
It was then that I risked the balance of my tiny legacy on the
career which was to bring me in touch with G.B.S. I have now
forgotten what led up to my embarking on it; I think I must
have read of the positions open to women who qualified as
chemists or dispensers to country doctors. Anyhow I found out
how long it would take me to pass the necessary examinations,
decided I could afford it, and then announced the new departure to my parents, who received the news with their
customary calm. We were now living at St. Leonards-on-Sea;
two days before I left, my father, who had retired, told me that
he thought he would pay half my fees. This was to me very
welcome news; but, alas, next day he changed his mind and
said he could not afford to give me anything. Poor old dear, he
forgot that I should be costing him nothing for the next nine
months. None of us realised how his health was failing: he died
six months later.

Sometimes I wonder where I found the courage to persist in
becoming a dispenser. Even had there been a G.B.S. visibly
beckoning at the end of the long road, I doubt whether that
would have kept me going, for I could not have realised the
fascination of that later journey. My first setback was in the
house of a doctor who trained pupils for dispensing. I was given

one of two lumpy beds in a comfortless room shared with another aspirant. The dining-room was entirely papered with
news cuttings. Our meal the evening I arrived was fried fish and
chips, brought from a van which came to the village on certain
days. Breakfast next morning, I was told, would be served in
the garden—weather permitting. It did permit; but before
sitting down to it I made the unhappy discovery that there was
no hot water anywhere, and that the only bath was littered
with boxes and other junk. Later in the morning, the doctor, a
kindly but insignificant little fellow, explained how he proposed
we should pursue our studies; but after a week of it I decided
that this was no place for me. The poor little doctor tried to
persuade me that it was; but I have usually known what I
wanted, so, although it meant forfeiting much-needed money
paid in advance, I remained firm, and went.

Chastened, but, after a week or two at home, resilient, I
passed on to a school in Westminster, living first with some
friends in Battersea and latterly at a club for working ladies
near Regent's Park: it could be done in those distant beatific
days for thirty shillings a week, all-in. After some nine months
of study I achieved the Certificate of the Apothecaries' Hall,
a goal which I would commend to anyone of faulty memory.
The course beats Pelmanism hollow. After several weeks'
recuperation at home, a friend asked me to go to a doctor in
the country who needed a dispenser. In later years G.B.S.,
as was his way, exaggerated considerably my adventures
with this man. His most imaginative flight, an absolute invention, was that I refused to become his secretary until I had
made quite certain that he did not throw his boots across the
room when he was in a temper, an unattractive trick to which
my doctor was addicted. As few had ever seen G.B.S. in a
temper, the stipulation would have been wholly unnecessary;
and, of course, I never made it. But I will own that I found the
boot-thrower a terrifying person. The house, run by several
servants, was most comfortable, but, to an absolute novice
such as I, the doctor himself was a bewildering creature,
talking much too fast when dictating prescriptions, and, if he
wrote them, doing it, like so many doctors, in characters which
even a practised pharmacist would find unreadable.

I worked from 9.30 to 1 p.m. in a well-equipped surgery
opposite the house. Panel patients were expected to be there
at ten o'clock; the doctor himself did not descend from his

bedroom until mid-day or later. Meanwhile I had to send up to him lists of the names of those present, and from his window he would survey the surgery entrance and send me a peremptory message to be more particular if he saw someone arrive whose name was not on my lists. Crossing to the surgery, he would polish off the patients in double-quick time, dash off in his car to visit the more lucrative private patients, and return in time for dinner, after which he would dictate prescriptions to be made up before I crept wearily to bed. After two months of it, I screwed up my courage and gave notice, pleading that I was too inexperienced for the work, and, if anything, those final four weeks were even more difficult than those that had gone before.

Luck came my way at last. When passing through London on my way home to Sussex for the week-end, I looked in at my dispensing school and heard that Dr. Horace Debenham, the village doctor of Presteign, county town of Radnorshire, was in frantic need of a dispenser. He wired asking me to go on a month's trial. At this point in time, when I had almost made up my mind to abandon dispensing, I was offered a missionary job in Jerusalem. As my father was a clergyman, it seemed to be taken for granted that I should automatically be interested in missionary work; but I was not, and on thinking the situation over I decided that on the whole it would be better to take a chance and go off to Wales. My predecessor had been an old man, and a woman dispenser was a topical novelty in those days, for the suffragettes were industriously adding to the general excitement of the 1914 war; indeed, while qualifying as dispensers, a friend and I used to loiter with our book satchels in front of shop windows whilst vigilant plain-clothes men were deciding whether these held hammers and stones.

When I arrived in Presteign I found it warm with its own domestic squabble. The Welsh church had just been disestablished, and, voting as a border town, Presteign had chosen to remain within the Church of England. With its thousand or so inhabitants, Presteign must be the country's tiniest county town, yet, being a county town, when the judge came there for the assizes the Rector had to find a couple of men to greet him with appropriate bugle blasts. Dr. Debenham's old uncle, then still driving about in a high gig, had chosen Presteign for his practice because of the good trout-fishing in the River Lugg flowing through one end of the lovely village and dividing

Radnorshire from Herefordshire. I never heard Welsh spoken
there. There was no policeman, I came to know, on the English
side of the Lugg bridge, and when cycling home from the Holts'
without a light I knew I was safe when I got so far without a
challenge; anyhow, as there was only one policeman, the
chances were that he was not about in the late evenings.

Molly Holt and her sister Mrs. Russell lived a mile on the
Herefordshire side of the border, where they had built themselves a pleasant house. I came to know them as patients of Dr.
Debenham's; they were about my age and we were soon fast
friends. Their mother was one of the nine famous Potter sisters,
daughters of a wealthy Liverpool merchant, Richard Potter,
chairman of the Canadian Grand Trunk Railway and friend
of Herbert Spencer. All of them married well. Mrs. Holt was
Laurencia Potter, wife of Robert Durning Holt, the Liverpool
shipowner. Another sister was Lady Courtney; a third, Lady
Parmoor, mother of Sir Stafford Cripps, who was thus my
friends' cousin. Most important for my own future, Beatrice
Potter, who could have become Mrs. Joseph Chamberlain but
who wisely preferred to be Mrs. Sidney Webb, was one of their
eight aunts.

Beatrice Potter had gone to London to investigate the working of the Poor Law. She was always determined to get at the
facts for herself, and I remember her telling me how, in order
to do so, she got herself apprenticed to a tailor as trouser hand,
fortunately, she said, under a very kind forewoman, for she
was a bad trouser hand; but she learned all she wanted to
know. It is odd how she and Sidney Webb, both magicians
with statistics, were hopeless with their hands. G.B.S. was not
much better, but he at least delighted in fiddling about repairing torn papers; or he would fuss away over tying up a parcel,
and, although he took a long time about it, he did do it securely,
if not as well as I. But Sidney Webb was completely useless.
At a picnic once I amused the others by doing some paper-
folding. Everyone else tried it and Mr. Webb was most anxious
to do it too. He just couldn't. The other mechanical gift of
legible handwriting had been denied to Beatrice; and of public
speaking to him. In later years when I was living with the Shaws
a letter from her would be passed round the table to see which
of us could decipher it. I remember, too, Molly Holt's disappointment that her uncle spoke so unimpressively when she
and I went to hear him at a Fabian Society meeting.

Like Mrs. Shaw, Mrs. Webb was wooed in the Fabian Society. All four were Fabians together, and the two couples had much else in common. Like Beatrice Webb, Charlotte Payne-Townshend was the child of wealthy middle-class people. Her father was Irish; her mother, English; and she was born in Cork. Her childhood, spent entirely in Ireland, was not exactly a happy one. Her mother, so she told me, was domineering, and, being English by birth, had always a hankering for England, whereas her father loved to be in his own country. When the Payne-Townshends came into money they moved to England, and by then Charlotte's education was finished. She and her parents and her only sister went to live in one of the houses at the top of Queen's Gate, Kensington, whence she emerged every morning to ride in the Park. The little shops, still standing in Bute Street, gave the neighbourhood a village look. Both Charlotte's parents were dead when she married G.B.S., and he had not much personal knowledge of her family.

So, just as with Beatrice Potter, it was from a comfortable middle-class home that Charlotte Payne-Townshend strode out to emancipate the workers. The proletariat have reason to be grateful to the bourgeoisie which has given them Lenin, H. G. Wells, Edward Carpenter, Hyndman, Cunninghame Graham, Shaw and Karl Marx himself. The two women had many qualities as well as a similar background in common. They lived simply, dressing sensibly but without gewgaws. Again like Beatrice Webb, Charlotte Payne-Townshend was a strong character with no use for fools; scorning frivolity; a very retiring woman even with those immediately around her. She translated into English *La Femme Seule* by Eugène Brieux; called it *Woman on Her Own*; and saw it presented at the Coronet Theatre, Notting Hill Gate, with Lena Ashwell and Nancy Price in the cast. She denounced Lloyd George's Insurance Bill in a preface to a Fabian tract. She knew her own mind; a determined creature, to a few perhaps almost grim, with something of her mother's domineering strain in her. She certainly took G.B.S. in hand. She found him living in Fitzroy Square among stacks of dusty papers and a clutter of dirty dishes; orating at dock gates and street corners. Charlotte stopped all that. She set about tidying Shaw up. He left his unwashed cocoa cups in Fitzroy Square for her well-scrubbed rooms in the Adelphi. He abandoned the soap-box for the Memorial Hall duels with Chesterton and Belloc. She saw to it that he was regularly fed.

Sidney Webb once remarked to me how thankful he was that
all his life he had had a good woman to put food before him
three times a day. Shaw from the day of his marriage was
equally lucky.

In their way, the two men were as similar as their wives.
Neither of them could begin to appreciate the pleasures of ordinary mortals. Each had his set aim and neither would tolerate
any interruption of it; neither, therefore, had much use for
those he could not use. Both of them, too, had absorbed a range
of knowledge which was encyclopædic, and they could draw on
it at once with assurance. In their attitude to other human
beings there was neither superiority nor the reverse; they
accepted men and women as they found them, without a trace
of envy. The parallel between the pair ran even to how they
handled their writings; each did his own publishing, retaining
the nominal publisher simply as an agent.

The Holt girls would tell me about their famous uncle and
aunt when I pedalled into England of an evening, returning
after dark across the Lugg to the Radnorshire Arms where I
lived. It was a fine old inn, said to have been built by John
Bradshaw, who conducted the trial of Charles I. The landlord,
Monty Kemp, was a huge man weighing, some said, 28 stone.
His habit was to get up about 9.30 and waddle from his bedroom to a front sitting-room where, with a good view of the
street, he could gossip with passers-by. Opposite us was a cottage in which a man used to store furniture bought at local sales,
and I remember one morning Monty calling out, "What's the
weather like to-day, Jarvey?" "Nice and sunny." "Bring out
the sofa." And out it came that Monty might take the sun for
the rest of the morning. The Webbs were simple in their tastes,
but not so simple as Monty hoped. On their first visit to the
village they had lived in the chauffeur's cottage near the nieces.
Next time they put up at the Radnorshire Arms Hotel, living in
the old ballroom turned into a bed-sitting-room for them.
Monty was delighted, for he was given to gambling and never
too well off. He could not afford more than one servant, and he
thought that, as the Webbs were Socialists, they would need
next to no attention. The poor fellow was soon disillusioned. As
it was summer time, he had concluded that they would not need
a fire, but, like G.B.S. himself, the Webbs, even on holiday,
worked all morning, and their first demand was warmth. Moreover, in the years during which the ballroom chimney had not

been swept a family of jackdaws had been nesting in it, so it was not long before Monty had to admit that his new guests were giving him more trouble than any others he had ever had.

Sidney Webb, unattractive in appearance with his little goatee beard and pince-nez, was a very gentle creature, serenely indifferent to what people thought about him. Beatrice, thin even in those days, was most distinguished, with a slightly gipsy look. She had a deep religious side: they were, I think, both Unitarians, although neither of them ever talked about it. She astonished Presteign with her ceaseless energy. The day after they arrived, off she raced round the village at eight in the morning in search of ration cards (Lord Rhondda's Food Control Board had just been set up) and was most caustic on the indolence of Welsh country folk when she found that nothing could be done about it until, at the earliest, half-past nine. The Webbs were great trampers. After giving up their mornings and early afternoons to work, they would be seen in the evenings walking briskly along the lanes arm in arm. One night a moonlight picnic was held among the remains of a Roman camp on a hill-top to which the Webbs drove me in a governess cart. On the way Mrs. Webb told me of her early married days. Sidney and she had always intended to have one child, she said. It was to be a "Sunday baby." Sunday was the only day they could spare from work, and the baby was to be something they could play with then. As time went on, they found that there was none of it left over for this relaxation, so they did without the baby. Mrs. Shaw did not want children either; in fact, when she was a young woman she shrank from marriage. G.B.S. told me that Beatrice Webb had tried to marry off Charlotte to Graham Wallas, and that this had broken the friendship between Wallas and himself.

"You say you are fond of kittens and small animals," I once remarked to Charlotte, "yet you don't like babies."

"Babies!" she exclaimed, "who could like them? Disgusting little things!"

She was thankful she had no children. They seemed to frighten her: perhaps the memory of an unfortunate childhood turned her against all children. With Beatrice Webb, on the other hand, childlessness left an affection to lavish on her many nieces and nephews, to say nothing of great-nieces and great-nephews too. She was "Aunt Bo" to all of them: to one another she and her husband were plain "Beatrice" and "Sidney."

They rented a small house in the village when next they came
to Presteign, and I was rather alarmed when they asked me to
supper there. I was indeed flattered by the invitation, for Mrs.
Webb never allowed herself to be troubled with those whom she
looked upon as bores; but I was afraid I should be hopelessly
out of my depth as I was not particularly interested in politics,
and thought that Socialism and the Fabian Society would be
the only subjects they would talk about. Molly Holt told me not
to worry about the conversation but to take care to eat quickly
and not stay too long: so I finished each course at a dead heat
with my two hosts and left at nine o'clock.

"Splendid!" said Molly, when I reported this feat to her.
"You will always be a popular guest." Of the conversation at
supper I have not the least recollection.

While the Webbs were living in their cottage, G.B.S. came to
visit them. Mrs. Shaw was not with him; possibly she was on
one of her trips abroad, and he had most likely come to us from
the Fabian Summer School in Wales. Mrs. Shaw was very keen
on foreign travel, and up to the time I joined Shaw she used to
go abroad on her own account while G.B.S. joined the Fabians
at their Summer Schools. She was not as enthusiastic as he
about the Fabian Society, and did not care for some of the queer
people he mixed with at the Summer Schools. You would never
find Sidney Webb going off on trips by himself; although the
Shaws were attached to one another in their own way, I always
felt that the Webbs were more devoted than they.

It was in the summer of 1917 that I met G.B.S. at a garden
party given by the nieces one Sunday afternoon. In those days
the nieces were looked on as somewhat unconventional, for they
asked the tradespeople along to mix with their own friends, and
there was a certain amount of doubtful whispering before they
all decided that they might safely meet one another. We were
joined by a number of convalescent soldiers from the local hospital. These soldiers knew very little about the dislike Shaw had
brought on himself by his views on the war. Some said he should
be lynched; Herbert Asquith thought he ought to be shot, and
Sir John Squire proposed that he should be tarred and feathered.
The hubbub began with his *Common Sense about the War*. He was
all for the war; but he was all against the Foreign Office and
Sir Edward Grey. Clubland did not like it, and when he followed up this manifesto by putting the sinking of the *Lusitania* in
its correct perspective clubland threw him out. He was, to his

great hilarity, expelled from the Dramatists' Club. Even H. G. Wells and Arnold Bennett looked down their noses. He called *O'Flaherty*, *V.C.*, his next war effort, a "recruiting pamphlet". Augustine Birrell, Secretary for Ireland, viewed without enthusiasm its main idea, which was to get ignorant Irishmen to fight by telling them that England, not Germany, was the enemy.

"I have read your play with interest," remarked Mr. Birrell, "but it won't get a single recruit unless you are thinking of joining up yourself. And as for my doing away with oaths, you might as well ask me to do away with the Thirty-nine Articles or the 'not's' in the Ten Commandments. Do use a little common sense."

But the troops gave the playlet a great reception when it was produced by a British Army unit on the Western Front. They knew that Shaw was on their side. When he came to us at Presteign he had been on a week's tour of the Flanders front by invitation of Sir Douglas Haig. C. E. Montague, who took him round, told in the *Manchester Guardian* how Shaw had asked to be allowed to drive his car alone across the square at Ypres because he did not see why a serving soldier should risk his life on his account. He had done the full round—Arras, the Somme, and Vimy Ridge; so when he arrived at the Holts' in his trim knickerbocker suit he got on famously with the convalescents, entertaining them with stories of his own behaviour when bombs fell near, but not near enough to harm him. After a bomb actually fell, he said, he was always fifty yards away from the spot where he and Sir Douglas Haig had been standing before the explosion, an illustration of the truth that one's mind works subconsciously and moves one's body to safety.

"Later on," he said, "you tell everyone that you stand firm as a rock and never flinch when the bombs explode; that is, if they don't hit you."

He spoke to us in the dining-room after tea, although as a rule he did not take tea. The quick, witty, friendly way he talked was new to me then; for I must admit that at this time I knew very little about Shaw. *Fanny's First Play* was the only play of his that I had seen. In my young days I was not so lucky as G.B.S. in the way of theatre-going. Before he came to London, he told me, he had seen many of the operas and much of Shakespeare in an old Dublin theatre, the Royal. As a youth he shouldered his way into its pit at two shillings, or four when it had its opera season. There were no stalls; the pit ran right forward to the orchestra.

Stalls arrived with the Gaiety, a new theatre which went up in Dublin before he left for London, and here he first saw Gilbert and Sullivan. He still remembered how like church music, after Offenbach, Sullivan seemed in *Trial by Jury*. Gilbert and Sullivan came early in my own experience of the theatre. I saw both *The Mikado* and also the light opera *Dorothy* at Hastings, and I have a very dim recollection of being taken as a child to a pantomime on Hastings pier. We had no theatre at Winchelsea; Hastings had the nearest one, which meant quite a trip to see a play. We were not a family of playgoers; my elder brothers went and my mother may have done; my father certainly never did. In those days he would never have dreamt of going to London to a theatre, but I do seem to remember an uncle taking me to *The Tempest* with Tree as Prospero. I enjoyed *Fanny's First Play* very much, although the friends with whom I went to the Little Theatre were sure that I only said so out of politeness, and that I was as bored with it as they were.

After the garden party I walked back into the village with the Webbs and G.B.S., yet neither then, nor when I met him in London three years later, can I recall the conversations with him. I went back to London in 1918, a few weeks before the war ended, for the landlord of the Bull Hotel, where I was then living, had decided, after a confabulation with his wife, that they wanted no more paying guests. So we were all given six months' notice, and, as it was difficult to find rooms in the village, I felt that a complete change was called for, sorry as I was to leave Dr. Debenham, an ideal employer, and the people of Wales, from whom I never had anything but kindness and hospitality. I decided to train as an officer in the Wrens and I was accepted, although not for foreign service: I did not get full marks in the medical examination. They asked me to stay at home for a bit as they did not want to send any more women forward for training, and while I was waiting the Armistice came along. My only regret was that I did not get the uniform: the three-cornered hats were rather becoming.

After a couple of temporary dispensing jobs, I felt that I did not want to go back to that type of work, so I returned to London and lived in a women's club with my sister, working as a secretarial pupil in a Victoria Street office. Here I learned typing, but I had no great speed at shorthand: indeed, I must own that I never have had any. They say I am too tetchy with the vowel signs. Fortunately, I have never needed shorthand speed. G.B.S. did not dictate. Like Pepys, he wrote shorthand, but, whereas Pepys had a secret system, Shaw used simple Pitman outlines, done slowly, passing the result along to me for transcription. Nor did I need shorthand for my first secretarial job which was with an oculist in Devonshire Place who liked to have his letters taken down in longhand that he might refer to them easily in my notebook when I was not there.

I was helping him while his secretary was ill when Mrs. Webb invited me to lunch at 41 Grosvenor Road, that centre of Fabian strategy acidly etched by H. G. Wells in *The New Machiavelli*. A manœuvre was even now in progress around one so humble as myself; for Mrs. Webb added that "Shaw" would be there and she thought I might like to see him again. She had already asked me to help her in getting a pamphlet round to Members of Parliament, paying me half-a-crown an hour for my work. I imagine that in her goodness of heart she did so that she might be able to say to G.B.S. that I had worked for her, and it occurred to me afterwards that I had been invited to Grosvenor Road so that Mrs. Shaw, who was also there, might have a look at me. Be that as it may, soon after I had met them both at Grosvenor Road, I received the unexpected summons with which these memoirs open. He had not tested my ability in any way. He had just trusted Mrs. Webb's judgment. Probably he was much surprised when I wrote and declined his offer on the plea that I was very inexperienced as a secretary, and that I thought it might be unwise to throw up my job with the oculist for one at which I might prove incompetent. All my friends assured me that I was both rash and foolish because, for all I knew, my oculist employer might not intend to keep me on.

A week later G.B.S. wrote and asked me if he must take my decision as final. This is his letter:

10 Adelphi Terrace, W.C.2.
8th June 1920.

Dear Miss Patch,

May I take this as quite final? My reason for asking is that your misgiving about your capacity is all nonsense: much less capable people than you have been able to do all I want. If that is really what is standing in the way, come along.

However, you may be right on other accounts. I am 64; and my wife is 63, which means that your engagement might not be as long as with a younger principal. The occupation is a blind alley one, except to a woman who had her eye on a theatrical agency. But, after all, you cannot become a dentist; so perhaps there is nothing in that.

As to shorthand you will have to pick that up anyhow; and transcribing for me is not a bad way, as you can do it as slowly as you like: I practically never dictate, as it is easier for me to write a draft in shorthand myself.

My wife, on whom you made a pleasant impression, is very anxious that I should not accept diffidence as a disqualification, etc., etc. I am much more impressed with the plea that your present engagement can be made permanent, as I hardly like to steal you away from another man. Still, I will not take your first No for an answer; so will you let me have a second one, or a Yes, before I let loose a general announcement that the post is vacant?

Faithfully,

G. BERNARD SHAW.

By now I was beginning to find my work with the oculist most monotonous, so, thinking that, should I fail to please G.B.S., he had only himself to blame, I told him that, if he would wait so long, I would come to him in six weeks' time. He agreed and I eventually became his secretary in July 1920. Many years later, when giving me permission to use the correspondence, he handed it back to me with this covering note:

The engagement as my secretary negotiated in the enclosed letters has now lasted 28 years and has never been regretted by me.

G. BERNARD SHAW,
Ayot St. Lawrence.
7th March 1949.

It was a kind of accolade.

I once mentioned to G.B.S. that people were surprised that I, who had no degree, had been chosen for the job.

"You would have been absolutely useless to me if you had been a University woman," said he.

Graduates, as a class, he regarded as "politically and scientifically obsolete and ignorant". As far as real education is concerned, the native of Panama is assured in *Buoyant Billions*,

University degrees "are usually the falsest of pretences". You cannot hope for a degree at Oxford "unless you are a hundred years behindhand in science and seven hundred in history". The insistence, recurring throughout the years, that he was as good as any graduate does suggest that he was not quite sure about it, a startling thought, when you put him alongside any one of the horde of B.A.'s echoing one another round the world. Perhaps it began when he was a lad in Dublin and had to go into an office instead of getting to a University. Yet he politely declined the honorary degrees which were offered to him. What he would not realise was that you must have some standard of education, and examinations to measure it, for positions in the public service. He was very largely self-educated: he could sit in the British Museum reading-room and speedily absorb whatever he wanted to know about any subject he was writing on. His concentration was intense and his memory, until he was past eighty, unusually exact. It faltered latterly when he would repeat, with a certain self-pity, that he could not remember anything for ten minutes. Just as he had educated himself by reading what he wanted to know, so he believed that I had qualified myself by doing what I wanted to do. I once told him of a discussion at the club where I lived about the writing on the wall. I had an idea it was connected with Daniel but a woman from Cambridge had no idea where it came from at all.

"I could believe anything of anyone who comes from Cambridge," he remarked.

When I arrived at 10 Adelphi Terrace the Shaws had left London, as they always did in August, for Ireland. Ann Elder, the secretary who "had gone and got married on him" had sailed for India, leaving in charge a locum who knew as little about the work as I did. G.B.S. confided in me later that he always thought this young lady resembled "a very attractive bullfinch".

CHAPTER II

WHERE WE WORKED

"GO ROUND AND SEE the horribly pokey room in which we have to work," G.B.S. advised me from Dublin.

10 Adelphi Terrace had been Charlotte Payne-Townshend's flat when G.B.S. married her in May, 1898. She had settled there twelve years before to help Sidney Webb establish the London School of Economics, "the greatest one-man achievement of the kind since the Middle Ages", as Shaw told the students of Glasgow University when Sidney was candidate for their Lord Rectorship. An ex-town clerk "who was a good judge of men", said G.B.S., had bequeathed a few thousand pounds to Sidney Webb "to do some good with"; and out of it he had built up the London School of Economics and added it to the University of London.

The Webbs had housed the School at 10 Adelphi Terrace, and Charlotte Payne-Townshend came in as an ally by taking the rooms over the School at £300 a year for rent and service (quite ample, in that era of mild rents, for a flat with only cold water laid on), not to mention her subscription of £1,000 to its library and the endowment of a woman's scholarship. No. 10 was soon to be swallowed up by the huge office block which now takes to itself the name of the whole quarter; but in 1920 there were still bits of Adam elegance in Adelphi Terrace, a ceiling or two, a few fireplaces, although in the main it had surrendered to offices and wine merchants, with the Savage Club in their midst. No. 10 was on the corner of Robert Street and the Terrace itself; the top flat on the corner over the way was occupied by J. M. Barrie. The *Nation* staff now had the ground and first floors of No. 10, with H. W. Massingham, a friend of Shaw's earlier years, in charge: when T. P. O'Connor was editing the *Star* it was Massingham who had suggested that T.P. should take on G.B.S. as music critic. The stories about G.B.S. and Barrie tossing nuts, biscuits and epigrams to one another across Robert Street are probably a playful invention by Barrie himself. I can imagine nothing less likely on the part of either of them. Barrie did say that, after Mrs. Patrick Campbell had called to try to get a play out of him, he would watch her cross the street to try to get one out of Shaw.

The Shaws occupied the second and third floors. The kitchen was on the third, with the bedrooms and our study, "the horribly pokey room" to which G.B.S. had directed my attention. It looked out over the Terrace and the Water Gate arches upon Hungerford Bridge and the Thames, a long narrow room, with Shaw's desk at one end and mine at the other. It had no reference library: books were just stowed away on shelves all over the place. On the second floor was the dining-room and a large drawing-room, part of which had been curtained off for some of Shaw's books, including dictionaries and every imaginable work of reference. He had such a craze for dictionaries that, whenever he saw a new one advertised, he bought it. Apart from these stood authors' copies of all the Webbs' books and most of H. G. Wells', Chesterton's and Maurice Baring's. Mrs. Shaw had no study of her own; she would write wherever she happened to be. The flat did not possess a bathroom. Mrs. Shaw used to have cans of hot water taken to her room for a hip-bath, as did most women of the Victorian generations, including Queen Victoria herself: even Windsor Castle had no bathroom until Edward the Seventh became king.

There were Adam ceilings in both the drawing-room and dining-room, with its "They have said. What say they? Let them say", carved on the mantelpiece, a challenge which Shaw himself might have done for the good Queen Bess to whom it is credited. Rodin's bust of G.B.S. was in the drawing-room. It went with us to Whitehall Court whither, when she heard the rumour that the Terrace was coming down, Mrs. Shaw at once made all arrangements for moving. I had been with G.B.S. almost seven years when we left the Adelphi. "We are in a fearful crisis just at present," Shaw told a friend, "as we are leaving Adelphi Terrace after 20 years; and the rooting out is appalling. Hence the unearthing of The Mouse's Repast." This was a well-nibbled article from a magazine. "It wasn't our mouse," G.B.S. explained; "it was one belonging to the late George Standring, who gave a bundle of old *To-days* to Charlotte. Your article must have been exceptionally appetising; for none of the other numbers were attacked."

Whitehall Court is a large block of service flats, next door to the National Liberal Club, from which we still looked across the Embankment Gardens to the Thames. There we took the corner fourth-floor flat which had belonged to the Countess Russell who wrote *Elizabeth and Her German Garden*. H. G. Wells had lived at Whitehall Court too, but he went off to Regent's Park before we arrived. The playwright and dramatic critic, St. John Ervine, was next door, and he and his wife used to come in and see the Shaws. From the balcony running round our five rooms we surveyed the Houses of Parliament, a panorama broken, after G.B.S. had retreated to Hertfordshire, by an ugly War Office building rising to the west of his bedroom. But the Admiralty Arch and any Royal progress up Whitehall still lay open beyond his balcony eyrie. Eastwards ran the line of big modern blocks along the Thames to St. Paul's; over the Thames to the south-west was County Hall by Westminster Bridge, and, directly across the river from the study, a great heap of rubble from the blitz lay lumped for a time on the spot dedicated to a dream of Shaw's later years, the National Theatre.

In the study stood his big flat-topped desk, my smaller desk, a table, at which each morning I typed the daily batch of shorthand from Ayot, and half a dozen filing cabinets. Books, of course, everywhere: the *Encyclopædia Britannica*; the Bible in French, German, Italian and Spanish as well as in English; Shaw's plays in all their editions, including his rehearsal copies and foreign translations; the two large volumes of the *Oxford Dictionary*, seldom opened, for, as Shaw once boasted, the whole vocabulary of English literature was so completely at his call that he had never had to consult a thesaurus except for a third or fourth synonym. Although he admitted that he could never learn languages, he would patiently tackle one when driven to it. Thus, when he was twenty-six, he had plodded through Deville's French translation of *Das Kapital*, not then available in English, and in my day he wrestled with Siegfried Trebitsch's *Frau Gitta's Sühne* and produced *Jitta's Atonement* from it. So there were French, German and Italian dictionaries on the shelves among the Bibles, the plays, the encyclopædias, and the usual miscellany of books in general. Of the pictures, my own favourite was an oil of Waterloo Bridge done in the Impressionist manner by a Belgian refugee. There were Dürer prints over the mantelpiece; several watercolour landscapes of

Sartorio's, an inheritance from Mrs. Shaw's unmarried days, with much of her Chinese pottery; in the hall, a terra-cotta bust of Lady Astor by Strobl which, Shaw would always declare, flattered her; a print of William Morris; many photographs, including one of J. M. Barrie, inscribed to Mrs. Shaw; and a caricature of G.B.S. himself.

These various possessions, with Shaw's own bed, the clavichord by Dolmetsch, and other treasures, were scattered by a sirocco which blew up from Ayot just before his ninety-third birthday. In his latter years G.B.S. had become obsessed by the idea that he was not only living beyond his means but on the verge of bankruptcy. The introduction of the Capital Levy was the final blow, and he decided that he must begin to economise by giving up the over-large flat at Whitehall Court. As he had lived only at his country house for more than three years, there was a certain amount of wisdom in this decision. The only difficulty was that, although he wished to retain my services, he did not want his solitude at Ayot invaded by my continual presence in the house and at every meal. In any case I should have refused such an arrangement. Eventually it was decided that, as soon as a tenant could be found for our flat, costing round about £1,000 a year, we were to move into another two-roomed furnished one in the same block to be used by me as an office. It faced the War Office building and was not very light; the rent unfurnished was £350 a year, but Shaw decided to take it furnished and sell all his own furniture, books and other possessions (the things I needed being excepted), so that "on my final removal to Golders Green", as he put it, there would be nothing for his Trustee to do but hand back the two-roomer ready for re-letting. I nearly passed out when I received a letter from him notifying me that Sotheby's were calling two days later, and adding "Everything MUST be got out that day". As it was impossible for us to move into the new flat for another three or four weeks, and as the tenant for ours did not want to come in for another three months, this haste seemed to me quite unnecessary; so I got in touch with Sotheby's who agreed to write to G.B.S. saying that they found it impossible to remove his goods before the following week. This threw G.B.S. into a fury and he telephoned to Sotheby's that he insisted on them keeping to the original plan and everything must be taken *at once*. At the same time he wrote to say that he had disposed of my procrastinations!

Turmoil raged around me for the next three days while Shaw sat like a potentate at Ayot, vetoing every suggestion I made, and evidently imagining me sitting peacefully high and dry in the study. One of my suggestions was that I should send a file stacked with papers direct to Ayot so that Dr. Loewenstein, his bibliographer, could go through them at his leisure. This brought the command, "No: this is nonsense. Empty the drawers out in a heap on the floor higgledy-piggledy. Loewenstein will sort them out. Everything must go TO-MORROW. It must be possible for you to go to bed on Wednesday and stay there for a week or so until you are thoroughly rested".

Of course I did *not* throw them out, but left them packed, and the following week-end the unfortunate Loewenstein arrived, intending to complete the task of looking out what he needed in two days. But when I got to Whitehall Court on the Monday I found a pathetic note from him informing me that he was a physical wreck and that it was impossible for him to go through the papers under four to six weeks. It was just what I had expected: I must admit that I gave way to laughter, as I tidily parked the files in the bathroom. I never knew the Sage to be so unlike one as he was over this episode of the Whitehall Court removal. I had a certain feeling of responsibility for his possessions and those which had been Charlotte's; but he just tossed everything into the sale. Nothing must go to Ayot: one little sofa he said was too hard; two Oriental rugs which actually got down to Hertfordshire were judged too valuable and came whizzing back to Sotheby's. It was only by good luck that I rescued from the auctioneers a marble hand of G.B.S. done by Strobl, which Shaw himself considered precious.

The sale was spread over several weeks both at Sotheby's, who took what might be generously described as works of art, and at Phillips Sons and Neal's who had the remainder. By an error the Strobl bust of Lady Astor went with the latter and somehow got listed as a "terra-cotta bust of Mrs. Sidney Webb", which would have pleased Beatrice Webb even less than it did Lady Astor.

"Do I get my bust or do I buy it?" she telegraphed to G.B.S. when she heard of the slip. He at once had the bust taken out of the sale to give to some Institute in Lady Astor's old Plymouth constituency.

G.B.S. made one or two half-hearted efforts to exploit the Shaw name, offering to inscribe a number of the books;

signing on a label attached to the Dolmetsch clavichord the story of how he had got it from Arnold Dolmetsch for £40; and so on. In my opinion he was all wrong about the value of the clavichord. He thought it was wonderful that Dolmetsch should have revived clavichord music. He seemed to forget that Dolmetsch was a modern maker of clavichords and that nowadays there was no great demand for them. Anyhow it went for £110 and his four-poster bed was picked up for £18 by an Ilford dealer who observed very wisely that, although there were plenty of four-posters about, there was only one G.B.S. Shaw complained that if the bed had been a Hepplewhite and thoroughly uncomfortable somebody would have given hundreds of pounds for it; but I was inclined to agree with his housekeeper that he was so pleased about getting rid of these possessions of his that he was really indifferent about what they brought in. Certainly he put no reserve price on anything sent to the salerooms.

The first batch of furniture, thirty-six lots, brought in £837; and I imagine that he was quite pleased with what he got for the rugs and carpets. The pictures did not go well. Among them were two portraits of G.B.S. by Feliks Topolski, and two pencil and wash sketches of Charlotte by Rodin, inscribed "Hommage à sympathique Madame Charlotte E. Shaw": yet these and ten others fetched only £150. The books did best, yielding £2,570. I took Gertrude Lawrence along to the sale of them. She sat scanning the catalogue as the bidders gravely assembled, and suddenly a low gurgle came from her direction. She had lighted upon the H. G. Wells inscription in his *Short History of the World*, "G.B.S. To improve and steady his mind".

"I must have this", she whispered; and it went to her cheap at £8 10s. 0d. She bid boldly up to £163 before getting a facsimile set of the four folios of Shakespeare's plays, and she paid a further £58 for a *Mort d'Arthur* illustrated by Aubrey Beardsley. Rather overcome by her merriment at the opening of the proceedings, she faltered "Gertrude Lawrence" in a tiny voice when the auctioneer's clerk, one Samuel Patch, but no relative of mine, came over and asked for her name.

Four caricatures by Max Beerbohm which had never been hung in the flat did not go to the sale. G.B.S. presented the originals to me in, so to speak, a written deed of gift. Perhaps, like the play, he regarded them as too true to be good. One of them shows "Mephisto Bernard—influential friend of Aylmer

Faust". Aylmer Faust (Aylmer Maude) is the betrayer of Marguerite Tolstoi, standing in the background, with a beard to reinforce her pigtails. Max himself is her angry brother and G.B.S. holds a drawn sword between Valentine Max and Aylmer. The drawing is inscribed "To G.B.S. from Max. Saturday, January 10, 1905". It is all a trifle involved; perhaps the years between have rubbed away an edge of wit. Another is yet more obscure. A. B. Walkley is displaying to Shaw his pear tree growing against a wall. "So these are your pear trees?" says G.B.S. "Now I see why you don't like my plays." In a third, Rebecca West is "La Femme Shaw", after Max had read her brilliant articles in the Star: "And perhaps erroneously as I dimly imagine her," adds Max. One James Timewell appears with Shaw in the fourth, a "Historic scene at 10 Adelphi Terrace Dec. 10. 1903". James Timewell is seated on a chair gazing up at G.B.S. perched on a stool and saying, "But here I stay till I find something he *is* sound on." They probably had a good chuckle over that in 1903.

Along with these caricatures Shaw gave me one of Mark Twain signed "Max 1908"; a photograph of Max under which he has written "Max—with apologies to all concerned", and a drawing of Max's Old and Young Self talking to one another thus:

Young Self: "Did you ever manage to articulate the bones of that microglamaphoid lizard?"

Old Self: "I'm not sure. But I've articulated the whole past of mankind on this planet—and the whole future too. I don't think you know very much about the past, do you? It's all perfectly beastly, believe me. But the future's going to be all perfectly splendid . . . after a bit. And I must say I find the present very jolly."

Wilde and Whistler could not have found it difficult to snatch a reputation from competition of that quality.

An oil painting, in red coat and powdered wig, of Robert Shaw, the great-great-grandfather of G.B.S., hung at Whitehall Court until the blitz, when it was moved down to the country. Both Thomas Hudson, who did this portrait of Shaw's ancestor, and Thomas Patch, an ancestor of my own, had worked with Reynolds, the first as teacher, Thomas Patch as a student in Rome. Thomas lived most of his life in Florence. He made quite a name for himself: not so long ago I was offered one of his works at a figure, specially reduced because of the family connection, of £480. I declined the offer.

G.B.S. was obliging enough to settle a point which arose out of a painting of Thomas Patch's father, my own great-great-grandfather, Dr. John Patch, who was surgeon to the Old Pretender in France. Several friends told me that I was the only living Patch bearing any resemblance to Dr. John, who, I imagine, must have settled in Devon and become a hospital surgeon, for his picture hangs in the gallery at Exeter Hospital. One day when G.B.S. was visiting Exeter while on holiday at Falmouth he went to see the portrait and sent me his verdict. The strongest resemblance he detected was between my ancestor, and, of all people, Harold Laski.

"If it be true," he wrote to me, "that those who resemble the same person must resemble one another, then you must resemble Laski, though I have never noticed it. Laski is the flattered party."

He did, however, add that a likeness was to be traced between Dr. John and me. Better there, I thought, than between me and his son Thomas, said to be one of the ugliest artists who ever lived! The Patches of those days were inclined to be eccentric. One of them, Claude, ran away from home, joined the gipsies and became their king. The chronicles of Devon and Cornwall refer to him as "the worthy King, Claude Patch". When my father was at Rugby under Arnold, it may have been a descendant of this Gipsy King who, to the delighted jeers of the boys, pitched the tent of Patch's Travelling Menagerie in the town with the skeleton of a whale for its main attraction.

"I had no notion you have a Gipsy King up your sleeve," said G.B.S. when he saw this ancestor referred to in a magazine article. "I almost regret he was a runaway Patch and not a Romany." One of the few occasions I have known Shaw plump for romance.

Although G.B.S. had been an art critic (or it may be because of that fact) he was no patron of the arts; but at Ayot St. Lawrence hung a portrait of Mrs. Shaw by Sartorio. The Rodin bust of G.B.S. was also moved on to Ayot, where there was another by Prince Troubetskoy, both of them now bequeathed, together with the house, to the National Trust. Mrs. Shaw would have none of the Epstein bust, to which a workman and a press photographer gave a fleeting fame when it was shown at the Leicester Galleries. The workman clapped his bowler on the head (or more probably the photographer clapped it on for him); the picture was published, and Epstein,

very naturally, was so annoyed by this impertinence that he
was on the point of taking proceedings. Anyhow, although
G.B.S. assured Epstein that they were conferring immortality
on one another, Mrs. Shaw so disliked the bust that she said
she would go out of the house if it were brought in. So we never
got it; but the Shaws' friend and neighbour, Mr. Cherry-
Garrard, had a work of Epstein's at Lamer Park nearby.
Charlotte's favourite bust of G.B.S. was one by Strobl which
Shaw also thought good: some said it made him look too tidy.
It used to stand in the drawing-room at Whitehall Court,
but latterly it went with the Rodin down to Ayot. Just before
Shaw's ninetieth birthday, Feliks Topolski brought a large
picture of G.B.S. to Whitehall Court; and there are of course
many others. Dame Laura Knight did one, which I believe is
still in her possession. At Knebworth, Neville Lytton has
another of Shaw as Pope Ignatius, and there was one in the
sitting-room at Ayot by Augustus John.

In pre-war days the Shaws motored down to Ayot, about four
miles from Welwyn in Hertfordshire, every Saturday, returning
to Whitehall Court after a long week-end. Ayot was Shaw's
country retreat for more than forty years. The story of the tombstone is authentic. When Mrs. Shaw and he were looking for a
house near London they came upon a woman's grave at Ayot
St. Lawrence, "Jane Eversley. Born 1815. Died 1895". "Her
time was short," said the stone. "Then this is the place for me",
said Shaw, oppressed as ever by the menace of death. Ayot
St. Lawrence, a mere hamlet, is some three miles from Ayot
railway station, which the Shaws themselves never used. A lane
twists through woods and bracken and open country past the
trim brick church of Ayot St. Peter, and, a mile or two further
on at the top of an incline, after passing through a tunnel of
trees, you come on what appears to be the ruins of a church
standing among overgrown tombstones. A former Rector started
to demolish this church because it obstructed the view from
what was then the Rectory, building the present church in a
field some 200 yards from the main road in the style of a Greek
temple. There are fewer than a hundred tenants for the handful
of cottages, many in brick and timber, scattered around; among
them is an inn with a magnificent version of the old Brocket
arms dangling next door to the village Post Office. During the
war, when the old Rector died, the two parishes of St. Lawrence
and St. Peter were joined together and the Rectory at St.

Lawrence became a private house. This meant that there was no place for the meetings of the Sunday School, so the Brocket Arms came to the rescue and offered them the lounge, which was still being used for the Sunday afternoon meetings when I visited the village.

Along with picture postcards of Ayot and its famous tombstone, the post office, a tiny general shop, used to offer the tourist Karsh's photograph of G.B.S. and another of Shaw's Corner. Shaw's considerable mail came with the rest of the village letters direct from Welwyn in a van which cleared the letter box, but Shaw bought his stamps from the village postmistress, Mrs. Jisbella Lyth, in £5 lots, with several dozen stamped envelopes at a time. He liked stamped envelopes, partly because he did not have to waste a second or two licking stamp gum, partly because of his fastidious palate. For these two reasons he was much given to tucking in the flap of an envelope without securing it, until I explained to him that, if an envelope were above a certain size, the Post Office did not approve of flaps being tucked in as smaller letters might easily slip into the bigger one. From what some of the newspapers said, one might have thought that Shaw was never out of the Post Office; in fact, as often as not, if he wanted anything he would send Jisbella a little note. But he and she were great friends. He took her photograph at her cottage gate, and she once told him that she had to point out his house so often to the faithful that she thought of charging a penny a head. "Make it half-a-crown and I'll come in with you!" said he.

It was a pretty hamlet for disciples to amble round on a holiday, but as a permanent abode it was deadly dull; at least, so I found it when I lived there during the 1939 war, with nothing to do but go out for a short walk after mid-day and in the evening. For G.B.S. the seclusion was ideal. Sundays were like weekdays and week-days like Sundays. When I knew it, the bus service it once possessed had abandoned it to its isolation; most of the pilgrims came by car or bicycle, content to gape and go away. School was so remote that small children were taken there by car and bigger ones given bicycles on loan. The nearest shops were at Wheathampstead and Welwyn, both a few miles off. The water supply was not at all good. The taps in Shaw's garden were run from the town main, but the house water was pumped by an oil engine in the garage, tended by the chauffeur, and some of the cottages had to wind theirs up by hand from

B

the well at the village inn. Here G.B.S., at the age of ninety-two, broke out as a public figure and proposed that a water tower, "straight and stable, masked by a colonnade of pillars", should be set up in the middle of the church meadows "as a kind of village ornament". When he was about it, he invited a parish meeting to demand the demolition of "two ugly and obsolete cottages that cut off the view of the tower of the Abbey Church" and their replacement by "two modern pre-fabs." Perhaps he was coming to look upon himself as the big man of the neighbourhood, which indeed he was. Until this outburst the tendency of the village had been to regard him more as a legend than a human being, although I would say that the villagers were proud in their way that they should have such a famous man living in their midst. Now and again there would be an effort to consult the oracle, as, in 1940, when a farm labourer found him hedge-clipping. "Will 'Itler get 'ere?" he asked. "Napoleon, you know, tried it and couldn't." Clip-clip. I was stranded at Ayot when the Nazis marched into Paris and Charles Morgan sent out to me there with a very charming letter the rough proof of an ode to France which he wrote at the time of her collapse.

It was the villagers who first called the house Shaw's Corner, and in time the collector of rates did so too. Eventually G.B.S. himself accepted the local name for his house and had "Shaw's Corner" worked into the centre of a new wrought-iron gate by the blacksmith at Wheathampstead. Charlotte would have strongly resented drawing public attention to their establishment in this fashion. She disliked having people gazing in upon them. During the war some lively young men going home one night lifted the wooden gate of those days from its hinges, and, to the gardener's annoyance, left it up the lane. They would have found it difficult to repeat the trick with this embellishment which brought the weight up to 6 cwt.: to carry the new gate, G.B.S. had to have the posts replaced by two squat pillars in red brick, not out of keeping with the architecture of the house itself which was in the less attractive manner of English rectories.

The future of the place as a Shavian museum under the National Trust is unsure. Shaw's Corner is only a fair-sized suburban villa with a study, drawing-room, dining-room and seven or eight bedrooms, including, in the Shaws' time, rooms for the two maids and the housekeeper, who also had a sitting-room upstairs. When I went to Ayot the gardener was the husband of the housekeeper of that day, and an under-gardener and chauffeur completed the staff.

The Rodin bust used to be in the drawing-room which even in Shaw's lifetime was a museum of trophies: it was his intention that the room should be the actual museum under the National Trust. The drawing-room was Charlotte's room when she was alive, and after her death it was rearranged and remained unused except when Shaw happened to have visitors. Her own desk still stood there among the Shaw trophies. On a small table by itself was *The Seven Pillars of Wisdom* which G.B.S. was horrified to find Lawrence selling at £30 when it had cost him £90 a copy to produce, with its special paper and printing and all the famous Arabs done in colour by the more expensive artists. Dominating the room from above the mantelpiece was the Sartorio portrait of Mrs. Shaw, rather pale and dim I always thought, with landscapes by Sartorio around it. On one side of the mantelpiece below was a statuette of Joan of Arc; on the other, the "Oscar" awarded for *Pygmalion* as the best film of its year; and, in the middle, a china figure of Shakespeare, his arm resting on a pile of books. Charlotte, Joan, Shakespeare, and the "Oscar"—these may have been his household gods. He picked up the Shakespeare ornament in a curio shop at Frinton-on-Sea where Mrs. Shaw and he, then aged eighty-two and eighty-three, were when the war broke out. They had gone to Frinton in the midst of the war rumours because it was an easy car journey for Mrs. Shaw, who was not at all well. Writing to me then about my own welfare, he said: "There are no shelters in Frinton. When that wicked false alarm was sounded on Sunday night I was wakened and urged to get up and crowd with the other people downstairs, where one lady was proclaiming that 'passages' are safe. I absolutely refused to budge. As there are no safe places in Frinton and the beds are very comfortable, besides being respectable places to die in, I advised everyone to follow my example. Presently the All Clear sounded and settled the question, except for the people who took it for a fresh alarm. I slept in peace for the rest of the night. I should have done the same at Whitehall, as I have no reason to believe that the club basement is bombproof; and your account of it confirms my guess at its horrors." But Mrs. Shaw "has been in bed all day with a bad relapse, possibly the result of Sunday night". Next day she is much better, although there was "another alarm at 7 this morning. Nothing happened except a flight of British planes along the coast. I slept through it. Heaps of children here carrying gas-masks," he adds. "They are having the time of their lives. They do not understand bathing, but take to paddling like ducks. Mrs. D. . . . has had one planted on her. Mrs. C. . . . has twenty-eight on her hands at her son-in-law's place in Somerset. Her comment is 'They smell awful'."

G.B.S. himself must have been one of the few people in England who never carried a gas-mask: someone did bring gas-masks round, but that was all that happened. He was right about the gas-masks; but he was wrong about the blitz. In September 1940, on the eve of the earlier raids on London, he gave me his reason for believing these would never occur:

"There is no safe place during a bombardment except (doubtfully) the public shelters", he wrote, "and the belligerents so far dare not bomb any Power that can retaliate. Spain, China, Poland and the North West Indian hills can be bombed with impunity; they cannot hit back; but to bomb London or Paris with the certainty that Berlin would be for it by return of post is quite another pair of shoes; so we need not be very uneasy."

I was staying in Kensington at that time, and one night, just after the Shaws had returned to Ayot, we had a particularly bad raid during which one bomb passed so close to the ceiling of my bedroom that it sent me on to the floor, whistled past, shattered a house in Cromwell Road, and damaged the roof of the Imperial College. Next day G.B.S. telephoned me, saying that he thought I had better become an evacuee and go to them at Ayot which was, in comparison to London, fairly quiet.

"But," reported G.B.S., "as the I.C.I. has left Ayot, our searchlight has been re-established; and on Saturday morning's raid a bomb landed in Blowey's field, rocking this house and shaking Maggie out of bed. But the two raids since were nothing worse than firework displays of great splendour."

However, one night, soon after my arrival, eight bombs fell in the roads and fields around us. No particular damage was done, and although the house shook, and I heard shrapnel rattling on the roof, none of us left our bedrooms, probably pretending next day that we had been quite calm. To be honest, I felt just the opposite and wondered if my last hour had come. It was during one of these early raids that a bomb blew up some thousands of Shaw's plays waiting at Leighton-Straker's to be bound. They were insured against war damage and we got between £2,000 and £3,000 for them very quickly. The cheque arrived about the same time as the demand for his surtax, which G.B.S. promptly cleared with his insurance money.

There was never really any serious suggestion, even in those first days of the war, that the Shaws should take in evacuees at Ayot. People would come and inspect the house to see if it was suitable for billeting young children, but there was no room to have them with someone to look after them too, and the Shaws were beyond doing that. Despite the fact that it appeared to be as safe as most places, no children were in fact evacuated to Ayot, although one or two families did take cottages which happened to be empty. During the war G.B.S. made all sorts of suggestions, such as that he should live in one room to save work, and so on. No one took any notice of him. The chief signs of war to be noted in the village were one wartime reserve policeman, lately a gardener, now in uniform; desultory manœuvres now and again in the Park; and, in the early days, Imperial Chemical Industries used Ayot House as a kind of week-end refuge. Latterly it was handed over to the Women's Land Army. It was a pleasant place with a hard tennis court, a swimming pool, and glasshouses. They sold its garden produce to the neighbourhood. Ayot House belonged to Lord Brocket. As far as I know, G.B.S. and he never met, and I myself never saw him. He did not live at Ayot, but his mother, old Lady Brocket, used to come to the village for various functions. Neighbours at Ayot had long ceased to leave their cards on one another as they did in the old days.

Marking the entrance to Ayot House were two tall square pillars of red brick on each of which a black cat, with a human hand between its paws, reared on hindlegs. They were from the Brocket family crest. Passing between the pillars one afternoon, along the right-of-way to a house on the other side of the park, I was challenged and asked for my identity card by one of some men on manœuvres. I had not brought it with me and offered Jisbella as an alternative witness to my impeccability; but he relented and let me through. On another afternoon walk an R.A.F. officer stopped his car and asked the way to Ayot House. We had been warned against giving information to strangers and I told him I knew but was not sure whether I should tell him, at which he produced his Service identity card and all was well. These were mild excitements in drab days. Until the war I had not been down to Ayot, for there was never any need for me to go. Before he left the place to the National Trust, G.B.S. asked me whether I would like to live there after his death. I could not face it. The existence would be utter banishment for anyone used to the amenities of a town life. Charlotte may not have felt so strongly about it as I did. She probably did like it when she was younger, and she was never there for any stretch of time: they went down only for week-ends and they had frequent trips abroad. She did realise that G.B.S. could work better there, and G.B.S. and his work always came first with her. But as she grew older she felt the cold intensely, and, except in the height of summer, it was always cold at Ayot.

Thus, although Shaw's Corner was a haven for me in wartime, it was a chilly one: Hertfordshire is a cold county in any circumstances and my own room looked out upon the north and east walls of the house. I stayed at Ayot until July 1943, when, as there was a temporary lull in the raids, I returned to London, and the Shaws came to Whitehall Court so that the staff at Ayot could have a holiday, which they needed badly. Their intention was to return at the end of August, but they were obliged to prolong their stay owing to the illness of the housekeeper, Mrs. Higgs, who had been with them for many years. Mrs. Shaw had been in failing health since 1939, and while at Ayot seldom went further than the garden. The move to London, combined with the worry over Mrs. Higgs' illness, seemed to weaken her even more, and she died rather suddenly on the 12th September. All this trouble made it necessary for G.B.S. to remain in London much longer than he had intended, but before Christmas he went back to Ayot, while I kept on at Whitehall Court until the following June when the V-bombs started, and the blast from one which fell near Charing Cross blew in the study window, shattered the grandfather clock in the hall, and covered the place with dust. After costing us £30 to have it restored, the clock, designed by Euclid Neale of Aylesbury, fetched only twenty guineas at the sale six years later.

So I again retired to Ayot, and I had only been there a few weeks—in fact just before midnight on the eve of Shaw's eighty-eighth birthday—when I awoke suddenly, thinking that something had struck the wall under my room. I got up and went out of the room to see what had happened, but G.B.S., for all his eighty-eight years, was there before me, reconnoitring in his dressing gown. A V-bomb had fallen some half a mile away in a coppice and the blast had blown in the glass of one of his windows. The glass flew clear of his bed, to which, finding that the rest of the household were safe, he retired unruffled.

All through the war his nerve remained steady, and often in the late evening when we heard the wail of the Alert siren, and the planes were droning overhead, he would sit down at the piano and play and sing the old Italian operas. The piano was an ordinary upright; he hated grand pianos, as, so he told me, did William Morris. It was always in the hall because Charlotte liked to lie in her room upstairs and listen to him. One day he asked me if his playing disturbed me and I said it did not, although it really did for I used to try to hear the planes and the banging of the raids on London, which were quite audible from my room. At Ayot after breakfast G.B.S. always went off to put in a full morning's work in the shelter, often mistaken for a toolshed, which he had set up at the foot of the garden, about three minutes' walk from the house. It will remain for the Ayot pilgrim one of the most interesting features of this National Trust property; in Shaw's day the visitor doing the round of the garden of a fine afternoon usually had a peep at it when G.B.S. was not at work. He liked it because he could get down to his writing there undisturbed, and the housekeeper might honestly inform callers that Mr. Shaw was "out"; Charlotte would, of course, go down and talk to him if she wanted to. The popular belief that Shaw himself was as talkative as Polonius is wrong. Ordinarily he was a silent man, though I could imagine that when he was younger he would talk a great deal, especially among his cronies. The shelter was entirely his own idea. It was built so that it could be turned to face the sun, but in fact it was never to my knowledge moved at all: he kept it always in its original position. He did not go to it in winter, when they were compelled to be economical with their electrical current. The electric heater had to be on in the dining-room whether he was working there or not, and if he went down to the shelter it meant an additional heater. When asked once whether he needed peace and quiet for writing, Shaw replied that he had begun his literary career, like many others, without the means to choose his surroundings.

"I had either", said he, "to write under all circumstances or not to write at all; and I have retained this independence of external amenities to this day. A very considerable part of my plays has been written in railway carriages between King's Cross and Hatfield; and it is no worse than what I have written in the Suez and Panama canals". He might have added, as Macqueen Pope records in his *Haymarket, Theatre of Perfection*, how he hired a chair in Regent's Park one summer and sat there writing, wet or fine, until he had completed *You Never Can Tell* for Cyril Maude. What Shaw did resent, wherever he might be, was the inquisitive intruder, whether in a railway carriage, or on board ship, or at Ayot, where his shelter, hidden among the bushes, gave him the solitude which he preferred. There he would sit all morning in his wicker chair by the window at a simple flap table fixed into a corner, with a thermometer on the wall and his paste pot, paper clips, red ink and alarum clock tidily deployed in front of him as he wrote his neat shorthand. He loved his red ink, paste pot and paper clips; to make a correction he would type the altered line or two on a slip of paper and paste it over the deletion. Although he carried a watch, the alarum clock was set each day to remind him when it was time for lunch. He never took any notice of it, and had always to be summoned. For this purpose a hand-bell such as porters used to clang on railway stations was installed, not without feeling in the village during the early days of the war when all other bells were banned. The bell was wielded by Maggie who came to the Shaws from Ireland. She was a great favourite of Charlotte's, and would always take her breakfast up to her. An intrepid young woman, she cycled off quite fearlessly in the air raids to dances or to the cinema and to Mass every other Sunday. I got on very well with her, but Shaw was, as usual, shy about embarking upon a general conversation and spoke to her only when he wanted something. I should think that it was Maggie who darned the Sage's socks: latterly, whenever the housekeeper was away from Ayot, she would look after G.B.S., tackling the cooking which at first she declared was beyond her. After sixteen years' service, she went off in Shaw's Rolls Royce to be married to an insurance agent; and it was they who rescued G.B.S. when he broke his leg in the garden.

In the shelter on another small table stood Shaw's portable Remington. He had always played about with a typewriter. I imagine that he got one in his early London days as soon as typewriters were to be had and he had the money to spare: he was ever curious about any new device, whether typewriter or atom bomb. He toyed with the idea of a dictaphone, and at one time looked forward to a day when an author would speak into a dictaphone and the dictaphone would work a linotype without the intervention of a compositor. Then he decided that meantime his own shorthand was more fascinating. He also joined the British Interplanetary Society whose ambition was a flight by rocket to the moon. So, before he had a secretary, he did for some time do his own typing. He did not "touch" type: he used two fingers. Latterly, for personal letters, or, to save time, he might want to add an extra page when revising a script. Before deciding to buy his last machine he went round a trade exhibition. "Could that typewriter type a play?" he asked a young woman demonstrator, perhaps somewhat unnecessarily. "Of course it could", said she, rather annoyed. "It could type anything". For all his interest in the most up-to-date mechanical devices, G.B.S. himself was baffled when faced with having to put a new ribbon on his machine: he had actually to bring it up to London to let me fix it for him. So too, although his enthusiasm for photography, especially during the Malvern Festivals, was unbounded, it would be unusual for him to get more than ten successes out of fifty exposures.

Latterly at Ayot G.B.S. looked after his own files, although in his more active days most of the filing was done in London. When he did have a burst of energy and tidy things up, he never knew where he had put anything when he was finished; and he would leave letters lying around anywhere, quite oblivious of the fact that some were marked "Confidential". He went through his files pretty thoroughly when he was bringing out the collected edition of his works, selling at thirty guineas the set. One volume which he put together for it was *Scraps and Shavings*, made up of odd writings, some of which had never appeared in book form. Then there were the three volumes *Music in London*, articles from his days as a music critic which had been published only in the *Star*. Work on the collected edition meant also short prefaces for those plays which had none, with small additions to the plays themselves.

In his later years at Ayot, G.B.S. would breakfast before nine o'clock, but before the war, when he was in town, he was up even earlier to go for a morning swim at the Royal Automobile Club, stalking off down Pall Mall from the flat. Over breakfast he would read the *Daily News* as it then was (in later years the *Daily Herald*), while Mrs. Shaw read *The Times*. At ten o'clock he began the day's work, and never failed to carry on from then until lunch-time at one o'clock. He always had a rest in the afternoon, settling down to work again about six o'clock for an hour's work in the study before dinner for which he would, as a rule, change into a dark suit. When Charlotte was alive he had to be up in his room by eleven o'clock; latterly when he had, as he said, returned to bachelor habits, he would sometimes continue writing in the dining-room, but he usually read or listened to the wireless, seldom going to bed before midnight.

My own day began at 9.30, and I had the morning post open and ready for him by the time he had finished breakfast. In the early days at Whitehall Court, before he began hoarding so greedily the handful of time that remained to him, he had no objection to giving up an hour to a visitor before lunch if we did not have too much work on hand. He was indeed glad of the chance to fit in a talk with someone whom he might otherwise miss. While *Pygmalion* was being filmed, for example, there was much to discuss and Gabriel Pascal would drop in to clear the latest problem up; or Feliks Topolski would sit around making sketches while we worked. I would keep on typing while Shaw interviewed people, disturbing them much less than they disturbed me, for my noiseless machine did not break in upon their talk, whereas their talk did not make the transcription of Shaw's shorthand any easier. Occasionally I lunched with the Shaws, but usually I was glad to get out and go off at one o'clock to my home, returning about two o'clock and finishing at five. But if they were not in town and there was no great pressure of work I did not go back after lunch.

When Shaw was out of town he forwarded to London work in his shorthand which I transcribed and returned to him typed. One advantage of this arrangement was that it let him keep in touch with me through the post while he was down at Ayot or abroad. The largest accumulation of words given to me to tackle in this way was *The Intelligent Woman's Guide to Socialism*. It began as a leaflet for a Women's Institute and it finished up as a tome of 200,000 words. It went on and on, one grim instalment following another. Charlotte's sister was godmother, so to speak, to this monumental work. She had married General Hugh Cholmondeley and lived in Shropshire where he survived her, marrying again when he was eighty and living to a great age. There was one daughter who used to visit her Aunt

Charlotte at Whitehall Court. Mrs. Cholmondeley had written to Shaw asking him to do a leaflet for her, as she wanted to explain Socialism to her Women's Institute. G.B.S. began the leaflet and soon found the task colossal. On and on it went for three years, to be finally dedicated to Mrs. Cholmondeley "the intelligent woman to whose question this book is the best answer I can make". He gave a copy to Winston Churchill, for whom, as much for his mother's sake as for himself, he had a liking. Winston he regarded as a romantic militarist who throughout the war "quite splendidly kept up the spirit of the nation". What made him dangerous in the politics of peacetime, Shaw maintained, was that he sincerely and honestly believed what he said and did not know that he was talking nonsense. G.B.S. therefore did not agree with those Labour critics who kept denouncing Churchill as a hypocrite and humbug.

The book jacket for the first edition of the *Guide*, designed by Eric Kennington in four colours, was not popular: it showed a nude female looking down a well, presumably for truth. "You may not know", protested somebody from Dublin, "that the paper cover of your book presents the picture of a female making a copious display of bare breasts and indolently scratching a swelling on her right forearm. She does not look Intelligent." I remember Lady Lavery wrote chaffing him about it too. "If this intelligent woman," said she, "is meant to be a portrait of Mrs. Shaw, she should not have allowed you to publish it." Frequently during these three years Charlotte told me she was tired of hearing about his intelligent women and their socialism. Both of us implored G.B.S. to hurry up and finish the thing.

"The more I get into it," said he, "the more there is to write."

When it was at last completed, I remember he came to town one day and asked me, "Did you notice that on the last sheet I sent you I wrote 'The End'?"

"I wonder how you felt?" said I.

"I threw down my pen," G.B.S. replied, "and said to Charlotte, 'It's bloody well finished!' "

CHAPTER III

HOW WE WORKED

"THIS, THE FIRST play on which we were engaged to-gether", G.B.S. wrote on the fly-leaf of my copy of *Saint Joan*. Many Shavians maintain that it is his best play; neither Shaw nor I agreed with them. "I shall be able to form an opinion on the Judgment Day, not sooner", he told somebody who asked which of his works would live longest. At other times he was more explicit.

"Rightly spotted by the infallible eye of Frank Harris as My Best Play", he inscribed that queer man's copy of *Heartbreak House*; and *Heartbreak House* is the American favourite too. I remember once going to the Savoy Hotel in search of an Ameri-can visitor. The page boy, thinking he knew him, did not bother to call his name and came back to say that he was not in; but I, having noted a man sitting in the lounge reading *Heartbreak House*, was able to say he was. It was before he wrote *Back to Methuselah* that Shaw preferred *Heartbreak House*. He liked his biological pentateuch; and he sent Thakin Nu, the Premier of Burma, a copy describing that as his masterpiece. Yet I don't think he really had any first favourite; I have, in fact, heard him say so.

Although it was Charlotte who suggested a play on Joan of Arc to G.B.S., the central idea, that Joan was an early Pro-testant, had been in his head since reading a report of her trial years before. Shaw often said that when he began a play the fate of the characters was not predestined. That may have been true of the discursive plays where the characters sit round and talk; of these, as G.B.S. once remarked, "it is unnecessary to disguise the fact that there is no play". In the plays of action he may not have known precisely what everybody was going to do, but clearly all of them, like Joan, are the creatures of a dramatic situation already determined. There could have been no *Devil's Disciple* without a gallows. *Heartbreak House* grew from a story of Lena Ashwell's about the character who became

Captain Shotover. *Pygmalion* grew out of the idea of an illiterate flower-girl, trained to speak correctly, conquering Society.

G.B.S. went off to County Kerry to write *Saint Joan*, and while there he cracked his ribs when scrambling over the rocks. A Birmingham osteopath soon put him right again. *Saint Joan* was the first of twelve Shaw plays which I have been the first person to read. I found the work of transcription fairly easy, for, as I have said, Shaw's shorthand was simple Pitman's in outline and there were not many corrections. Before he had a secretary he wrote all his plays out in longhand. *The Doctor's Dilemma* was the last to be so written, and I was surprised when I came upon the three small notebooks which contained the play at the back of a filing cabinet at Whitehall Court when I was having one of my periodical fits of tidying up. Each notebook held one act. I wrote to G.B.S. and told him of my find and he asked me to send on the books to Ayot. As Sir Almroth Wright had helped him with the play, he was thinking of presenting the notebooks to Sir Almroth's hospital, St. Mary's. Our publishers suggested that the College of Physicians would be more appropriate, because more doctors likely to be interested would see them. Shaw would not agree. Some months later when I went down to Ayot I asked if the notebooks had ever been sent on. He replied (he was now ninety-two) that he did not know what I was talking about, and when I reminded him of the notebooks I had found and forwarded to him, "The Lord only knows what has happened to them", said he. I wonder where they are to-day: I would be surprised if Shaw did not succeed in losing them once more.

While he did not write it very quickly, his shorthand was definitely quicker than longhand would have been. It was clear and accurate, with all the vowel signs filled in. He told me that in his teens he had easily learned Pitman's phonetic alphabet in six weeks, and that he had then dropped it because he was appalled by being told that, to be fully qualified, he would need to take down 150 words a minute. To do that, said he, meant contorting the Pitman alphabet to a reporter's code, omitting the vowels and contracting the consonants, and an author had no use for all this. What an author needed was a writing speed of twelve words a minute, and to him the overwhelming advantage of this Author's Shorthand as he called it, was that it "saved manual labour". He estimated that, by writing each word phonetically, he cut down by almost one-half the number of letters needed. But he insisted that each word must have its clear phonetic symbol. He would scorn shorthand contractions and grammalogues which skipped the definite spelling of each single word: these he regarded as corruptions invented for the convenience of verbatim reporters, which, indeed, they are. G.B.S. was justly proud that any stenographer could read his shorthand. On occasion, when time pressed, he might send it direct to a newspaper office, where he would be delighted to find that the typists could invariably transcribe it with ease; and he would advise young men who proposed to write for a living to learn his phonetic shorthand, and not reporting shorthand which "would take years to master". But there were disadvantages in this labour-saving device of his. Transcribing to a typewriter from short-hand is often rather difficult. Looking at a page of words in longhand, you automatically take in and read a line at a glance, whereas with shorthand you move warily from one word to the next. I used to rest his manuscript on a stand, such as violinists have, placed behind my typewriter and raised to eye height.

Although Shaw would always write in longhand any words which he thought might be difficult to decipher, he would sometimes slip up. Even if I could transcribe the error so as to make sense, it might not be the sense that he had intended to convey. Once, when he was writing to someone on theatrical matters, I translated his symbols as "the profiteers of the theatre", and happened to see the letter before it was posted. "I meant this for the proprietors of the theatre," he had written in the margin, "but my secretary has seen fit to translate it for what is, I think, a better word." On another occasion I puzzled for some time over a sentence in a letter written to someone in domestic difficulties. All I could make of it was "the woman got nothing but *porter* out of it". It seemed to me rather queer, but, knowing the couple were in poor circumstances, I thought that perhaps porter was the only drink they could afford. It happened that Shaw was in town when he came to sign the letter and presently I heard a shout of laughter. He turned to me and asked for the shorthand script as he couldn't remember what he had meant to say instead of *porter*. Imagine my delight when he found that he really had written that word and it took him some time to remember what it should have been. Finally it came to him as *torture*. Anyone who knows Pitman's shorthand will guess that he had made a slanting stroke instead of an upright one. I think this was the one and only occasion when he admitted that my mistake was excusable and could not be attributed to what he called my habit of "jumping to conclusions, just like most women".

When one thinks of it, it is something of a feat to write a play like *Saint Joan* straight off in shorthand, even although this was the play Shaw said he found easiest to get down on paper. True, his thoughts flowed easily; yet, when all is said, it must be uncommonly difficult to write dialogue in shorthand which cannot be visualised as you go along. Noël Coward once told me that as, like Shaw, he could not dictate he "wrote" his plays straight on to the typewriter where he could see what was being said and correct where necessary. I don't think G.B.S. ever went back to correct a word, and, although he did occasionally make mistakes, there were never many alterations in his shorthand as it went on from line to line. Apart from that and the clarity of each outline, transcription was all the simpler because Shaw would not write a few pages and then revise what he had done. He would go right ahead to the end, sending his shorthand script to me in small batches and running through my typescript when it was completed. So I had always something already done to refer back to if need be; nor was there any hurry to get a play finished. On the contrary, I would often have to put it aside for the articles and long letters which rained upon me in a torrent when I first went to him.

He used blocks of water-lined paper of a green tint to rest the eyes, and on them he would turn out, between break-fast and lunch, an average of 1,500 words a day. The rate would depend on the intricacy of stage "business", and with that he never had much patience. He once told me that he would rather write the whole dialogue of *Hamlet* than manage the entrance and the exit of the Ghost. He would complete the dialogue of a long play inside two months, aware, roughly, of the number of words done as he went along. All his readers know that with punctuation he could not have been more precise. He always put a comma before "and". He never used an apostrophe or a hyphen, writing "cant", "dont", "Ive", "tomorrow", "today": personally I would prefer "can't" to save confusion with "cant", the noun. He would grow restive over his colons and semicolons. He was one of few writers to use the colon: he picked the habit up, I imagine, from his Bible reading.

Colons are to be found most frequently in the Bible and the works of George Bernard Shaw.

"Please get three copies of this typed", I find an instruction from him. "You had better put it out and not interrupt your transcription of the play: but you must impress on them that they must put it on a machine that has a colon as well as a semicolon, and that they must follow my punctuation and paragraphing exactly."

In thirty years I can recall only one spelling error: for a time he omitted the third "i" of "millionairess", but he had reformed before the curtain went up. There were small deliberate efforts at spelling reform—"program", "cigaret", "vigor", and, occasionally, towards the end, "fotograph". He split his infinitives defiantly. Every good literary craftsman, as he once assured *The Times*, did so when the sense demanded it; and he invited that journal to dismiss a busybody who spent his time chasing them, it being "of no consequence whether he decides to go quickly or quickly to go or to quickly go".

A double-spaced typescript was the working copy for his revision. Carbons of anything that was to be published were made on yellow paper: he seldom kept a carbon of a letter. After the typewritten copy had been made, signed by him, and put in the post, the original shorthand script was torn up; and that was the end of that. When he had run through in typescript his first draft of a play, he himself would send it off to the printers. Like Sidney Webb, Shaw, as I have said, did his own publishing, dealing personally with printer and binder and paying direct for the paper, setting up of type, machining and binding work. It might be suggested that Shaw's early misadventures with the tribe of publishers were the motive for this decision to be his own. Blackwood, Chatto, Macmillan and Smith Elder had all refused his novels. In my opinion neither that fact nor Sidney Webb's example was what decided him. Shaw stood guard over his works like a hen over her chicks. Nobody dared disturb a comma. It was because, at first, he would not have a line of his precious dialogue cut that he held out so long against any play being filmed. He became his own publisher in order to have absolute control over the form in which his work was to be finally presented.

He met his match in William Maxwell. William, managing director of R. & R. Clark, the Edinburgh printers who became the Edinburgh University Press, was a Scot who knew his own mind and frequently made Shaw's up for him. Thus, when the collected edition was decided on, G.B.S. wanted the type to be set up by hand: in the William Morris tradition, he scorned machinery and the usurping monotype. William Maxwell hastened down to London with two specimen pages, one set by hand, the other by machine. "Choose"! in effect William commanded, not telling Shaw which was which. The monotype won. G.B.S. preferred the page set by machine; and William Maxwell convinced him that for close spacing it was as good as hand-setting. Shaw was fussy about equal spacing between words, although he would have none of William Maxwell's story about the division of a "the" into a "t" with the "he" in the next line. The two came to hold a firm respect for one another, and ambitious young Scots doubtless contemplate William Maxwell's career with awe. Beginning as a shorthand clerk in 1892, he became, fifty-five years later, an honorary LL.D. of Edinburgh University and the host of G.B.S. when he stayed in that city.

The wide range of Shaw's knowledge included a very fair acquaintance with the different sorts of type, and his ideas about the format in which his books should be published were as autocratic as usual. None the less, he bowed to the advice of the master printer and declared that his firm, to whom in 1908 he was sent by the Webbs for the printing of his first plays, was "as natural a part of my workshop as the pen in my hand". Shaw himself read the printer's proofs of the millions of words which gushed from his successive fountain pens: at an average of fifteen hundred a day for only seventy years there would be more than 40,000,000 of them. It almost stuns me to face the fact that I myself must have transcribed at least 10,000,000. Even with articles he would insist, if they were at all important, on seeing a proof before publication. I myself did no proof-reading, although if a double set came along he would occasionally ask me to make his corrections on the second copy, when Charlotte was too busy to do this for him. He was meticulous in correction, altering the punctuation, taking out a word here, adding one there, or even, in the first proof, fretting the printer by slashing out whole lines. He would usually tear up the corrected typescript when it came back from the printers with the first proof, although he did keep the originals of a few of the plays. In a second proof, which always followed the first, he could not have been more considerate, calculating the exact number of words, or even letters, to balance further cuts.

Before final publication, fifty copies would be struck off for rehearsal, titled as "By a Fellow of the Royal Society of Literature". Older actors did not take kindly to this idea of reading a play and fitting their own part in to it; formerly they had only their own lines and cues, a system which most of them much preferred. Shaw was a benevolent tyrant among his actors. Roy Limbert, the kindly manager of the Malvern Festival, has a lively story of how Shaw, then approaching his eightieth year, put them through *You Never Can Tell* at Malvern. G.B.S. remarked that he was far too old to have a long rehearsal. They began at eleven o'clock. Shaw acted every part and produced every passage. At a quarter to two somebody dropped a hint about lunch. Shaw apologised. "Certainly; we'll go now," he said, "and we'll be back at a quarter past two sharp."

Few playwrights are really competent to produce their own work, although Shaw held that all of them ought to do so; but he was a supremely able producer. He looked upon the production of a play as a duel between actors and playwright, and he accepted the challenge with glee. So long as he could stand up to the strain of it, he was always his own producer, never ruffling the actors but never allowing them to steal the play. Some say that in his earlier days, and before my time, his feuds with Irving, Mrs. Patrick Campbell and Beerbohm Tree arose quite simply out of their determination to put on star turns of Irving, Mrs. Pat and Tree and let the play go hang. Some plays might be all the better for being twinkled by the stars into oblivion but not, he vowed, a play by George Bernard Shaw. He held the whole cast firmly to the axiom that any play of his must be given as he saw it when he wrote it. On his own rehearsal copies of the plays he had worked out the precise mechanics of each. Saint Joan must stand just here; Dunois there; the Dauphin over yonder. Each must speak as directed, each when silent must be silent in a natural way. The audience had to be convinced that they were looking at actual men and women behaving as men and women behave; the actors must be coaxed into believing that in this way they were getting the best out of the play for themselves. Shaw had a gift for seeing other people's point of view (except perhaps, now and again, my own). He realised the abnormal sensitiveness of actors and actresses. He accepted it and he was careful never to ruffle any of them. He would rehearse, again and again, a passage which was not just as he wanted it; yet he would chide no one. His tact was equal to his patience and there was no limit to either. I have confirmed in talks with actors and actresses what I have gathered in this connection from G.B.S. himself. I was never allowed to be present at any rehearsal. No outsider ever was. Rehearsals were a ceremonial performed by Shaw and his cast: upon all others the theatre doors were closed. Corrections would invariably be made in the rehearsal copies of the plays, and there might be more when the run had begun. Shaw could not comprehend the sentimental interest, or, it might be, a mercenary one, in rehearsal copies, typescripts and first editions. Surely, he would ask, the latest editions were the best? Had not all corrections been made in them? The published plays have been bound in two styles, the Venetian sail-cloth red of the later Standard Edition superseding the original pale green because G.B.S. was annoyed by the way it faded. Most of us regretted the change.

The terms for the ordinary professional performance of the plays were on the same fixed percentage for any theatre, large or small, at home or overseas. At one time the rates for amateur and professional performances were different; a sliding scale of percentage on takings for professionals, and a fixed five guineas for not more than three consecutive amateur performances. Galsworthy was understood always to allow small amateur companies to perform his plays without fee and, although many of them requested that privilege from Shaw, he would never give it: he said it would be blacklegging. When I handled the licensing I regularly checked up our press cuttings for reports of any amateur performances which had not been licensed, passing on infringements to the Society of Authors to deal with. Shaw did relent when the Birmingham Municipal Players asked him to reduce his author's fee. He told them they could have performing rights as professionals if they would use the money towards building a Municipal Theatre. The objects of the Players were thereupon amended to include "the building of a civic theatre", and six years later the first performance was given in the Crescent Theatre, built by themselves. In 1949 it celebrated its silver jubilee. Shaw made this same concession to other amateurs: they could call themselves professionals if they worked for their own dramatic funds, had no reports in their local papers, and gave nothing to charity. Latterly he put both amateurs and professionals on the same percentage basis on takings, which was much cheaper for the amateurs than a gross five guineas.

Several sent him only half a crown and once we found a single shilling in the post. Shaw was quite satisfied. It was not the money he wanted: his aim was to build up amateur theatre societies everywhere.

I shall discuss later his attitude to money: however out of the ordinary it may have been, he was not, fundamentally, mean. The reason why there are three plays in most of the published volumes is that he thought people would feel they were getting better value for their 8s. 6d. It would never occur to him that many people do not enjoy reading plays at all. In the usual way I myself prefer to see a play before I read it, and, if I wanted something to read, a play would not be my own choice. Indeed I gave up *Back to Methuselah* when I was halfway through. On the other hand, many have remarked to me that they enjoyed reading *Heartbreak House* more than seeing it because on the stage the lines are spoken so quickly that their meaning escapes the listener. As a rule you do not get much idea of a play when concentrated upon typing it and reading through the typescript for corrections. I would complete this mechanical work and post the result off to Ayot without any coherent notion of what it was all about, but I, of course, saw the plays as soon as they were produced on the stage and always found that my impressions of the characters were very different from those I received when typing the play. When I was transcribing *Saint Joan*, for example, I thought the scene after the burning of Joan where de Stogumber, the chaplain, rushes in and cries he will be damned for all eternity, would be most impressive, yet when I saw the play on the first night, March 26 1924, it somehow disappointed me. Perhaps I should not have gone at all: I had just heard of the sudden death of a friend and was not really in the mood for the theatre.

G.B.S. had read my typescript to Sybil Thorndike and Lewis Casson down at Ayot. There was never any question of anyone but Sybil playing Joan. In those days Shaw himself would do much of the casting and he had an eye for just the right person for any part. I imagine Sybil Thorndike will be one of the few who possess an autographed copy of the large *de luxe* edition of the play, brought out at about 30s. and illustrated in colour by Charles Ricketts with all the designs, stage settings and costumes. G.B.S. would autograph his books occasionally, but he was reluctant to do so because the more of them he autographed the less would be the value of the others distributed among his friends. Following their usual custom, Charlotte and he were both at the New Theatre for the first night of *Saint Joan*; but they stole quietly away before the final curtain, when it might then be truthfully announced that the author was not in the house. Shaw was much more indifferent to applause than are those who charge him with a passion for it. If it interrupted any play of his he looked upon it as intolerable. No printer, no actor, no film producer, no audience must presume to come between the creator and his creation. Ten years before, when *John Bull's Other Island* was running at the Kingsway Theatre, he went the length of circulating a broadsheet scolding the audience for their "most generous and unrestrained applause". The more applause there was during the performance, he told them, the angrier he felt with them for spoiling their enjoyment and his own. Had they noticed, he asked, that if they laughed loudly and repeatedly for two hours, they got tired and cross, and were sorry next morning that they had not stayed at home? Nobody would applaud every bar of a piece of music which happened to be pleasing, and an act of a play, like a piece of music, was intended to be heard without interruption from beginning to end. Although he civilly assured them that, at each fall of the curtain, they could not possibly applaud his plays too much to please him, he would almost always slip off before he himself could be caught up in it. He would not often take the stage on a first night. At his first nights in London Charlotte and he usually had a box; but at Malvern he always had a seat in the front row of the dress circle. If he invited friends to see his plays, either at first nights or during the subsequent run, he always paid for their seats, not approving of the custom of giving complimentary tickets. *Saint Joan* was Shaw's biggest box office success to date. A critic who found the epilogue wordy and fantastic got his knuckles rapped. "When disapproval of the epilogue persists after witnessing a second performance," chid G.B.S., "the case is one of mental defect, and is hopeless." He had a trick of attributing mental defect to anyone who did not agree with him.

While *Saint Joan* was running at the New Theatre, theatregoers kept asking for copies not only of the play itself but of the preface to it. The play was not published until after it had been performed, nor did Shaw ever write his famous prefaces until he had completed the plays which were their text. The first night of *Saint Joan* in London, for example, was on 26th March

1924 and the preface to it was not written until the following May. His prefaces, as he explained to one playgoer, were essays, quite independent of the plays, written when their subject was too large to be fully dealt with on the stage; and it was nonsense to think that they were meant for playgoers to read before the plays could be understood.

During the run of the play a succession of young women called at Whitehall Court, each wanting to play the name part. One of them, who told us that in her dwelt the spirit of Joan, refused to leave the doorway. She was a rugged young woman, as if from the London School of Economics. Although a porter told her that Mr. Shaw could not see her, she hung about the hall, dodging him and standing around outside the flat. Several times I went out to say that it was no good waiting because Mr. Shaw would not see her: she insisted that, if he did not, he would be making a great mistake. Finally I had to warn her that the management would object to her hanging about and that if she did not go I would have to have her put out. After a talk with another youngish claimant, who came by appointment, G.B.S. shook hands with her as she left. When I saw her to the door I held out my hand too. She shook her head. "No one else will touch that hand again to-day," said she. Yet another aspirant to the part tried to demonstrate the excellence of her elocution by reading to G.B.S. and me the chapter about Jezebel from the Bible. The performance embarrassed us both. But Shaw had a practical sympathy, ready to serve anyone who showed the least promise. On one occasion he took a girl into the church at Ayot and told her to stand up and read from the pulpit while he sat in a back pew to test her voice for carrying power.

Any young person determined to go on the stage was always directed by him to the Royal Academy of Dramatic Art: he regarded a sound training as indispensable, and he knew that, after a stiff entrance test, the Academy had it to give. When the war ended, several American students, including former G.I.'s, took the Academy course on a United States grant. Other overseas students came to it from the Argentine, Australia, Canada, Czechoslovakia, Egypt, Greece, Holland, Iceland, Iran, New Zealand, Norway, Poland, South Africa, Uruguay and Yugoslavia: all told two hundred and fifty young people were learning to be actors and actresses from ten in the morning until half-past five daily in the building in Gower

Street put up in 1931 from a fund which G.B.S. himself opened with a cheque for £5,000. The tiny theatre, where Shaw in person used to rehearse members for the Academy's public shows, was smashed by a German bomb in April 1941. Here many a star had taken the first cue as a stage recruit: Meggie Albanesi, Richard Attenborough, John Gielgud, Cedric Hardwicke, Celia Johnson, Charles Laughton, Vivien Leigh, Margaret Lockwood, Robert Morley, Stephen Murray, Basil Radford, Flora Robson, Lydia Sherwood, Valerie Taylor. More than any of the honours for which men strive, G.B.S. prized the placing of his bust opposite Shakespeare's in the Academy's foyer; for, in the scale of things which he truly valued, the theatre came second only to his reformed alphabet. It was with him a passion stronger than most men's religion. In his active days he was one of the keenest men on the Academy's Council, and was punctilious in attending its meetings. I once went with G.B.S. to the opening of an Academy term. As part of his speech I remember he said: "You young people probably think there will come a day when you will get to the top of the tree. I have had that feeling myself, and sometimes I have said 'I am there; I am up at the top'. And then Joey the Clown pops out between my legs and I could never resist him".

It seemed to me at the time to show how he would spoil a useful speech by some unexpected remark which appeared to confirm the widely held belief that he took nothing seriously. There was another example of his facetiousness a few weeks after I went to Adelphi Terrace, when Charlotte and he had returned from Ireland. A friend of mine asked him how his new secretary was getting on.

"What chiefly impresses me," he said, "is her wonderful knowledge of canaries."

Mrs. Shaw had asked me to look through the telephone directory for a dealer in canaries, as she wanted one to take to Ayot St. Lawrence, where the gardener bred them. It occurred to me that Gamage's stocked canaries, so I rang them up, and sure enough they had a very nice cock bird which Mrs. Shaw went off to look at and bought there and then. The gardener was delighted with it and G.B.S. pretended to be much impressed by my resourcefulness. But even if he had thought me useless he would not have given me away to anyone else.

After *Saint Joan* I saw the *Methuselah* cycle; and rather hard pedalling it was at times. In this case the play was published

before it was produced. I had nothing to do with the typing of
it, for G.B.S. had just got it off to the printer when I went to
Adelphi Terrace. While writing it, I don't believe he imagined
it would ever be performed, and, but for Barry Jackson, it
probably never would have been. Twenty-three years Shaw's
junior, Barry Jackson had come into the theatre with a troupe
of amateurs, the Pilgrim Players, whom he led round the
Birmingham halls for a performance a week. After five years of
this he was responsible for the building and equipment of the
Birmingham Repertory Theatre, and it was when he found
G.B.S. in the stalls at a matinée there that the oft-reported
conversation about the production of *Back to Methuselah* took
place: how Shaw asked him whether he wished to see his wife
and family in the workhouse, and how Barry Jackson replied
that he was not a lunatic.

Far other, as it turned out. After the production in Birmingham, where both G.B.S. and Charlotte saw it, *Methuselah* came
to the old Court Theatre in Sloane Square. I went to the
matinées. You took a set of tickets for the complete play and
could use them for any performance during the three weeks'
run, which gave you a day or two to spend in cogitation
between the acts, and eased what might have been an exhausting experience. For myself, I found the Pentateuch most
interesting on the stage, particularly *In the Beginning*, and *As
Far as Thought can Reach*. London liked it: all seats were
sold for the run and Shaw was exultant. If Barry Jackson, he
said to me, would produce a play for the love of it and make it
a success, he was just the man for him. So it was *Back to Methuselah* which led to the pair of them working together in the
annual Festival at Malvern.

Sir Barry hired the Malvern Theatre for six weeks and put
on a different play, not always by G.B.S., for each night of the
first week, beginning the programme over again in the succeeding weeks. The seats were at ordinary provincial theatre prices
and there were season tickets for the whole Festival. London
stars would take the leading parts, and some not yet stars began
there: Ralph Richardson, Robert Donat, even Errol Flynn.
Afterwards there might be a London run. The Festival drew
great crowds; it was claimed that it left between £50,000 and
£70,000 a year in Malvern. I was always holidaying while it
was on, but I sometimes went over if I happened to be staying
in Herefordshire or at Presteign. The shops all put up a great

show, with special displays of Shaw's works. Sir Barry would organise garden parties and concerts, and it was altogether a gay occasion. In the early days the Shaws stayed at the Malvern Hotel throughout the affair, and, attended by the news-reel people, G.B.S. might plant a mulberry tree; or they would go off by car to visit Sir Edward Elgar nearby.

The first of the Festivals opened on August 19, 1929, with the première of *The Apple Cart*. Before that came to me for transcription, I had done another play of slight importance: there must be many Shavians who have never read it and only a handful can have seen it played. *Jitta's Atonement* was done by G.B.S. in gratitude to the man who had made his name for him in Europe long before he became "box office" at home. As he has confessed, it was not until the middle of the first decade of the present century that he could have lived by what the London theatre brought him, although for ten years and more he had been drawing a good income from the United States and Central Europe. It was Siegfried Trebitsch, his translator, who, then a young man of twenty-five, had opened up this market for him. Each took one-half of the profits, a generous concession on Shaw's side, and made at a time when he could not have guessed how much it was going to mean to him. He had begun by pooh-poohing the whole proposal, and it was only Trebitsch's faith and drive that carried it through and won the world for Shaw.

In Vienna before the 1914 war, Trebitsch, an Austrian, some thirteen years younger than Shaw, had been a novelist and playwright of standing, and G.B.S. now decided to turn into English for him his *Frau Gitta's Sühne* which had been put on at the Burgtheater Vienna in 1920. It was a heroic decision; for although Shaw had been to Bayreuth, and to the Passion Play at Oberammergau, he had no more than a tourist's German. Laboriously, therefore, with a dictionary, he plodded through the original script, word by word. The result, *Jitta's Atonement*, was not Trebitsch's play; but it pleased them both. Herr Trebitsch imagined that Shaw's name was sufficient to give it a run, nor did Shaw disagree, for latterly he did come to regard his name as a key to the box office. All of them were swayed by the names in neon lights: Gabriel Pascal even contemplated trying *Buoyant Billions* on the United States. Roy Limbert would, I think, have produced anything at Malvern if it had a good name behind it. The public, they would tell you, are like that. They are wrong. The public may be rather foolish, but they are not so foolish as their servants make them out to be. As I ran through the transcription of *Jitta's Atonement* I asked myself why Shaw had done it. Can he, I wondered, see this as a West End success? It never was. It ran for a week at Fulham Grand Theatre with Violet Vanbrugh as Jitta. I went to the first night while G.B.S. was in Madeira.

"When Jitta is produced at the Grand at Putney Bridge," he wrote to me from there, "buy the next day's papers and cut out the notices and send them to Trebitsch. If there are any pictures so much the better. If you have nothing better to do some evening you might buy a couple of tickets and see what is happening for yourself: the first night for choice, as you could tell Trebitsch how many curtain calls (if any) Miss Violet Vanbrugh gets."

I cannot remember anything about the production, except that I thought it rather dismal. It had a short run at the Shubert Theatre, New York, with Bertha Kalich as Jitta. Afterwards, when the persecution of the Jews began in Vienna, Trebitsch and his wife, a lady of family, had one or two narrow escapes. At first they did not take much notice, but one day, when they were motoring home, they were stopped and their car was confiscated. Then, during the night, they began to hear terrifying sounds. They grew alarmed. As it happened, Herr Trebitsch had arranged to go to Switzerland to lecture, and to take his wife with him. Using these passports, they stole out of Vienna one night each carrying a suitcase, and succeeded in making the frontier. Nevertheless, all their considerable property was seized and Herr Trebitsch's publishers in Berlin disappeared. From Switzerland they crossed into France where they were given naturalisation in recognition of Herr Trebitsch's translations of French poets into German, returning, when war broke out, to Zurich where they continued to live when it ended. Herr Trebitsch then came to England several times and on each visit he went down to Ayot where the venerable pair (Trebitsch was now almost eighty), would sit discussing their vanished royalties, for Trebitsch was no longer rich and his health was going too.

As far as his work as playwright went, Shaw's mind lay fallow for four years, between writing *Jitta* and beginning *The Apple Cart*. After finishing that, it was more than two years before he began his next play, and then he would rattle off something, however slight, every year for the next seven years. He began *The Apple Cart*, the play which blows up Demos, on Guy Fawkes' Day, 1928, and worked steadily at it until he had finished it off on December 29 while staying with the Astors. Mrs. Shaw and he were two of a house party at Cliveden. I still have a note which Mrs. Shaw wrote to me then.

"Mr. Shaw read the play," she says, "(all we had of it) to the party here and had an immense success. All that political part went splendidly: better than the love scene! They are wild to hear the last Act which he has just finished. Have you any of it typed?"

G.B.S. himself thought it was "a frightful bag of stage tricks". He sent me the shorthand of the whole of the last act with a covering note begging me to let him have it by return of post, if possible, as he was eager to get back to town and could not do so until he had read the rest of the play to his Cliveden audience. I remember I spent the whole of the last day of that year transcribing and typing the Act, scarcely pausing for a mouthful of lunch. I was mentally exhausted before I had finished; but I got the typescript off by the country post, and G.B.S. was able to return to London in a couple of days. Not one word of thanks or praise did I ever get for what was really a stupendous effort. G.B.S. was like that: he took one's work for granted.

It is the strict code of the theatre that no one shall let slip a hint of a play's plot before the curtain rises, and for the opening of the Festival they were being more than usually secretive about *The Apple Cart* when, on June 14, it was produced at the Teatr Polski in Warsaw and Floryan Sobieniowski, Shaw's Polish translator, innocently cabled the whole story to the *Observer*. Great was Malvern's consternation. The Polish version was still running when the curtain went up in Worcestershire two months later, with Cedric Hardwicke as Magnus and Edith Evans as Orinthia. I went to the first night when the play came to the Queen's in London. Ramsay MacDonald, Prime Minister of the day, was sitting behind me with the American Ambassador, for *The Apple Cart* found much favour with those in authority, appealing as it did to the feeling of importance which authority usually confers upon those who possess it. In Warsaw too the President of the Polish Republic had been to the first night; indeed the only person with a grumble was a coster who wrote and told G.B.S. that he was disappointed in the play because after buying a ticket he could not find a single reference to apples anywhere.

CHAPTER IV

HE TAKES HIS PEN TO SEA

WHEN HE WAS sixty-five years old, G.B.S. learned to dance the tango at Madeira. Just as a new typewriter would arrest his eye, so he may have been fascinated by the mechanics of the new dance. Charlotte and he had no sooner returned from Ireland to me at Adelphi Terrace than she decided that they must go off again for Christmas. They left in a mild domestic breeze, for they found that they could not get away until Boxing Day and the daily help lost her temper when the housekeeper asked her to come in on Christmas Day.

"Well," said Shaw genially as they stepped out from No. 10, "I hope we shall enjoy this holiday; we seem to have succeeded in upsetting everybody."

They had, in fact, as he told me by postcard, "a most frightfully tempestuous voyage"; and "except for a few hours in the middle of the day, I have found this place cold. However, there is evidently something seriously wrong with the weather here as elsewhere." Both Charlotte and he brooded over the prevailing state of the weather and seldom failed to report upon it, frequently with a sympathetic comment on what they could hear of England's weather at the moment of writing. Thus, in a week's time, although they had found Madeira "all flowers and maize and bananas and bathing (in the Gulf Stream), to-day and yesterday it suddenly turned tempestuous and rainy in fits of fifteen minutes or so with a high sea, no bathing possible and great difficulty in landing from the steamer which brought your letters, one tourist being snatched from the deep just as his collar was disappearing". The high sea even burst open my budget to him "with letters and cheques protruding".

He must have been apt as well as picturesque at the tango, for his instructor invited him to demonstrate it with him on a world tour. Perhaps it was his success here which decided Shaw to learn Spanish. As he did not want them to know who their pupil was, he applied in my name for a course at a Correspondence School. He got bored with it, and in a few weeks the

Director of Instruction wrote to me regretting my lack of perseverance with my studies. When I showed Shaw this reprimand he told me to ask them to remove my name from their list of students and to say that the press had got hold of the fact that I had enrolled and were ringing others up about it. G.B.S. had somehow been detected as the Spanish student; perhaps his handwriting gave him away.

"*You* are becoming too famous," he wrote to me.

In the late summer, after they got back from Madeira, Charlotte and he went off to Strathpeffer. The big toe of my right foot now became the main subject of correspondence between us. In my school days I must have injured the joint; gradually it stiffened, and by the time I had settled in Adelphi Terrace it was causing me agony. In a letter to him I had made a passing reference to it. He was full of concern.

"You must tell me something more about the toe," he wrote. "I don't know what is the matter with it or which toe. By wearing high heels women used to get their middle toes into such a condition that the approved surgical remedy was to cut off the top joint of it. Is that your case? If so, I should think *both* middle toes should suffer. . . . As you know, I greatly mistrust the operation panacea. . . ."

His conclusion happened to be wrong; yet how many men not actually shoemakers or surgeons would possess this specialist knowledge of my sex's middle toes? "Miss Bullfinch", my predecessor, and now my deputy, had meanwhile gone off for an operation. Shaw was in a mock rage, for his work looked like being held up.

"Miss Bullfinch has put the lid on the situation," he cried. "I throw up my hands and ask desperately, is there ANYBODY who is not being operated on? Who is your proposed *locum tenens*? You will probably find her on the table also." Then, "Is the toe very bad?" he asks, adding that he had recently heard from a Scandinavian who claimed to be able to cure all ailments by natural methods; and there is "no harm finding out what this Naturopath has to say at my expense". Not too hopefully, I went to the man two or three times and had hot fomentations applied to every part of my body except my foot, after which I was told that all I needed was to visit a chiropodist for an ingrowing toenail! "That villain you would insist on going to!" Shaw snorted when he saw I was no better. I was finally disabled by too much walking during the General Strike, so they operated on me at St. Thomas's Hospital and I passed a peaceful convalescence at Frinton. G.B.S. wrote to me there offering to foot the bill. "By the way," he asked, "what about the former affair with the Scandinavian? Did I pay? I promised to. You must not be shy about dunning me as I forget everything I possibly can. I am distracted and lost without you."

He found that he could work much more easily at Strathpeffer than during the succession of trips on which Charlotte hustled him out of England. "I have some thoughts of staying here until I get the *Guide* MS. off to the printers," he wrote. "I am getting desperate about it."

The pair of them are away to Mexico on the *Arandora Star* next spring, and in the late summer they are at Stresa on Lake Maggiore. It was the beginning of a long series of tours which included South Africa, the United States, China and New Zealand. Had Shaw had his way, he would never have roamed further from Ayot than Whitehall Court. The passion for travel was Charlotte's, and in all things he humoured Charlotte, who for her part hovered over him like a guardian angel. Wherever they went she would take with them a menu of what suited G.B.S. I typed out a list of the dishes he would eat, giving her several copies of it whenever they set out from London. She would hand one to the chief steward on their boat, and one to the head waiter when they stayed at a hotel. For a time, Charlotte herself tried a vegetarian diet, but she did not care for it: she felt she needed meat.

Her ultimatum to the world's chefs ran:

Mr. Bernard Shaw does not eat MEAT, GAME, FOWL or FISH, or take TEA or COFFEE. Instead he will want one of the undermentioned dishes at lunch and dinner. He will eat green vegetables, puddings, pastry, etc., cheese and dessert like other people. He likes oranges and salads and nuts—especially walnuts.

For breakfast.	Oatmeal porridge or other cereals and always grape-fruit. For drink "Instant Postum".
Other meals.	One of the following dishes at lunch and dinner.
(Haricot Beans dry, white)	May be plain boiled, with a sauce; or curried or formed into cutlets.

(Butter Beans)

Lentils	(as above)
Macaroni	*au gratin*: or with tomato, cheese or other sauce—or curried.
Spaghetti	(as above)
Welsh Rarebit	
Yorkshire Pudding	
Rice	Savoury: or Milanese (no ham): or curried with haricots or eggs or nuts, raisins, etc.
Pease pudding	
Eggs (not too often)	
	Curried: cutlets: mayonnaise: *Espagnoli: en cocotte à la crème:* omelette, etc.
Gnocchi	
Sweet Corn	
Curried Chestnuts	
Minced Walnuts	
Soups	Any thick vegetable soup such as

      Lentil
      Haricot
      Pea (*St. Germain*)
      Barley (*crème d'orge*)
      Rice (*crème de riz*)
      Artichoke (Palestine)
      Celery
      Onion
      Tomato.

Mexico and Stresa were both too much for Shaw's pen. Charlotte and he "came through the Mexican excursion pretty hardily", he reports from the Gulf of Panama, "but the heat here is infernal (86 in our cabins). I try to write plays, falling asleep between every sentence." There follow civil regrets about London's winter record. At Stresa the weather "holds up miraculously. I am getting stronger; but I can't work in this climate which is perhaps just as well."

A postman robbing him of odd francs for postage stamps offers an interlude in the meteorological survey of Cap d'Antibes during the summer of 1928. They arrived "at the crest of the heat wave and almost died of it. Now the weather is more reasonable and we are acclimatised; so life has become possible with plenty of sea and sun bathing. But the nervous vicissitudes are trying: one never knows whether the morning will find us smiling in a paradise or groaning in a purgatory." Then he is off after the wretched postman when I tell him that I am having something to pay on all his letters. "Please send me the envelopes when there is excess postage to pay," he exhorts. "The postman here takes them unstamped and charges up the stamps against the hotel; so the stamping is official and ought to be right. I shall have to buy a letter balance," he adds, resigned to it, "and do my own stamping, I expect." He would have gladly paid a few hundred francs for a letter balance rather than be robbed of ten a day. He was not mean; he was finicky.

Next, on the way to Geneva, for which they set out from Cannes, he is attacked by the brute creation. "Some poisonous creature bit me", was how he put it, leaving me puzzled until Charlotte told me that a kind of spider had stung him. "It caused great swelling," she said. "Finally we got a doctor and after a lot of poulticing he lanced it. Now it is really getting well; but it has been quite serious!" Charlotte had an old-fashioned partiality for the exclamation mark. To Shaw the bite was serious not because of himself but because it slowed down his output. "I have been going about with my hand in a sling," he wrote. "This has hampered me in writing, though it is fortunately the left hand that has suffered."

He must have been run down, for, four months later, in January 1929, he was still somewhat troubled by the boils caused by the spider bite; so off he went to a doctor who was experimenting with Abram's Box. Shaw was so drawn to any treatment which challenged existing practice that I believe he would have joyfully consulted a witch doctor had there been one in the neighbourhood. I have told how he commended my big toe to the Naturopath. So once he sent me to Lillah McCarthy's sister to try out, in a spirit of sympathetic inquiry at his expense, a new system for teaching elocution. Our first lesson was on breath control and one of the pupils was a man, unskilled in using his breath properly, who proposed to go round speaking on behalf of some charitable institution. Marion McCarthy explained to him that he did not expel his breath correctly. He tried her method and expelled it with such force that he blew a cough lozenge right across the room. I only went twice or thrice, and when Shaw asked how I was getting on she said I had done very well but I was not continuing my attendance, on which he commented that he supposed I knew all she had to teach me.

Shaw's most fantastic "cure" was one which he passed on with perfect seriousness to Lady Martin Harvey for loss of sight. Loss of sight through shock sometimes cured itself, he told her. What the victim must do, apparently, he explained, was to buy "a nice white wig, which looks well at all ages". Then, he went on, "get your head shaved completely and utterly. You will have a fearful shock when you see your shoulders surmounted by a bladder of lard with your well-known features carved on it. I have witnessed this phenomenon in the case of a very handsome woman; and I nearly fainted. So you must have a wig ready to clap on immediately. The reason for the wig being white is that, when the hair grows again, it will grow white or grey long before it would have changed colour if let alone. This also is a shock; and the total effect is to wake up the head and produce physical and psychological activities which may react on the sight or on anything else".

Charlotte, who had a healthy scepticism for these strange treatments, was horrified when G.B.S. and I went to see the doctor who had the Abram's Box, a device with quite a passing vogue in the United States. In a darkened room a specimen of the patient's blood was put on a slide; an indicator then diagnosed the illness, and treatment was thereupon prescribed. Shaw was treated five or six times, and either his boils were vanishing anyhow or the treatment indicated speeded them out of his system.

In the spring of the same year he and Charlotte were away again, this time to Istria, and from there to Split—"a wonderful place, we are delighted with it and Ragusa", Charlotte remarks—and so by steamer to Venice and by the Orient Express back to Paris, "to have a look at the city which we have not visited since 1906", and, he adds, to see *La Charrette de Pommes*, *The Apple Cart* in French: they might, it seemed to me, have given idiom for idiom in the translated title.

G.B.S. liked the French more than the French liked him. He accepted with equanimity the preference of the Comédie Française for Molière and affably saluted his French critics. Discussing English critics with a man whom they annoyed, he

C

compared them with those of Paris. Many years before, said
Shaw, when *Candida* was first performed there, he used to hold
up Catulle Mendès as a model to English critics. If English
critics dislike a play, as, he alleged, "they always dislike mine,
they set to work to prove that it is wrong: wrong technically,
wrong morally, and in fact not a play at all. Catulle disliked
Candida very thoroughly; but he described it carefully and
politely, and said that, though he was able to follow it in-
tellectually and to recognise that it had a duly constructed
story with a purpose and meaning which I apparently thought
interesting and dramatic, he could not share that interest, and
had been chilled and repelled by it. He could only state this
effect on himself apologetically without pretending to assign
any general validity to it. Shaw was for him an unacquired
taste: that was all. That was fine of him don't you think?"
asked G.B.S. "I said to the London critics, 'Why can't you be
gentlemen like Catulle Mendès?' "

This presentation of *Candida*, put on at the Théâtre des Arts,
Paris, on May 7 1908, had a queer history. It had been done
fifteen months before at the Théâtre du Parc, Brussels, in the
same translation by Augustin and Henriette Hamon, when it
was the first performance of any of Shaw's plays in French.
Augustin Hamon was a scientist who had never before dabbled
in literary affairs, and Shaw, taken by the lively way he had
written up a Socialist Congress in London, promptly assured
him that he was just the man to do all the plays into French,
acting on impulse much as he had done when he rushed me into
becoming his secretary. The scientist protested that he had only
lived seven months on our side of the Channel, and that anyhow he had no technical knowledge of the theatre. G.B.S.
would not listen to him. He told him that he had a knowledge
of modern society and human nature, that his wife knew
English, and that all would be well. It was, but not before M.
Hamon had imagined that all was lost when he first heard the
audience bursting into laughter. He thought that he had
ruined Shaw by bad craftsmanship until his wife explained to
him, what he had not noticed, that he had been translating a
comedy and that it was quite amusing.

The Shaws found the gay city of their earlier middle age
"abominably depressing". It rained, and Charlotte caught a
bad cold which developed into congestion of the right lung.
G.B.S. was manifestly concerned. It was a sharp attack and

their departure had to be delayed. In a day or two, however, "the patient," he reported, "is happily convalescent, but she has had a full-dress illness, with doctor, nurses and all complete, and is still in bed."

It was on their way back to Venice two years later, to be exact between the islands of Corsica and Sardinia on March 5 1931, that G.B.S. began to write *Too True to Be Good*, the Malvern play which followed *The Apple Cart*. He worked on it in Venice and I should not be surprised if he kept at it on the way home, when eventually they were able to embark. They appear to have been delayed by workmen who were not getting ahead quickly enough with repairs at Ayot; for, "if you think it will hurry up the repairs," I find a postcard from Venice suggesting to me in mid-April, "if you intimate that Mrs. Shaw is furious at being kept abroad by them when she was promised a clean house by 1st April you need not be afraid of exaggerating her indignation."

On June 30 Shaw completed *Too True* at Ayot St. Lawrence and I finished the typing of it on July 4. It went to Malvern by way of Poland after its first performance in the spring of 1932 by the Theatre Guild of the United States. In Poland there was a censorship comedy rivalling the earlier one in New York twenty-nine years before when the whole company playing *Mrs. Warren's Profession* were marched off to the police station, and the judge, after taking a week off to "read this play by this blackguard", came back and said he could see nothing wrong with it.

Shaw's own most adroit assault upon the censorship was when he went up to Harrogate and talked the Chief Constables of England and Wales into resisting any attempt to impose the handling of it upon them. He told them how, on coming back to England from Italy where he had been taking a sun cure, he, "a respectable, dignified, white-bearded member of society", found to his utter amazement that the illustrated papers were full of pictures of him with nothing on but a bathing slip. Someone had snooped. At one time, said he, that would have been regarded as indecent exposure, and it might be so regarded in the future unless Parliament defined exactly what indecent exposure meant. To-day it and a number of other misdemeanours were all a matter of opinion; and to add to these the censorship of plays would be "the most impossible and the most odious" duty of all. He urged the Chief Constables to declare that they were "not prepared to be Plato and Calvin and Moses and the Prophets rolled into one". They agreed that they had never heard sounder common sense, and that it ought to be the theatre and not the play which should be licensed. With *Too True to Be Good* the Polish censor was even more detached. He passed the play without reading it and was promptly dismissed from his post; for the Polish Government were scandalised by Shaw's comments on war: by the John Bunyan Sergeant who remarks that London, Paris, Berlin, and Rome will all be burning "in the next war", and is not attracted by the idea of blowing up in its cradle a baby "that might have been your own"; and the Elder who would have been a conscientious objector had he been of military age; and the chaplain flying ace who won "a very poorly designed silver medal for committing atrocities which were irreconcilable with the profession of a Christian clergyman", and the objection to dropping bombs on sleeping villages.

For once, G.B.S., whether he liked it or not, had to accept cuts in his text. These and other commonplace remarks about war went out; the censor came back; and in three days *Too True* began to run again. For Malvern, Shaw produced a special leaflet explaining what the play was about, telling young people that he wanted them all to have a good time; yet remaining a trifle vague about the sort of good time he meant them to have. The critics were flown down from London, somewhat grudgingly on their part, for Malvern's opening performance, arriving in the stalls in the middle of the first act. Sir Barry Jackson had assembled for them a cast of stars—Cedric Hardwicke, Ernest Thesiger, Leonora Corbett, Scott Sunderland, Margaret Halstan, Ralph Richardson and Walter Hudd. In the casting one girl, fair with an attractive lisp, rather stumbled through her lines. But she was chosen to play Sweetie, her first part. She was a success. Her name was Ellen Pollock and she and her small son became friends of the Shaws. Walter Hudd played Private Meek. He was rather like T. E. Lawrence in appearance; and the chatter went round that Meek was meant for Lawrence.

None of us, including Lawrence himself, ever had any doubt about it. Meek's long head with the Wellingtonian nose and chin under the *pagri*, or head-dress, giving him a feminine air of having a veil, is exactly the painting by Augustus John. He is insignificant-looking, gritty and windbitten. He rides a powerful motor bicycle at eighty miles an hour. He speaks dialects. His Colonel tells him to confine himself to the duties of his station. He tells his Colonel he can become a private if he wishes; that he himself has done it again and again. He was "mostly a sort of tramp before he enlisted"; and, as G.B.S. says of Lawrence, "when he threw up his Colonial Office berth he found himself destitute and, after a brief experience of actual hunger, enlisted as a mechanic in the R.A.F."

Private Meek is Lawrence transposed from life, and Lawrence himself was as pleased as Punch about it. It would indeed have been easier to believe that Lawrence had walked off the stage into real life than the other way round. He was barely credible. No playwright could well ignore such a gift; and Shaw was assiduous in collecting human beings. Boanerges in *The Apple Cart* is John Burns caricatured (and Boanerges was Lawrence's name for his motor cycle). Shaw once described Cunninghame Graham as "a story writer of genius: he figures in my play *Arms and the Man* with Webb in strong contrast". Sidney Webb is the innkeeper there; Professor Murray, the Oxford professor in *Major Barbara*. Dubedat is an elaboration of Edward Aveling, who cut out G.B.S. with Karl Marx's daughter Eleanor. Stopford Brooke suggested the Reverend James Mavor Morell. The name Candida is borrowed from an Italian lady who became a Marchioness. Professor Henry Higgins is Henry Sweet, a phonetician friend of Shaw's. The Elder in *Too True to be Good* is probably founded on Dr. Inge.

The idea of the bomb which ends *Heartbreak House* comes from the bomb in the first world war they heard at Ayot bringing down the Zeppelin at Potter's Bar. Orinthia detains Magnus in *The Apple Cart* much as Mrs. Patrick Campbell, to annoy Charlotte, used to detain G.B.S. at *Pygmalion* rehearsals. The scene where Mrs. Warren justifies herself to Vivie is borrowed from his own *Cashel Byron's Profession*, from which *Mrs. Warren's Profession* also gets its title. *Buoyant Billions*, about which nobody was too polite, is a dish of odd bits. The reason why it is such a rattlepate of a play is that its Act II, "The Adventure", written years before the rest of it, was almost certainly suggested to Shaw when steaming through the Panama Canal where its scene, crawling with alligators and serpents, is set. This scrap lay around until G.B.S., happening to come across it, told his thrifty self that something had better be done about it. So he tacked

"The World Betterer" on as Act I, added "The Discussion" and "The End" as Acts III and IV, spiced it with the views of one who, like himself, found it impossible to stop making money because of the Commissioners of Income Tax, and sat back beaming like little Jack Horner. The idea of a drawing-room in Belgrave Square being shown as a Chinese Temple seemed to me to be rather unreal; nor would a solicitor of the standing of Sir Ferdinand Flopper call there; the client would call on him. And I suppose that the reason why a native from Panama announces a visitor in somebody else's house is to save another character. There are already too many of them.

It may be my fancy, but I have always felt that two of Shaw's next three plays, all written at sea, were the result of the famous ten-day glimpse of Russia which he had with the Astors and Lord Lothian in July 1931, a week or two after I had finished typing *Too True to Be Good*. T. E. Lawrence looked in to bid him farewell just after he had left for the Golden Arrow at Victoria. Shaw's last instruction to me was to search for a photo of Mrs. Pat Campbell's dog Twizzles, a griffon, and send it to her. I did find one, but Mrs. Pat wrote to say that it was of another dog which had been dead for at least fifteen years. Twizzles' picture remained lost.

The newspapers held a spirited gambol round the Russian excursion: how the visitors took tins of food with them; how Lady Astor was discovered washing Shaw's beard; how at last they met Lenin's widow; and so on. Shaw came back even more impressed than he had been prepared to be. A Mr. A., an incredulous American, was foolhardy enough to hint that the visitors had been too well conducted.

"Russia," Shaw told him, "is a country for whole-hearted Communists. For people with American commercial ideals like Mr. A. it is neither a happy country nor a safe one. And America is neither a happy country nor a safe one for people with Russian communist ideals.

"If anyone were to suggest that Tammany could camouflage New York so as to make Mr. A. mistake it for an earthly para-dise, he would probably form exactly the same opinion of that person's credulity as I form of those Americans who are good enough to explain that what I saw was a camouflaged Moscow and Leningrad."

I have heard G.B.S. tell how Lady Astor swept through the Kremlin "like a flying bomb" and went off before the astonished

Stalin on the subject of child welfare, and that Stalin promptly had someone sent from the Russian Embassy in London to the Margaret Macmillan Centre in Deptford to collect the facts. To me G.B.S. never said much about the Soviet, for he knew that I was not versed in political matters. I must own that I should have liked to know what Moscow and he had to say to one another about equal incomes, a question on which he was at that time a much sounder Communist than they. Perhaps it was Stalin who began the work of conversion which was to lead to Shaw's climb-down. The only reference to the Moscow outing that I had from him was a picture postcard from the Hotel Metropole there of a pleasant young woman with auburn hair, a red tie and an armful of books. There are five titles in the type of various Slav tongues and one in French, "Guide des pionniers (Propriété de la Section Culturelle du Conseil Supérieur des Syndicats de l'USSR) N. Kassatkine".

"In spite of the list of printed titles," Shaw comments, "I have not the least notion of who the red lady is: I select her because she looks so Russian and revolutionary, though there is nobody here like her."

The Shaws were seventy-six when, as cheerful as a couple of children off on a picnic, they set out for South Africa aboard the *Carnarvon Castle* in December 1932. It was touch and go that Charlotte ever came back. I got a picture of their ship from G.B.S. on a postcard (with a penny to pay) saying,

"Please send a copy of *Too True* to Colonel Lawrence: address 338,171 A.C. Shaw, R.A.F. Mountbatten, Plymouth" (this a second thought to Lawrence's "Myrtle Cottage, Hythe" address which Shaw had scribbled out: T.E.L. lived there, near Southampton, while testing seaplane tenders). "We are now through the Bay, with almost smooth sea all the time. I haven't missed a meal; and neither of us is any longer qualmish." I posted the play to Lawrence and ventured to ask him for his autograph. "Dear Miss Patch," he replied (from Myrtle Cottage after all) almost by return of post. "Not even an autograph proper, I fear: paper has been short, and to-morrow there will be no proper ink. With the last in the pen I am writing to G.B.S. to say that *Too True* pleases me beyond measure. . . . Hythe keeps me week after week. In Plymouth are some perfectly good books, waiting my return. Here life is too broken for reading seriously. Yet I have done *Too True* three times already, with vast gratification. It is really good, I think. Yours, T. E. Shaw".

I found *Too True* improve with age. In 1932 it bored me a bit, but I liked it much better sixteen years later when Esmé Percy produced it for the Arts Theatre to celebrate Shaw's ninety-second birthday and Cedric Hardwicke spoke a prologue. In the years between the two productions, the stage must have grown more sensitive over uttering "certain disgusting truths", as the chaplain flying ace calls them, "that no lady would throw in the teeth of her fellow creatures". G.B.S. was invited to cut the reference to the idle rich being inefficient fertilisers who do nothing but convert good food into bad manure, and Sweetie's, "if chambermaids were as dainty as you, you'd have to empty your own slops". But the nonagenarian would not relent.

Charlotte's misadventure occurred after they had been some weeks in South Africa. Towards the end of January, G.B.S. had written to me to say that in a couple of weeks they would be leaving Cape Town on a three or four days' car journey to Port Elizabeth from where they proposed to take ship for Durban and home. On February 14 he announced that on the way they had had "a mishap" in which "Mrs. Shaw was so badly knocked about that for a day or two she was as helpless as after her accident in London". In the interval she had begun to mend quickly as "the injuries are only bruises and sprains and a troublesome hole in her shin plus two black eyes"—quite enough, one would say, for a venerable lady of seventy-six. Shaw gave the whole affair an air of mystery. It was just, without any details, a "mishap", and I was strictly enjoined not to tell anyone about it, especially Mrs. Higgs, who then kept house at Ayot.

"Mrs. Shaw," he remarked, "will probably tell Lady Astor only about the accident, which has so far miraculously escaped the press. I got a clout on the jaw and a clip on the knee, both quite negligible. Keep it utterly dark or we shall be overwhelmed with inquiries and reporters. It will be all over and Mrs. Shaw quite well before we arrive."

The reporters won, nevertheless. I was in a nursing home at the time, very ill, and I read all about the accident before the letter arrived; nor was I too worried, for the newspapers said that Shaw's injuries were not serious. What had happened was that G.B.S. had been driving a strange car, with a friend beside him and Mrs. Shaw with some of their luggage in the back seat. Not knowing his car, G.B.S. had pressed the accelerator instead of the foot brake, at the same time turning it, not, as he thought, right, but left, which was the way it went, "leaping," as Shaw said, "a bank and careering into the veldt." His friend told him to brake, which he did with such force that poor Charlotte was thrown forward with some of the luggage on top of her. She was laid up for some time, and at that not fit to do the journey by road. "Any further racketing," as Shaw remarked, "is out of the question," adding, three days later, that travelling for her was not to be thought of; so, "I have cancelled our passages and made up my mind to stay here until the wound in her shin heals, and then remain at a very pleasant place in the neighbourhood called Wilderness until she is quite herself again. The case still threatens to be slow and troublesome. It has not yet taken a decisive turn." The prospect of doing nothing in the meantime was not to be tolerated; so, while waiting for the wounds to heal, G.B.S. sat down and wrote the 17,000 words of *Adventures of a Black Girl in Search of God*. When they were ended and Charlotte was fit to travel they decided that the only way to get to their boat was by air. She had never flown before, and to begin now at the age of seventy-six left her at first, as she told me afterwards, a trifle scared. Then she determined not to be a coward and agreed. Flying delighted her.

"Last Saturday we flew!" she wrote to me. "It was glorious! A perfect day. We flew over two oceans, and back over a chain of mountains—one being Table Mountain. We were about 5,000 feet up, and we went about 120 miles an hour. It is not true to say the country looks like a map: the view was glorious. We were up about 40 minutes. . . . I believe I shall be very sorry to leave!" They even thought of quitting the boat at Marseilles and taking a plane home, "because," said G.B.S. "we have had an hour's flying over the Cape and Mrs. Shaw liked it immensely and no longer dreads it." When they got home and someone asked G.B.S. whether she was any the worse for her accident, "Oh no!" said he. "It took a little time, but on the whole I think she was all the better for it". South Africa, within an ace of being a double tragedy, became a happy memory for them both. "Mr. Shaw," said she, "looks five years younger already."

Not long after their return, G.B.S. was invited to attend a luncheon given by the All British and Empire Nations' Foods Exhibition in London. He was unable to go, but he told me to write and say that in his opinion the nations' foods were wrong foods, and that "the spectacle of this unfortunate little island, like an overloaded locomotive, struggling to drag along an Empire which is sucking her blood", was one which he contemplated with pity and misgiving, and he felt he would be entirely out of place at a luncheon which was intended to create an entirely contrary impression.

Before the year was out they were off again, this time on the *Empress of Britain's* world tour. He got to work at once on *Village Wooing* and finished it in the Sunda Strait. By February he was able to write asking me to "Tell Barry Jackson—but no one else—that my efforts to write resulted in nothing at first but a very trivial comedietta in three scenes for two people which only Edith Evans could make tolerable; but I am now well into a more considerable political play, rather in *The Apple Cart* line, but contemporary. But I cannot hold out much hope of its being any use except to fill up the *Too True* volume into bulk for money."

Four days before, Mrs. Shaw had complained to me from the China Sea of the heat coming down upon them "like a blanket, and seeming to stifle all energy. Mr. Shaw," she said "has written a lot! He has not been really himself, slack and often very tired, but all the time we have been on the ship he has done his morning's work, and there is a lot to show for it. As it is in Shorthand," she added demurely, with a capital 'S', "I am not able to say what the quality is."

So out of the heavy heat of the China Sea emerged this brace of playlets, *Village Wooing*, the "very trivial comedietta", and *On the Rocks*, good to pad out *Too True* "into bulk for money". Neither is a pot-boiler: Shaw never wrote a pot-boiler in his life. He only wrote because he must; and, having written, he had to tidy the result away between book covers. *Village Wooing* had its first production at Tunbridge Wells with Christopher Fry, who wrote *The Lady's Not for Burning*, playing the Man. Sybil Thorndike and Arthur Wontner appeared in it some months later at the Little Theatre. I thought it quite an amusing trifle. Sybil said it was one of her favourite parts, and Ellen Pollock also liked it and, with Walter Hudd as the other "voice", did it both on the stage and by television. This playlet about a cruise is one other example of Shaw's thrift in using up odd bits of life: the idea of it obviously came to him because he himself was cruising and, as I suggested earlier, the Ayot postmistress Mrs. Jisbella Lyth may have completed the outline of the comedietta in his mind.

Charles Macdona, who produced *On the Rocks*, the study of a Prime Minister bound up in red tape, was allowed to get the layout of the Cabinet room at 10 Downing Street for his setting. The play was done into German with the title *England Arise*, Edward Carpenter's hymn, sung by the unemployed in the last act. G.B.S. did not like the first gramophone record made for the purpose. "The record," said he, "began with a very perfect performance by the Wireless Men's Choir. It would have done very well at a concert. The singers were much taken aback when I told them that mobs of the unemployed did not sing like that, and that every man of them must bawl the words in his native dialect at the top of his voice and the bottom of his luck. They threw themselves into it with enthusiasm, and produced exactly the needed dramatic effect, including the cheering. The words did not matter provided 'England, arise' got across."

On the Rocks did not have much of a run, and personally I found it rather dull. Its own preface and its successor, *The Simpleton of the Unexpected Isles*, both toy with the idea of exterminating those who are socially undesirable. It may be that Shaw picked up during his Russian visit this convenient prescription for those who defy established authority. He is always careful to explain that such dissenters are not punished; they are merely liquidated, a distinction which has never appeared to me to be of moment. Either motive leaves you dead; nor is there much question what would have happened during the 1914 war could this power have been exercised by those then in authority who, mistakenly it is true yet emphatically, regarded G.B.S. himself as socially undesirable.

CHAPTER V

LAWRENCE OF ARABIA

It was Augustus John's portrait of G.B.S. that brought
T. E. Lawrence and the Shaws together. The discerning famous
and Augustus John were in considerable demand by one
another in those years. Of Lawrence himself, John did five
drawings and two oils: one of the latter is in the Tate Gallery,
the other in the United States. Lawrence, always impulsive and
kind, offered to get John to do yet another drawing of himself
specially for me. I had asked him to send me a signed photograph and "Not being a film queen," he had replied, "I daren't
send autographs or photographs (and have no photographs!)
to inoffensive persons. They might resent it. However, something must be done. I will find Augustus John and have a
modern drawing made and copied. That will (let's hope) be
flattering to respect, if not to looks."

I fear that I must have grown importunate, for, when the
drawing failed to arrive, I sent Lawrence a reproduction of his
portrait by Orpen, enclosing a stamped and addressed envelope,
telling him that I would be satisfied if he would autograph the
reproduction for me. Lawrence looked upon Orpen as mere
"house furniture", so it was civil of him to respond with:

> Plymouth.
> 20 . 2 . 33.
>
> Dear Miss Patch,
>
> Indeed, the envelope was a kindly thought. Usually I
> have to steal an O.H.M.S. effort!
>
> The portrait is no great shakes. I remember it as better
> than that. Orpen was a bright surface and that's all. Some
> day I'll find in my baggage something better, surely.
>
> I can't write to these wanderers of yours! Somehow the
> feeling that they are nowhere in particular breaks in—
>
> Yours ever, T. E. Shaw.

He wrote across the portrait "Painted in Paris in two sittings
of 90 minutes, which being done by Orpen was the then fashion-

able pastime. We were Peace Conference". And Aircraftsman Shaw carefully altered "Lieutenant-Colonel T. E. Lawrence" to "ex-Lieut.-Col."

I still possess the portrait, not to mention one autographed by Benito Mussolini. But that, as Kipling used to say, is another story, and I anticipate. The portrait of G.B.S. which brought Lawrence to us in Adelphi Terrace was one of which Augustus John had done three copies, naming the result "The Sleeping Philosopher". The Queen bought one copy, I imagine at an Augustus John exhibition. The second was the one which hung in the sitting-room at Ayot. Mr. S. C. (later Sir Sydney) Cockerell, who was to pay the last tribute to G.B.S. at Golder's Green crematorium, wanted the third for the Fitzwilliam Museum, Cambridge, of which he was curator. For a time G.B.S. held out against the idea, but at last he gave in, and, on Saturday March 25 1922, the curator came up to London to collect the portrait from Adelphi Terrace in person. As it happened, he and Lawrence were meeting at lunch to talk over how Charles Doughty's friends could best help him out of a financial tangle in which he had become involved. After they had discussed the purchase for £400 of the manuscript of Doughty's *Dawn in Britain* to present to the British Museum, Sir Sydney mentioned to Lawrence that he had now to walk round to Adelphi Terrace and collect Shaw's portrait; at which Lawrence remarked how much he admired G.B.S. Sir Sydney then suggested that Lawrence should go with him. Lawrence at first refused, because of a rule of his never to meet his heroes, of whom Shaw was one; but when Sir Sydney explained that G.B.S. would have gone off to Ayot for the week-end, Lawrence agreed, and they strolled across Trafalgar Square from the Carlton grill together.

Chance ruled again. For some reason or other, I cannot remember what it was, the Shaws were held up in London that Saturday, and they were just on the point of leaving when, round about three o'clock, Sir Sydney walked in with Lawrence to No. 10. He made the three of them known to each other, and they chatted away for twenty minutes, "friends from the first", in Sir Sydney's opinion, although Shaw and Lawrence were rather more guarded about the encounter. "You did not talk too formidably", said Lawrence later. "We hit it off together fairly well", said G.B.S.

There is a gap between that Saturday afternoon in March

and a morning in the following September when the postman dumped a parcel of 300,000 words upon us. It was Lawrence's history of the Arabian campaign in the 1914 war, the famous *Seven Pillars of Wisdom*. He wanted Shaw to read it, and to say whether it was any use. To read 300,000 words is a mass invasion of anybody's time; and these words were in newspaper type alive with printer's errors. Shaw flinched. In the next ten weeks he had not enough courage to dip more than his toe, so to speak, into the ocean of words. Lawrence became restive; then Shaw took the plunge, and by Christmas wrote to reassure him that this was indeed a great book which he had written. Perhaps Charlotte assisted G.B.S. to that opinion; Lawrence certainly passed on half-humorously to Lady Scott his own belief that it was Mrs. Shaw who had in fact read the proof for G.B.S. Charlotte was ecstatic. Here, she exclaimed, was a masterpiece! She read out bits from it to G.B.S. as he sat ruminating by the fireside. Masterpiece or no, each of them was quick with suggestions to improve it. Lawrence took most of these meekly enough. He has it on record that Shaw corrected his proofs for him and "left not a paragraph without improvement", and it was on Shaw's advice that he cut from the Oxford text the moving introduction where he tells why the men who fought were in a rage with the men who made the peace. "All the subject provinces of the Empire," he had written there, "to me were not worth one dead English boy." It was Shaw too who advised Lawrence on the contract signed with Jonathan Cape.

Charlotte, naturally, viewed the Arab tragedy more lightly than did Lawrence; but to her also he turned a respectful ear. Yet he must have winced when she proposed a preface to the *Seven Pillars* by J. M. Barrie over the way. Lawrence had no time for Barrie or for prefaces; he even evaded the idea of a preface, proffered by Charlotte, from G.B.S. himself. Nevertheless he dutifully accepted her suggestions for alterations in the *Seven Pillars* text. All the proofs came to her in batches, and Lawrence had no more understanding reader than Charlotte, diligently plodding through his 300,000 words. Out of that task of hers arose an intimacy which brought a glow to her later years. He ignored the gulf of time between them, and she became the only woman with whom he was quite at ease; she was probably one of the few who could have told why he became a humble aircraftsman. Regularly, letters came and went between Ayot and his different R.A.F. depôts in England. When he left for India she never missed a mail, and they kept in touch while G.B.S. and she were on their travels. At Whitehall Court I would get letters to forward to Charlotte in Italy or elsewhere, not to mention many a telephone call here and there about this and that.

For one who protested that he loathed letter-writing, the acreage of notepaper covered by Lawrence was prodigious. David Garnett has collected nearly six hundred of his letters, and among omissions noticeable in that volume of 300,000 words are the three hundred others which Aircraftsman Shaw wrote to Charlotte. She refrained from disclosing these to the public gaze, bequeathing the entire collection to the British Museum where they now repose. Of hers to him only a few survive: to keep his R.A.F. living space clear, he had to burn most of them. In addition to the letters, when Charlotte died there were found among her possessions a collection of newspaper cuttings about Lawrence made by her through the years; a copy, finely bound, of the original *Seven Pillars*, printed in the Oxford newspaper office and never published; and one of *Revolt in the Desert*, the abridgment of the *Seven Pillars* made much against Lawrence's own inclinations. This was the only copy, ran an inscription, that he had ever written in.

By the time that the last proofs of the *Seven Pillars* had gone off to the printers, Charlotte was securely installed as the Egeria from whom Lawrence received literary counsel. Two works followed *Seven Pillars*. First there arrived from Karachi instalments of a typed copy of *The Mint*, as Lawrence named his etching of the R.A.F., to be followed by the finished version. It was I, in fact, who performed the last act in the mysterious passage of this latter manuscript from Lawrence in India to his publishers in Bedford Square. The first notes for it had been scribbled five years before on a writing pad, propped against his knee, after going to bed in the R.A.F. Depôt at Uxbridge. It was to lighten the gloom of these earlier chapters that he added his impressions of Farnborough, whither he was transferred to the R.A.F. School of Photography, and of the R.A.F. Cadets' College at Cranwell in Lincolnshire. The book crept along, for Lawrence was a slow and finicking writer; he sorted out the notes at Cloud's Hill, his cottage near Bovington Camp, and took them off with him when he was posted to the R.A.F. Depôt at Karachi where he drafted the book in pencil; typed

out copies from it, and then wrote in ink the final version of
70,000 words, burning, he declared, his pencil draft. When he
told Charlotte about the book, she asked to see it, and instalments of the typed version came to her as Lawrence tapped
them out. The Cranwell section was not forwarded until the
final version had reached England, but both the complete
earlier draft and a copy of this final version were among the
possessions left by Charlotte at Ayot. The reason for the mystery
in which Lawrence enveloped the dispatch of his manuscript
is puzzling. He posted it to Charlotte direct, asking her, when
G.B.S. and she had read it, to send it on, within ten days, to
Edward Garnett, reader to Jonathan Cape the publisher, in
a plain wrapper, and with no indication of who was forwarding
it to him. By the same post he wrote to Edward Garnett
announcing that the manuscript had gone "by an official
by-pass for safety", and asking him to let him know what he
had to' pay on the parcel "if the first receiver does not put on
stamps", which will indicate Lawrence's views upon the
unreliability of womankind. Charlotte did keep the manuscript
for a few days longer than his stipulated ten; but she played her
part in the conspiratorial affair. She was in North Wales at the
time, and the postmark might have given a clue to the sender,
so she tied *The Mint* up in a plain parcel, with a second wrap-
ping addressed to me in London, and I posted it on to Edward
Garnett (correctly stamped), when I had got back from a
holiday I was having.

Charlotte thought *The Mint* a masterpiece, regarding its
conversational obscenities as merely incidental to the main
theme. G.B.S. did no more than, as he said, "sample" it; and
he took it rather primly. Neither of them liked a reference to
Queen Alexandra's funeral which even Charlotte thought
cruel, while Shaw found in it that touch of "the grinning street
arab" which Robert Graves perceived in Orpen's portrait of
Lawrence. Almost in Shaw's own phrase Graves said that the
portrait possessed "a seldom-seen element in Lawrence's
character—a sort of street-urchin furtiveness". Charlotte was
the first to read *The Mint*. To begin with, Lawrence limited its
audience to the Shaws; Edward Garnett; his son David; the
novelist, E. M. Forster, and Sir Hugh Trenchard, as he then
was. But in the succeeding months, and when Lawrence himself had come back to England, it went the rounds. It is on
record that H. M. Tomlinson, John Buchan, Maurice Baring,

Noël Coward and Sir Ronald Storrs were all among its early readers. Shaw remarked that he remembered "the horror of Ronald Storrs that Lawrence had given a copy to a lady and that she had perhaps actually read it". Although the range of what is defined as unprintable was wider in 1928 than it has become with the passing of the years, proposals for printing the manuscript were in fact made at the time. Lawrence toyed with the notion of setting up for it a printing press of his own. G.B.S. wanted twenty copies of it done for record, and although a number were struck in U.S.A., and priced for technical purposes at 500,000 dollars apiece to safeguard the copyright there, Lawrence decided against even a limited publication in this country. He was determined that nothing he had written should leak out: for one thing, he had promised to show Sir Hugh Trenchard whatever he might say about the R.A.F., and Sir Hugh had duly read *The Mint* and did not like it at all. Lawrence would do nothing of which the creator of the R.A.F. did not approve, nor would he publish anything which might conceivably damage the R.A.F. itself. But his main consideration was for his fellow airmen, several of whom appear in *The Mint* by name. They would resent being paraded before the public; therefore, until they had all gone, publication must be held up.

Lawrence the author was rather like a prima donna for ever trilling her last farewell. When he had completed his *Seven Pillars* he vowed that he would never write another line. Then he made notes, mere notes, of life in the R.A.F. They grew into *The Mint*. But never again. Yet I had no sooner popped that MS. into the Post Office than he was off once more, this time on a translation of the *Odyssey*. The test of a true artist is that he should be willing to remain anonymous: the work is what matters. Lawrence's motive was neither a desire for money nor a craving for fame, of which by now he had had more than he relished, but what the Romans diagnosed as a *cacoethes scribendi*, an itch to write. The date he set for the publication of *The Mint* was probably beyond his own expectation of life and he insisted that his name must not appear on the *Odyssey* translation. In one who weighed each word, it is surely astonishing that, when Lawrence had corrected what he wrote, and corrected it again, he should post off the latest batch for suggestions from Charlotte who, after all, was but a talented amateur. As for Charlotte, although all of us were at that time fully occupied in getting the

Collected Edition together, she gladly found the time to run
through Lawrence's translation, underlining bits in red here
and there and posting the result back to Karachi.

Lawrence welcomed these comments upon his prose. For a
writing man he was unusually modest. *The Seven Pillars* fell so
short of what he would have liked it to have been that his final
opinion of it was not high. Although he used words so adroitly,
he was oddly indifferent to misprints, and, like G.B.S. himself,
he never opened a dictionary. Lay-out was the one point on
which he was inflexible. Each page of the *Seven Pillars* must have
thirty-seven lines, beginning with a new paragraph and a small
capital letter, and ending in a solid line running to the right-
hand margin. The point at which a paragraph closed must not
be less than halfway across the line. Division of words at the end
of a line was banned; semicolons were anathema. Yet he
deferred to both the Shaws about what this meticulous lay-out
should contain; some thought, indeed, that he gave way to
G.B.S. too readily, as when he dropped his original preface to
The Seven Pillars. Nevertheless, although he venerated Shaw as
might one who gazed at Everest from afar, he would occasionally venture to indicate a flaw. He felt, for example, that too
much praise had been bad for G.B.S., and in one of his letters to
James Hanley he makes the foolish comment that Shaw is at
last "pedestalled, and not so good as you are".

Now and again he would toss an idea in our direction. Why
not a play about Venus and Adonis, or a biography of Sir Roger
Casement, the Irishman executed as a traitor in the 1914 war?
Shaw may have felt that *Man and Superman* adequately covered
the Venus and Adonis theme; and the Roger Casement proposition was a fantastic one to put to G.B.S. who eyed the whole
Irish rebellion benignantly as a squabble in the corner of the
Universe. He had Roger Casement in correct perspective too,
and I do not suppose that he regarded him as possessing any
more significance than the Chicago anarchists. But just as, years
before, he had rushed to their assistance, so now he rallied to
Casement's. After the latter had been caught landing from a
German U-boat off the West coast of Ireland, they brought him
to England and lodged him in Brixton gaol. There he was seen
by a woman cousin who then came along to the Shaws to find
out whether they could do anything for him. A kind of informal
defence committee, I am told, was thereupon assembled at
Adelphi Terrace. Shaw's advice to them was not to brief counsel

but to let Casement defend himself, acknowledge the facts, and demand to be treated as an Irish patriot and prisoner of war. Casement was a picturesque figure, and the escapade which our Secret Service had neatly scotched was like something out of melodrama: he had been trying to organise Irish prisoners of war in German hands into an Irish Brigade to fight against us. This was all highly romantic, but, suddenly, unpleasant stories began to get around about papers found upon the prisoner in which he described sex perversions of an unusually revolting nature. One side maintained that these papers were private diaries; the other, that they simply gave details of a trial which Casement had attended in South America. Whatever they were, they did not deter G.B.S. Shaw, with his gift for seeing things as they are, accepted the fact that in most individuals the sexes, in varying degree, mingle. "I am as much a woman," he once declared, "as Lady So-and-So is a man: say ninety-five per cent." Again, a broadsheet informed early audiences at Joan of Arc that, although Joan "inspired strong likes, and dislikes, and was not at all bad looking, she had no love affairs", and that "her complete neutrality in this respect was accepted as evidence of her divine mission by her soldier comrades". Shaw also agreed that "passionate attachments of the most devoted kind" between members of the same sex are "common and often very happy". But he would not have it that these attachments sprang from the balance of the sexes in each individual. That was "a fundamental mistake" he assured someone, who asked him for his opinion of Shakespeare and "Mr. W. H." of the sonnets. Attachments founded on the admiration of personal beauty had, he argued, nothing to do with sex. "Mary Pickford, ci-devant World's Sweetheart, was," he pointed out, "the sweetheart of normal women much more than normal men"; moreover, although the adoration of the beauty of children was very common, it was less common in the case of adults "only because beautiful adults are scarcer than beautiful children. Homosexual attachments are of an entirely different order, and are often inspired by damnably ugly persons. . . . The moment you remember the reality and popularity of asexual Mary Pickford love, the veil falls from your eyes and all the nonsense about Mr. W. H. being a Greek catamite to Shakespeare passes away like a bad smell".

Shaw maintained that the only writer on the sonnets who understood them was Lord Alfred Douglas "because his own

case was exactly that of Mr. W. H.: that is, he was an extraordinarily beautiful youth to whom men poured forth adoring
sonnets from sheer love of his beauty. But there is not the
slightest evidence that he was a homosexualist, or that Oscar
Wilde, whose homosexuality fastened on gutter-snipes, was
lying when he compared his affection for Douglas to the affection of David for Jonathan." Shaw and Lord Alfred used to
write to one another. In the American version of his *Life and
Confessions of Oscar Wilde*, Frank Harris had given Lord Alfred
a generous share of responsibility for the whole affair. Lord
Alfred revised the American edition for this country, absolving
himself with equal generosity, and G.B.S. accepted the absolu-
tion in a preface to the new version. Shaw never recanted, even
when the publication of letters from Lord Alfred's father seemed
to confirm the impression given by the appearance of *De Pro-
fundis* uncut. The appropriate receptacle for the letters, said
Shaw, was "the dustbin". The disgust of a man of Shaw's austerity with the irregularities of Wilde and Roger Casement must
have been much more intense than most people's; and the fact
that he could ignore these feelings of his, not to mention the
cruder public uproar, raises him high above the ordinary run of
men. Wilde was no friend of Shaw's, who once dubbed him a
"Dublin snob", yet he was with Wilde before the trial; praise of
him while he was in gaol can be noted in the collected dramatic
criticisms; he sent inscribed copies of his books to him when he
came out. So with Roger Casement. He wrote out his defence
for him. Casement had insisted on having counsel, but, after
sentence of death had been passed, he delivered Shaw's appeal
which was so eloquent that, according to Charlotte, members of
the jury declared that, had they heard it in time, the verdict
might have been otherwise. Perhaps Charlotte's testimony is not
altogether reliable. Both she and Lawrence, who was of Irish
stock, were under the spell of Kathleen ni Houlihan and her
martyrs. Shaw having failed them, Lawrence seems to have considered the idea of writing a memoir on Casement himself, but
Whitehall would not surrender the diaries.

Lawrence was more practical in his suggestions for *Too True
to Be Good* which Shaw read to him act by act. In the first draft
the Colonel asked why Private Meek was not at least a cor-
poral, to which Shaw made Meek reply that he was illiterate.
Lawrence, who was Meek, pointed out that this offspring of his
would not have put it quite like that. So Shaw accepted "Not

educationally qualified, sir"; and, later in the play, he allows Meek, again at Lawrence's suggestion, to describe himself as "intelligence orderly" instead of the "intelligence officer" of the first version. One gets the impression that Lawrence was more satisfied with the play as acted than when he heard it read.

He would discuss with the Shaws the affairs of everyday: their new Lanchester 8, which he liked; their trip to Palm Beach; how the Collected Edition should be presented—he wanted distinctive bindings in green, white, red and black for the novels, plays, essays and dramatic criticism. Charlotte's interest in his writing widened to discussions on books in general. His own preference was for the monumental sort: *Moby Dick*, *Don Quixote*, *War and Peace*, *The Brothers Karamazov* and the like. He did not care for Jane Austen. They went pioneering together among the new books. Charlotte sent him Wells and Conrad, James Stephen, André Gide and Brieux, all of which were passed round among his fellow airmen. He must have taken a small library out to Karachi with him, among them *Saint Joan* in proof, which was stolen from his box there. Fortunately he had left behind in England that copy which G.B.S. had inscribed "Private Shaw from Public Shaw".

While stationed at Karachi Lawrence sent to Charlotte a notebook in which he had written out a private anthology of poems that had pleased him. Music was a further bond. At his cottage in Dorset Lawrence had a splendid library of gramophone records which I once helped to augment by getting on the track for him of a Society formed to record the songs of Hugo Wolf. Elgar was a favourite when he went to Ayot and, for his camp gramophone, Charlotte got him Elgar records and others of Brahms, Delius, Bach, Beethoven, César Franck and Handel. Like Samuel Butler, she herself was devoted to Handel. She also sent Lawrence chocolates from Gunter's, China tea from Fortnum and Mason's; at Christmas, *foie gras* and peach-fed ham to Cloud's Hill; to Karachi, chocolates, cake and *marrons glacés*.

Both G.B.S. and Charlotte went to see him in his cottage, and Aircraftsman Shaw would look in upon them when on leave in London or by motor cycle to Ayot. "I would rather visit them", he told Lady Astor, "than read any book or hear any music on earth"; and to her, again, Charlotte was "as wise as 10,000 of you and me". Lady Astor was Nancy to him. He might stay the night with the Astors at Cliveden, or the week-

end with the Shaws at Ayot, or with other ranks at the Union
Jack Club in the Waterloo Road. When Colonel Lawrence
became Aircraftsman Shaw, many jumped to the conclusion
that the Shaws and he were kinsfolk. The story is fairly well-
known of how, when a clergyman caller remarked how "very
like his uncle" Lawrence was, the latter exclaimed, "A good
idea! That is the name I shall take." There was a similar misapprehension when he was with Barrie and the Hardys seeing
Tess acted down in Dorset and the rumour flew round that he
was Hardy's son by his first wife. Lawrence's solicitude for both
the Shaws certainly equalled that of any son for his parents, and
it was reciprocated by each of them. Although G.B.S. could not
persuade either Mr. Baldwin or Mr. Ramsay MacDonald to
grant Lawrence a pension, it was he who got Lawrence back
into the R.A.F. when he was so distressed over being refused
permission to rejoin that he was quietly contemplating suicide.
I believe G.B.S. would even have gone the length of helping
Lawrence's plan to become a night watchman at the Bank of
England, much as such a destiny would have been in apparent
conflict with any wise direction by the Life Force.

Lawrence on his part had a lively concern for the welfare of
both G.B.S. and Charlotte. He was quite alarmed when Lady
Astor mentioned to him that Charlotte, at her age and in her
state of health, might be going with them to Russia. In the
event, as I have mentioned, she stayed at home, and Lawrence's
relief was complete when G.B.S. returned from the adventure,
for he combined an unshakeable belief in the Soviet experiment
with a lack of enthusiasm for the experimenters. Again, when
Charlotte slipped and broke two bones in Hanover Square, he
pestered both Lady Astor and me for bulletins; and when the
motor accident in South Africa cut off Charlotte's weekly letter
he wrote to me anxiously for news of her.

Myrtle Cottage,
Hythe,
Southampton.
ii. iii. 32.

Dear Secretary-who-may-be-Miss-Patch-but-may-not-

Can you tell me anything of G.B.S. and Mrs. Shaw? They
told me the Llanstephan Castle: and then there was a crash:
and I am wondering. If they are coming by long sea to Southampton I would like to meet them here again . . . but if they

come east coast they will probably cross via Marseilles and Boulogne. Will you let me know how they are please? I have not heard for so long, and am hoping she is not hurt. . . .

Yours ever,

T. E. Shaw.

The Shaws were again out of England when I had to cable to them the news of that other accident which was the last earthly escapade of this human conundrum. Six .years before, when Lawrence came back from Karachi, it was Charlotte and G.B.S. who had sent to him anonymously the motor cycle on which he was killed. His death was Greek tragedy to them. They met it like Stoics.

CHAPTER VI

THEY GO ROUND THE WORLD

LAMENTATIONS ABOUT THE journalists of South Africa, India, the United States and New Zealand came to me from both the Shaws on their trips abroad. From South Africa, it is G.B.S., complaining that the pursuing newspapermen have been "frightful". From Bombay, it is Charlotte: "The drawback, as always, is G.B.S.'s terrible fame. We are really quite victimised—and are so helpless. The hundreds of passengers, when we are at sea, all want to know and talk to G.B.S.! The moment we touch land there is a violent rush from the shore. 'Mr. Shaw! Where is he? We *must* have an interview!' And really we are almost distracted!" As San Francisco comes nearer they warn her that "the arrival will be very arduous, (crowds and welcome!) and excitement and *journalists*. Poor G.B.S. has really suffered cruelly on this trip from journalists!" New Zealand overwhelms both of them. From Auckland G.B.S. writes: "We leave this town tomorrow after five days of public speaking and interviewing which have almost slain me". Charlotte corroborates: "Our five days in Auckland were a continual whirl of people and entertaining and sightseeing and journalists . . . especially journalists!"

Charlotte never got quite used to the publicity which dogged them by land, sea, and air. She would even do what she could to thwart the reporters, and she often said to me that press photographers ought to be fined for publishing pictures without the permission of the subject of them. She would either frown at a photographer or not notice him at all, and then be annoyed by the pictures in next morning's papers. Perhaps she was not photogenic. I once heard G.B.S. tell her that she would not see such villainous photos of herself if she would stop scowling at the photographers and try to smile. But she was naturally reserved, and those of us who knew her well fully appreciated how she must have resented attempts to invade their private lives, although indeed, once they went on board ship, their lives were far from private. While it is true that Charlotte could never

grow accustomed to the newspapermen themselves, she nevertheless got into the way of expecting to find in the papers the
results of their exploits: thus, after the car misadventure in
South Africa, "I wonder," she wrote to me from Cape Town,
"if you are seeing anything about us in the English papers.
We are having a wonderful time. . . ." She did not dislike the
actual publicity for G.B.S. but she would have preferred it
without any invasion of her own privacy. She wanted to be
left alone on holiday, and there were always strange men
rushing round taking photographs or picking up gossip. She
was interested in Shaw's press cuttings until there were so many
of them that they bored her. I had a press cutting book in which
I pasted his own articles and letters to the press. He might
glance through that, or take a desultory interest in the bundles
of clippings that lay around; for he did not go as far as Beatrice
Webb who maintained that it was bad for any successful person
to keep reading press cuttings about himself. What others said,
good or bad, would have small effect on G.B.S. Those who
thought that there was nothing he liked better than to engage
their attention flattered themselves; he valued their opinion of
him much less than they did. He was essentially too diffident
a human being to welcome advertisement for himself; when he
did dabble in publicity it was to draw attention to something
he wanted done: the reform of the alphabet, or the sale of his
belongings at Whitehall Court. Shaw was in fact rather an
innocent at the job. Public interest in his Whitehall Court sale
could easily have been trebled, and, as for his alphabet reform,
he got a negligible response, both from legislators and press,
out of the issue of hundreds of copies of an expensive manifesto
to all Members of Parliament in Britain and Northern Ireland.
The belief that he was as greedy for notice as a film star is
incorrect. He was proud to accept the freedom of Dublin, but
on condition that there should be as little as possible in the
papers about it: in the event, the High Commissioner for Eire,
Mr. Dulanty, went down to Ayot to confer the honour in the
quiet of Hertfordshire. So again he denounced as a "blazing
lie" the extravagant wording proposed for a plaque on 33
Synge Street, Dublin, stipulating that the announcement must
limit itself to "the unquestionable fact that I was born in the
house", with "no inscription of opinion as to merits or de-
merits"; and he had the unveiling ceremony itself cancelled.
The essential Shaw was a modest man.

"I never advertised," he once asked me, and with truth, to tell an inquirer: "advertisement, like success, has been shoved on me". If ever there was a man, said he, who succeeded in spite of his incompetence for helping himself, that man was himself. "I never went after success: it has to come to me, such as it is. . . . I have not made a tenth of the money that was within my reach at the cost of a little business energy and enterprise." He thought nevertheless that the country should be run "by imbeciles like myself, and all the energetic, shoving, self-helping chaps shot".

Shaw was kinder to journalists off the stage than on: I never knew him to be as unfriendly towards any of them as he was to his own loutish reporter in *The Doctor's Dilemma*; although perhaps he failed to be quite fair to the press in the famous incident of Harry Champion which he would repeatedly quote as an example of the low state of British journalism. Harry Champion, well known as a Socialist orator in his day, had been prosing away at a public meeting when, said Shaw, in the middle of a carefully prepared speech he suddenly remarked, "If the entire propertied classes of this country had only one throat, and I had a knife, I would cut that throat", and, having made this dramatic announcement, he promptly called the attention of his audience to the fact that reporters who had not been taking down a word of what he had been saying, now suddenly began "scribbling like mad". And who will blame them? If a bore unexpectedly makes an arresting statement, he surely cannot grumble when it is reported.

Shaw did have his complaints against the press as an institution, but he was invariably friendly to journalists as individuals. When Charlotte's illness held them up in Paris in 1931, he even tried to arrange a flight to London and back to keep an engagement to speak to the Institute of Journalists. When his branch of the more militant National Union of Journalists made an overhaul of its membership, he was the first, at the age of ninety-three, to reply (incidentally slipping up a century on the date of his birth), with . . . "Full Name . . . George Bernard Shaw (G.B.S.). Home address . . . Ayot St. Lawrence, Welwyn, Herts. Business Address . . . 4 Whitehall Court (116) London S.W.1. Tel.: No. . . . Codicote 218. Capacity . . . Free Lance. Where Employed . . . All over the earth. Date of Birth . . . 26 July 1956. Card No. . . . 1636

(Lifer)". One of his unpublished works is a lively survey of the North of Scotland, Orkney and Shetland, from the point of view of the motorist on tour. He sent to the Royal Automobile Club some six thousand words of it which had been passed on to me for transcription, and the R.A.C. risked offering typewritten copies to guide and entertain its members. Shaw's comments were occasionally rather too candid for public distribution. One hotel, for example, "is described by some reckless liar in a Club report", he remarks, "as comfortable. It is on the contrary, incurably uncomfortable. . . . The beds would be repudiated by the most hard-hearted Prison Commissioner"; and, while the proprietors are "amiable and anxious to make their guests comfortable, nothing short of burning down the hotel and building another as unlike it as possible could enable them to carry out their excellent intentions". Or it may be a hotel laundress who is "crazy and sends the washed clothes all over the country to various shooting lodges in mixed parcels according to her erring fancy". Yet again, although Shaw found the proprietor of another hotel, and his wife, to be most friendly, the hotel itself is "serenaded by screaming seagulls and honking steamer sirens. . . . The place is old and incurably musty; the cooking is plain to the verge of ugliness, and is clearly not done in aluminium saucepans; the bedding is penitential. . . ." Still another, in Orkney, "described locally as magnificent, looks as if it had been lifted out of the middle of Birmingham, and, except that it is profusely decorated with stuffed seabirds, its inside carries out that impression". He does not carp for the sake of carping. He found "a very nice little solitary hotel on the lake"; a second, "an eligible resting place", was once "a ducal shooting lodge and would be called a castle in England"; a third is "sacred to the memory of Queen Victoria"; the attendance at a fourth is "unsophisticated and to some extent idiotic, but the atmosphere is obliging and homely and one is happy enough there"; at another hotel the attendance, proffered "by braw Scottish matrons, is unpolished and occasionally turbulent but mostly obliging and efficient. The bedrooms are candlelit; the public rooms have petrol vapour lamps which can be lighted only by experts familiar with the alarming and explosive process". He dislikes candlelight, noting that, "although Loch Inver, which is a mile long, has at each end a river with a fall easily capable of lighting all London, the hotel bedrooms are

candlelit and the big rooms have petrol vapour machines".
Those who see their Shaw as a lithe figure bounding like a stag
from rock to rock may deplore his partiality for lifts: nevertheless he finds that an Orkney hotel "needs only a lift to be one
of the most comfortable hotels in the extreme north". And
practising Communists will receive with regret his distaste for
a common table at meal-times. He never fails to note the detail
with disapproval.

His judgment on the towns is as summary as on their hotels.
Inverness is "neither restful nor comfortable"; Dingwall is "a
horrid little place"; Strathpeffer is "restful"; "Wick is afflicted
with a stupendous smell of herrings", but its harbour is "a sight
worth seeing"; Stromness he finds "very fascinating as you
approach it by sea, but it has no internal attractions whatever";
Kirkwall "has excellent shops, one of the finest cathedrals in
Britain, a delightful situation and is a quite comfortable and
pleasant place for a halt for a week". Crossing to Shetland
"nine hours by sea from Orkney in fine weather", he damns
Lerwick as "an unrestful and rather crowded herring port and
market", but Scalloway is "quiet and pretty" and the island's
drives are "very attractive". Shetland is "a narrow zigzag
between the North Sea and the Atlantic, with many mountain
lakes in the peat moorland". (As its highest hill is some 1,400
feet above sea-level "mountain lakes" is over-generous.) "The
fiords (called voes) and bays occur every quarter of an hour,
either from the east or from the west, and they are all beauty
spots". He had the journalist's knack for appreciating the other
man's point of view. He notes when a locality is "dry (alcohol-
ically)" and wet, commenting that "this would certainly
determine the choice of many of our Members". Some kind of
local option had banished strong drink from Shetland at the
time (the report is made in 1925) and Shaw notes that "the
only drink available (except water) is buttermilk"; but he is
not above the hint that "tourists may carry as much liquor as
they please with them".

As happens in none of the published works that I can recall,
there is conveyed to us in this piece of reportage an unusual
picture of Shaw positively enjoying himself without a thought of
his fifteen hundred words a day. On the mainland there are the
salmon: Conal Falls "make a very pretty Salmon Leap", and
at Shin Falls "the fun of seeing the salmon leaping is in-
exhaustible". There are the Pictish remains, "a remarkable

Pict's House three miles beyond Brora", and "a very remarkable fragment of Pictish building in Strath More". There is the "piper on the premises who startles the guests at dinner by striking up in the kitchen". There is the scenery, "magnificent", "very fascinating", or "intentionally picturesque". There are the people of Shetland with their "good looks, good manners, good health (apparently) and soft speech". In Orkney they "are also pleasant folk"; and as none of them have been "spoiled by extravagant tourists they are neither servile nor rapacious". He revels in his actual driving, urging others to follow him past a notice board and ford a river with an island in mid-stream; commenting by the way that occasionally "the precipices make the driving rather like tightrope walking". None, in short, of the young men from Fleet Street, could better this report of "a leisurely exploring tour, with stops for rest and excursions, in a full sized saloon car (Vauxhall 23-60) driven by a gentleman of experience in mountain driving but on the verge of 70".

Shaw himself would instantly tell good reporting from bad; on one occasion when he assured a London newspaper man that he was no reporter, the latter countered with, "You say that I cannot report; perhaps you would care to come and report my wedding?", whereat G.B.S. sent him the fifteen guineas which he declared he would have had to pay for a new suit to attend the festivities. Another time, Tosti Russel, (he was named after Tosti of the "Goodbye"), then a young reporter with the United Press of America, called at Adelphi Terrace with a list of questions. "This man knows his job," said Shaw to me, telling me to ask Tosti to come back for the answers. After these had been handed over, and Tosti was preparing to go, G.B.S. inquired whether the reporter himself would be making anything out of the resulting article. No, said he; it was all part of his work for the agency, "But," Shaw expostulated, "I could sell it myself to America. You cannot have it unless you yourself are going to make something out of it." So the answers were left behind; but soon Tosti returned with the news that the interview had brought him a rise of £1 a week, and Shaw at once handed over the answers. Tosti went high in the service of the United Press but he never forgot that cub reporter's scoop. Quarter of a century later I got for him from G.B.S. answers to another catechism on international affairs ("*Jamais entendu parler de ce monsieur*", was Shaw's reply to a

question about Ben Hecht). Tosti was generous enough to
introduce them in a Belgian daily paper with, "*Blanche Patch,
sa fidèle secretaire—et celle qui, depuis des années, constitue un rempart
entre Shaw et les centaines de correspondants dans tous les pays du
monde, lesquels, les uns après les autres, écrivent des lettres tour à tour
insolentes, impertinentes ou de reconnaissance (rarement), selon que
Blanche aura réussi à convaincre son maître de leur accorder ou de leur
refuser satisfaction—a bien voulu, une fois de plus, me favoriser. Mais
elle m'écrivit pour me dire que si elle se proposait de lui envoyer mes huit
feuillets, il ne fallait pas compter sur une réponse.*" Tosti had charm;
he invariably welcomed one with a nosegay of pretty flowers,
and, had he only had a less unforgettable name, he might have
remained to the end as firm friends with Shaw as he and I have
been. He happened to find G.B.S. in a testy humour when he
was being rather persistent with another questionnaire, whereat
the Sage lost his temper, an event which did not happen more
than once in a decade. If Tosti Russel had been John Smith he
would probably have been welcomed back next week. As it was
his questions lay unanswered at Ayot.

The Shaws met most of the journalists of other nations when
they set out upon their world cruise on the *Empress of Britain*, a
month or two after they had got back from South Africa. First
they called at Naples, "still both dog tired", as well they might
be at seventy-six, "but picking up slowly. It was unlucky not
to have a few quiet days at sea before being plunged into three
days at Naples". They gazed down the crater of Vesuvius, and
in Egypt, adds Charlotte, "I did some *awful* journeys". There
followed a week of rest at sea, with a quiet time on board at
Bombay while the others scurried across India. "However,"
Charlotte reports, "we have made some delightful friends and
had some delightful moments, and I hope all will be well. We
are better able to protect ourselves now than we were at first."
After Bombay she finds it "too hot even to fill a postcard. It is
curious to be cut off from all our ordinary life. On the whole
we are very well and have enjoyed *some* of it very much! We
have made friends wherever we have been—some charming
people in India—natives. We went up to Kandy in the hills in
Ceylon and had some blessedly cool days and drove in the
jungles and saw some wonderful temples. The excursions the
bulk of the passengers do are amazing: I don't know how some
of the older people live through it! We only pick out a thing
here and there." In spite of that, both of them are obviously

exhausted. At Hongkong there is "kindly entertainment" with Sir Robert Ho Tung, a wealthy industrialist, as one of their hosts: more than a quarter of a century later he was to visit G.B.S. at Ayot, bringing him the gift of a Chinese robe, when they talked over the arrangement of the Chinese scene in *Buoyant Billions*. Charlotte found the cold after Hongkong "most bitter" and faced with dread the journey to Pekin, "after which it will be quieter". The pair of them were clearly becoming bored with their adventure. One symptom is that they are "rather starved for news. G.B.S. has read the *Times Weekly Sup.* you sent from cover to cover." Then, "I am a mere limp rag," says he himself. "We are just escaping from the tropical heat which has enfeebled us since the Red Sea." And there he sits, reading his *Times Weekly* and passing letters on to the ship's stenographer as the *Empress of Britain* bears them forward to Pekin and the Great Wall of China. Solemn Mr. Hsiung who wrote *Lady Precious Stream* was rather depressed when Shaw told him that he went to China to see the "old Wall" and relates how Shaw exclaimed "God help you!" when informed that a famous professor presented to him was "a great educator". I cannot quite follow Mr. Hsiung's other story of "the very polite fellow" who presented Shaw with a pirated copy of one of his own plays which he had translated. G.B.S. afterwards told Mr. Hsiung how greatly he had been impressed by the man's impudence, and, said Mr. Hsiung, Mrs. Shaw thereupon interjected that no Chinese could be so rude, and that it had all happened in Japan. But, "I was ill for a week," Charlotte wrote to me from the Pacific, "and saw almost nothing of Japan." Certainly there has never been an authorised translation of any of the plays into Chinese.

In Pekin G.B.S. had gone to a theatre, where, Charlotte reported back to me, "he picked up a germ and gave it to me". She was ill for a week, and, although Shaw himself threw it off, he slipped just afterwards and hurt his leg. "He is walking about now and our Doctor thinks it is nothing. I tell you because the papers may get hold of it and exaggerate it." "The papers" did in fact miss much more than they ever discovered. There was the battle over which G.B.S. unwillingly presided. He was not often scared. He did own that once, in the latter days of the 1914 war, the raids terrified him "into heartrending palpitations, and I am too lazy to go down into the excellent Adelphi cellars". Here in China, while they were flying over the Great Wall, they unexpectedly found themselves hovering above a battle which raged below. Shaw went dumb until the end of the flight, when "Thank God we're safely landed," he ejaculated.

A single star in the firmament was not enough for G.B.S. I have told how he joined the British Interplanetary Society, aiming at the moon; and he was quite serious about the possibilities not only of doing the trip but of finding the moon inhabited at the end of it. Established physicists he regarded with scorn, attaching no importance to the view usually put forward by "our professional biologists and physicists" that the limits of temperature to which life is subject on this planet are universal limits. "Neither the heat of the Sun nor the cold of the Moon," said he, "raise any presumption that both these bodies are not densely populated by beings adapted to their environment. The fact that men would perish in the Sun is no more to the point than the fact that a monkey would perish at the South Pole." It would have taken an uncommonly determined biologist to quench Shaw's belief in life anywhere; nor would G.B.S. have flinched from acting as the British Interplanetary Society's own messenger had their equipment been there for him. His courage matched his curiosity, and he had a zest for flying. At the time of his adventure in China he had been at it, off and on, for twenty years. I have a Passenger Flight Certificate, dated May 20th 1916 at the London Aerodrome, Hendon, testifying that "Mr. Bernard Shaw was a Passenger in a Flight made this day on a Grahame White biplane (80 h.p. Gnome Engine)", and duly signed "Bernard F. Hale Pilot Aviator". I remember telling him how one Saturday I had gone for a trip from Croydon Aerodrome with Mrs. Webb's niece, Molly Holt, and asking whether he did not hate his ascent. "I never noticed when the thing got off the ground", said Shaw. "I thought we were still taxi-ing when I looked down and saw the railway a hundred feet below me. But I had a qualm when we made the first dive downwards." As for me, although I quite enjoyed it, I shut my eyes tight, and clenched my teeth, and I am not sure if I should care for a long trip. Shaw's first flight, however, was not by plane, but in a balloon. In July 1906 he went up from Wandsworth Gas Works, which I suppose supplied the motive power, in the balloon "Norfolk" with the aeronaut Percival Spencer. It cost £20 for him and the companion referred to in a letter from the

Gas Works telling him how to get there. "There may be," it ran, "a short drive in an open trap to the nearest Railway Station, which might necessitate the use of a light wrap for the lady."

Ladies grew sturdier with the years, and Charlotte herself went flying with him at the age of eighty. Octogenarians, and undaunted, they were exploring the Welsh mountains at the time. They had gone on to Penrhyndeudraeth from Malvern, Shaw himself "rather distracted lately with food and work", wrote Charlotte, apologising for my not having been told of where they were. "It is *amazing* G.B.S. should not have let you know our movements. I can hardly believe it. He is generally so careful of that. . . . No, Mr. Shaw is so absent-minded I shall have to tell you our movements myself!" Their village was a surprising place. They lived in one of three cottages and had to go down a hill to their hotel for every meal. There was "no communication with the outside world. No bells, no telephone, no one living in the cottage. We might be *in extremis* and quite unable to get help. . . ." One can see the pair of them trudging from cottage to hotel and Charlotte's nerves daily getting the better of her. She urges G.B.S. to go home, "but he is mulish and only says 'Wait and see!' . . . We are both well on the whole though grumpsome! The food is very good when you get to it —that's something."

It was the mountains that held Shaw: landscape was wine to him. "I quite forgot to warn you of this move," he wrote to me. "It was a fearful packing and we arrived after a 150 miles drive in a half demented condition. The hotel is a crazy affair; and we swear every day to return home to-morrow; but the mountains are attractive when it is not raining cats and dogs; and we may stay another week." Next day, "the rain was *frightful*; but in the afternoon it cleared and became a series of enchanting pictures of sunshine. We alternate between feeling unable to bear another hour of the place, and planning excursions for next week. . . ." But will I get him the current Airways guide (with precise directions, "opposite the stage door of His Majesty's Theatre", where to find it) because "as our journey back will be a tedious business—two days if we come in the car—I feel tempted to fly if there is any available service within reach."

Meanwhile, Charlotte's misadventure there forgotten, they had again, the year before, faced the voyage out to South

D

Africa, suffering, she wrote, "tortures from cold" for the first
forty-eight hours, after which G.B.S. had gone to it, working
hard *all day* as if he was in harness." "Before turning into the
Mediterranean," said he himself, "we were caught by a hurri-
cane, and had to pass Tangier and scuttle into Gibraltar where
I caught a villainous cold from which I am just recovering.
Smooth seas after the Strait, Palma (Majorca) extraordinarily
pleasant and pretty." Then ("In the Red Sea") "I am
practically rewriting the wretched *Millionairess*."

Charlotte finds Durban "a beautiful city" where they are
"most kindly welcomed and taken to see the sights. . . . G.B.S.
is almost himself again and has at last thrown off the chill he
got on the dreadful ship! We did a little jaunt up country to
Pietermaritzburg and slept the night there. A dear little town,
the capital city of this province. The drive was lovely and the
drive into the mountains still more lovely. . . ." For G.B.S. too
the trip was, on balance, a success. While, as already noted, he
found the newspapermen "frightful", and he had been given
only £108 when cashing a letter of credit for £150, Charlotte
and he "absorbed sunshine enough to last us for some months";
moreover "I bought some shampoo powders in Capetown
which were the best I have ever found."

I had been introduced to *The Millionairess* almost twelve
months before as "the complete draft of a second play in three
acts called *The Millionaress*." It arrived from R.M.S. *Rangitane* on
which, in 1934, they were returning from New Zealand. It was
then that he began omitting the third "i", a mis-spelling which
he had corrected when he told me about it on his way home
from the second South African trip in 1935. The other play
which arrived with the first draft of *The Millionairess* was presented to me as *The End of the Simpleton* "the final title of which",
said Shaw, "will probably be The Unexpected Isles or something like that". It was produced by the New York Theatre
Guild in February 1935. "If Macdona should ask to know the
exact fate of *The Simpleton* in New York give him the figures",
ran Shaw's instruction from the Red Sea. "I presume it has
come off by this time". Macdona, the Charles Macdona who
had staged *On the Rocks*, was, with Esmé Percy as his very able
producer, blessed by theatregoers for the Shaw Players who
toured the provinces in those days.

G.B.S. did not often have to worry out a play as he did *The
Millionairess*. It skims the problem of the man or woman who

must be boss, a kind of prelude to Geneva which expounds the point of view of the totalitarians much more clearly than either Hitler, Mussolini, or Franco was ever capable of doing for himself. Shaw had a weakness for the big man who makes a show of tidying things up, and he could quibble in his defence of the conquerors. Any history, he once told the publisher of an unflattering book about them, which assumes that they killed millions of men, is "obviously nonsensical". Most of them never killed anybody. "They only organised slaughter for multitudes who delighted in it and honoured it. I should have faced Napoleon without the least apprehension; but if I had seen one of his grenadiers coming at me with a bayonet I should have bolted like a rabbit."

He began *Geneva* in the Panama Canal aboard the *Arandora Star* in 1936. During February a note headed "Approaching Miami Beach" came to me, enclosing a Dickens preface. "I have a Morris preface in hand," it said, "but it has not gone far enough to send. No play yet." A second note "Miami Beach, February 10th", brought the Morris preface and the news "We go through the Canal to-morrow. I hope to begin a play there." This was *Geneva*, put on at the Malvern Festival of 1938 with Eileen Beldon, H. R. Hignett, Ernest Thesiger, Cecil Trouncer and Donald Wolfit. After that it ran for more than two hundred nights in London, first at the Saville Theatre, then at the St. James's. Crowds were drawn to it much as they are attracted by a movie star in the flesh. They wanted in those days to hear Hitler, Mussolini, Franco and Chamberlain having it out with one another, and here, by the grace of the Censor, they were. Controversy rattled like a hailstorm on Whitehall Court and Shaw cheerfully took on all-comers, even to the length of placing Adolf Hitler among the great men of the world; for Hitler "had lifted Germany from the gutter, into which the Allies kicked her, into the most dreaded power in Europe; and a man who, himself starting in the gutter, has been able to do that without a single Napoleonic victory must be ranked among the great men (a fabulous species by the way)". Yet even then Shaw felt that Hitler would "have all his work cut out for him to keep out of St. Helena or Chislehurst or Doorn". He was just as fair to the Chamberlains when few outside the Carlton Club, or indeed within it, had much patience with either of them. Neville, he assured a Munich critic, was not a "sinister treacherous personality" but "an honest Liberal capitalist who did the best he

could under the circumstances. He naturally prefers Fascism to
Bolshevism without understanding either . . . and makes his way
through the maze of international politics as a conscientious
opportunist". Austen and he "are the most absurdly and naïvely
sincere statesmen on the face of the globe. Hypocrisy is the last
feat they could possibly perform, even if they thought it necessary for God's Englishmen to resort to such an expedient".

Apart from *The Millionairess* and *The Simpleton of the Unexpected
Isles*, one other playlet, *The Six of Calais*, came on to me from
R.M.S. *Rangitane*, as they returned from New Zealand. New
Zealand captured them both. "When I am dead", Shaw
advised me, "settle in New Zealand. The climate is first-rate."

At first, Charlotte found Auckland "not a very exciting
town", but a week later it is "bright, clean, sunny and happy;
all gay bungalows with brilliant little gardens—a garden city.
I was quite sorry to leave—only G.B.S. was really tired out. . . .
We got a very efficient and capable car which takes *all* our luggage," she writes from Rotorua, "and we have a very superior
young man as chauffeur who is also a 'guide, philosopher and
friend'! On our way down here we stopped one night at a comfortable Government Hostel, in remote hills, to see the mar-
vellous glow-worm caves, and here we are in a really first-class
hotel, seeing geysers and innumerable lakes, and fish in 100's
and 1000's in clear water where they are quite visible. In short
you may think of us 'in clover', for things seem likely to go on as
they have begun." Determined newspapermen compel Shaw to
"strike all cities out of my itinerary until Wellington", where he
sees the work of "a strange old genius Sir Truby King", who
brought down the infant mortality rate to less than half of what
it was in England: "the greatest man in New Zealand," said
G.B.S.

A mishap to one of the ship's engines in mid-Pacific slowed
down the voyage home for two days, then, says he, in a letter
flown from Panama to New York to catch the English mail,
"I have finished the play and begun another and had lumbago;
but our voyage has been remarkably free from mishaps and we
have not yet missed a meal on board". And so they steam peacefully across the Atlantic until met by "a heavily rolling sea" as
they near the Channel. "We hope to find you well," he faceti-
ously concludes, " 'as this leaves us at present: thank God
for it!' "

The play he had finished was *The Six of Calais* which came to me as "the complete draft of a scene called The Burgesses of Calais". During the summer of that year I saw Phyllis Neilson Terry and Charles Carson in it when Sydney Carroll put the playlet on at his Open Air Theatre in Regent's Park. It was probably suggested to Shaw either by Rodin's original group, which he once came across when motoring through Calais, or by the copy of the sculpture in the gardens near the Webbs' place in Grosvenor Road, Westminster. It is good fun with no moral. As with *In Good King Charles's Golden Days*, Shaw's fiftieth play, and the last to be written before the war, the novelty of *The Six of Calais* is that its kings and queens are allowed to behave "like unrestrained human beings". Malvern gave *In Good King Charles's Golden Days* in 1939 with Yvonne Arnaud, Eileen Beldon, Herbert Lomas, Cecil Trouncer, Irene Vanbrugh, and Ernest Thesiger, whom both G.B.S. and Charlotte thought much of, as King Charles, "the best of husbands who rules by his wits".

Shaw's Edward III, Queen Philippa, Charles II and Catherine of Braganza are all likeable creatures, for kings and queens never enraged G.B.S. as they did H. G. Wells. I think he felt rather sorry for them. Somebody once made the foolish suggestion that he should write a biography of King George V. He replied, with some restraint, that he was "the least qualified of anyone on earth" for the job. "We never met," he added; "and he never showed any consciousness of my existence. As he always kept strictly within constitutional limits, nobody not personally intimate with him could do more than produce a compilation of dates of his public appointments, of the most devastating dullness. The only really qualified person is Queen Mary."

At George the Fifth's Jubilee, Shaw himself ventured to direct his sovereign's gaze beyond these constitutional limits when the Authors' Society made His Majesty a loyal offering of books written by their members, all bound in a soft, dark blue leather. Shaw was away on a cruise, so the Society selected *Saint Joan* as his contribution, but when he returned to England he declared that *Saint Joan* would not have been his own choice, and that, if a work of his was to be included, it must be *The Apple Cart*. So the play about the king who dared to be one was hurriedly bound and went off to Buckingham Palace with the others.

Only once do I remember G.B.S. mentioning a meeting with

a member of the Royal Family, and that was at a reception when he did not know until afterwards to whom he had been talking. He had been trying to work out a suitable dress for a character in one of the plays when his eye lighted on a frock he liked. As he memorised the design, its wearer inquired what he was gazing at. Her embroidery, he explained; and it was only later that he got to know he had been talking to the Duchess of York who became Queen Elizabeth. The Queen was "quite a pal" of his, he would tell people on the strength of that encounter.

CHAPTER VII

OUR VISITORS

I HAVE HAD THE luck to know two of the most eminent women born in this country within the memory of anybody now living. One of them was Beatrice Webb; the other, Ellen Terry.

It is odd that, although my father lived to be an old man, and was always on quite friendly terms with all of us, my only specimen of his very excellent handwriting is an envelope on which he has written "Mrs. E. A. Wardell". Inside is a small handbill announcing a bazaar to be held in Winchelsea Rectory garden, on the back of which are the words "I shall contribute £5. Ellen Terry". I have also a letter to my mother, written by Ellen when she was in London, in which she apologises for not having returned my mother's "call" (she mockingly quotes the word) upon her. Again she proffers a £5 note, "a Christmas offering to your Church or to any charity for which you may think fit to use it". Another of her kindly thoughts was to give an order to the village grocer to send her a monthly supply of the coffee he stocked, a brand which she could easily have bought in London. And one winter she wrote to say that every child who needed them was to have a new pair of boots or shoes. The selection of the recipients was left to the discretion of the headmistress of the village school. Ellen Terry's daughter, Edy Craig, with whom we were very friendly, was at that time known to us as Miss Wardell, and I can only suppose that my father, the Rector, ignoring the most illustrious stage name of those days, must have thought that her mother had the same surname. It was Edy who gave me my first lesson in bicycle riding on a machine with bamboo rims which she had brought from America.

I never saw Ellen Terry on the stage when I was a girl, but we frequently saw and heard her rehearsing with Sir (then Mr.) Henry Irving in the meadow beyond the Rectory garden, and it was reported that Irving walked down to the beach, a distance of one and a half miles, one stormy night to watch the effect of a thunderstorm on the sea. Once, when he came with Ellen Terry to an entertainment in the Town Hall, a conjuror named Bosco undertook to hypnotise anyone who would "step up" to the platform. No one came forward until Irving stood up and said "I will give half a crown to any man who will go up". A young man then volunteered to submit himself to the experiment; but he was too much for Bosco who, after making passes over his head, cried "You can't speak, you can't move". The victim looked round at him, said "Yes, I can", rose from the chair, jumped from the platform and received Irving's half-crown amidst great applause.

As there were no motors in those days, and a visit to London was much more of an event than it is now, very few of the Winchelsea people were aware of Irving's fame as an actor: he was known by most as a guest staying with Miss Ellen Terry, and his presence in her house did not lessen the doubts of those ladies who held fast to Victorian taboos about whether a London actress was the sort of person who should be "called on". Evidently they overcame their scruples for she was soon very popular with everyone, and I remember she attended a bazaar which we held in the Rectory garden, subscribing to raffles and visiting every stall. My eldest brother, then an undergraduate at Cambridge, spent many hours helping her with her efforts at photography, and, in later years, when he had taken my father's place as Rector, she wrote to him from America. He had started the restoration of the fine old church, which dates from the reign of Edward I, by removing the ivy from the outer walls, and Ellen had seen a paragraph in an English newspaper denouncing my brother's work as "Vandalism at Winchelsea". The writer of the article said that it was unfair to the many artists who visited the little town, as the removal of the ivy made the church less picturesque for them, ignoring the fact that the walls were being picturesquely split. As far as I remember, Ellen's letter commenced "It is John, isn't it? I entirely agree with you". Another thing which caused some stir was the repairing of the canopy over the tomb of Gervase Alard, Admiral of the Western Fleet under Edward I. Before this could be started the workmen had to open the tomb, and in due course came on the Admiral's skeleton wrapped in lead. News of this find soon got around and sightseers began to arrive. My brother was obliged to tell the workmen, who were probably making profit out of their find, that the exhibition must stop, and the tomb was then surrounded by some sort of hoarding. The last visitor was Lady Maud Warrender. She tried to persuade my brother to let her see the remains, but he succeeded in showing her that it was quite illegal to permit the general public to view bodies buried in consecrated ground, even though they had been buried for many years.

The only stage celebrity who visited us more than once was Martin Harvey, but I never spoke to him until some years after I had been with Shaw, and I can honestly say that when I started working for the latter I knew nothing of his writings, or of the literary and theatre world in which he was such an out-standing figure. He himself told me more than once that this was the reason why we got on so well together, and perhaps he was right. Some of my friends who disliked his writings said they could not understand how I could work for such a man if I did not agree with him. My reply was that it was my job and that I simply did as he directed, just as I made up prescriptions for the doctors for whom I worked though I might at times think they were not treating their patients in what I thought the most suitable way.

One of the advantages of being brought up in a rectory, and my later work in a surgery, was that I learnt how to be at home with all classes; and, as all the world knows, G.B.S. was at ease with anyone. He neither accepted social distinctions nor had he any regard for them, yet he was aware of them and his guests were always chosen in the belief that they would get on well together. So when Einstein lunched with the Shaws in October 1930, Lord Samuel, at that time Sir Herbert, Postmaster-General, and his son, Mr. Edwin Samuel, were asked along to meet him. After lunch Sir Herbert took Einstein off to the House of Commons. That evening, or it may have been the next night, a banquet was given in Einstein's honour at the Savoy with Lord Rothschild in the chair. Mrs. Shaw sat between the Astronomer Royal and H. G. Wells and a speech by G.B.S., to which I am referring at greater length later, was broadcast and heard at Hollywood. He told Einstein that he had made a mess of science. "What does it matter?" Einstein retorted. "That is not your business!"

Another of our visitors from Europe, less well-known, was a Czechoslovakian, Mr. Ignacy Lilien, who brought with him, in

January 1930, the score of an opera he had composed from *Great Catherine*, Shaw's short play written seventeen years before as a picture of life at the Russian Court. The composer came to some sort of agreement with G.B.S. about its production, which was done at Wiesbaden in 1932, and, as far as I am aware, nowhere else, so that Shaw, not being able to go to Wiesbaden, never heard it. He wrote to the composer, however, telling him that he had studied the pianoforte score, but, as he found it impossible to play in twelve different keys simultaneously, and, as, even if he could, the effort would not be like that from an orchestra, he had not succeeded in learning the opera. Nevertheless, he added, he was satisfied that the score would be brilliant and witty enough to do more than justice to his unpretentious little play.

It has been remarked of Shaw that he knew everybody but had few friends, and certainly, at some time or other, he did meet almost everybody who might be said to be anybody. He would never give an appointment to a tourist who simply wanted to include him in a round of sightseeing as if he were the Tower of London or the Zoo or Madam Tussaud's. These he regarded as mere time-wasters; nor was he in the least flattered by their interest. It was one of my duties to make definite appointments for those whom he did agree to receive: in London they were occasionally made for the morning, but latterly at Ayot he saw no one until the afternoon, nor could that long pilgrimage be made on chance. Those who went by car to Hertfordshire, were, at the appropriate seasons, advised to come early "in this light", and when G.B.S. felt that he had had enough of them he would considerately suggest that they must be getting back as it was getting dark, and that they would need to have their car lights on; or, more abruptly, he would just pull out his watch and remark, "Well, I must get back to work". He had no time for bores.

Right up to the end, there was always somebody who wanted to see him. The Soviet story that he was living "lonely and forgotten near London" was one of their stupider myths. He refused, almost with ferocity, to admit that he was lonely, explaining that he had the gift of "solitariness". Save for occasional afternoon visits from friends, he saw very few people, and he usually refused to break the rule against being disturbed during the morning when he was at work.

He did give way when he found that Pandit Nehru, here in

the spring of 1949 for the Conference of Premiers, was only free for a morning visit. They had not met before, and G.B.S. was particularly anxious for a talk with him. The last time Mr. Nehru was in England a meeting had been arranged, but, through some misunderstanding, it did not take place. He now went down to Ayot on his return from Ireland, and, as it happened, I was with Shaw when he arrived. Like the Walrus and the Carpenter, the pair of them "talked of many things", from the religions of India to how many mangoes one might wisely eat. Shaw told Nehru how attracted he had been by the Jain temples which he had seen in India, adding that he was surprised to find so many folk still worshipping idols made in the form of animals. How, he asked, had they first come to be set up in India? Nehru explained that they had been made by Greek refugees in order that they might worship the images they had in their own country. Russia and the likelihood of another war was also discussed. Nehru did not think that Russia was ready for war, and G.B.S., agreeing with him, commented that no one would use the atomic bomb because, like the poison gas of the 1914 war, it would recoil on the user. What was needed, he contended, was a bomb lighter than air which would strike its offensive and then give off fumes. As Shaw had no great turn for scientific exposition, neither of us was quite clear about what he had in mind.

Mr. Nehru admired a bowl of tulips in the hall, and, remarking that he was fond of flowers, he asked me if I would show him round the garden. It was a beautiful spring morning and the garden was at its best, although I must confess that, apart from the statue of St. Joan, on which Nehru made no comment, there was nothing of any outstanding interest. I did not take him to the revolving shelter where at one time Shaw worked in the mornings, because in these latter years he remained indoors and the shelter had been abandoned. Nehru left a basket of mangoes for G.B.S., explaining how they ought to be eaten: it was afterwards reported, with what truth I cannot say, that the gift created an "airlift" of more than 1,000 pounds of mangoes from India over to Europe.

I had intended to return to town in our own car which had gone up to London in the early morning to pilot the visitors through the lanes of Hertfordshire: on a first trip few got to our remote village without losing their way. Nehru, however, protested that it was quite unnecessary for our chauffeur to escort him back, and insisted on my going with him. Naturally, I was only too pleased to accept, and we arrived in good time for Nehru to take a brief rest before going on to Buckingham Palace. He was easy to talk to. As is customary with distinguished visitors to this country, a detective sat with the chauffeur, and Mr. Nehru asked me if I knew why he was called a V.I.P. I had to admit my ignorance, so, with a smile, he explained that he was a Very Important Person. He also pointed out that the Indian flag flying from the bonnet had the same colours as the flag of Eire, though flying in a different direction.

When we had dropped Nehru and his secretary at Claridge's, the chauffeur took me on to my own hotel. But first, after fifty yards or so, he pulled into the kerb, rolled up the Embassy flag, and put a little cover over it. I was disappointed, for I would have liked the people sitting outside my "quiet Kensington hotel" to have seen me arrive with an Embassy flag fluttering at the bonnet. It was the Attorney-General, Sir Hartley Shawcross, who called it "a quiet Kensington Hotel" when he stated the case against John Haigh who murdered Mrs. Durand-Deacon. My table was opposite theirs, and for three years I dined almost within earshot of them. I had been there since my own hotel closed down at the beginning of the war; and a lucky choice it turned out to be, for a bomb on the Alexandra Hotel, which had been offered to me at the time, killed two of my friends who had gone to it instead.

Any acquaintance I had with Haigh was quite a casual one. We might meet now and again at the porter's desk when inquiring for letters; and once, I remember, he asked me for a clue in a crossword puzzle. His trial gave a particular thrill to a schoolboy, the son of an actress who sat with his mother at a table near Haigh's. He sometimes amused himself with one of those irritating toys which emit a bang when dropped on the floor. One day, while at dinner and the toy had been dropped two or three times, Haigh leaned over and said, "If you do that again I'll murder you!" He was an ordinary looking fellow, well-dressed, and in manner what one might call a bit of an exhibitionist. His belief that his sordid murders were the most remarkable in the history of British crime was characteristic. Whether or no he was legally insane is for the criminologists to say; but months before he was arrested I looked on him as an incipient lunatic. Poor Mrs. Durand-Deacon said she found him amusing to talk to, and, being a Christian Scientist and keen on the-osophy, it may be that she regarded her murderer as a possible convert, leading the conversation round to higher things while his mind dwelt grimly on the acid bath he was getting ready for her. As the name passed out of the newspapers, so the curiosity of the mob of sensation hunters ceased to pester us in Kensington.

It was rare in those days for a week to pass without Shaw's name bobbing up here and there. I should say that he grew indifferent to recurring references to what he was about: emphatically he resented those who were impelled to pry, and I can recall only two instances of people who did not want to meet him. One of them was a young lawyer, from the United States. "You can tell Shaw", he said to me, "that I am not one of those who want to see him", a reluctance which was probably mutual. Rudyard Kipling was the other who scorned G.B.S. When Shaw and he were pall-bearers at Thomas Hardy's funeral in Westminster Abbey on January 14, 1928, Kipling, it is recorded, "shook hands hurriedly and at once turned away as if from the Evil One". They would not have shaken hands at all but for the ubiquitous Edmund Gosse who pushed forward and introduced them, which is just what anyone would have expected Gosse to do. G.B.S. wanted to pair with John Galsworthy, but Kipling was alongside him, and Shaw said to me afterwards that he thought the arrangement was very bad stage management as he was so much taller than Kipling. The difference in height may have added to Kipling's exasperation with ideas which he imperfectly understood. One thing which pleased Shaw at this service was the organist's fine rendering of the Funeral March from Saul.

Whenever G.B.S. went to the Festival, he visited Elgar, who lived near Malvern, but Elgar rarely visited us in London. He dedicated his *Severn Suite* to Shaw, although the latter's active interest in music ceased when he gave up his work as music critic. Nor did we, in my time, see much of our neighbour J. M. Barrie. When he did come to lunch he preferred to be the only guest. Perhaps his approach to life and Shaw's were too diverse. As G.B.S., when a dramatic critic, remarked in a notice of *The Little Minister*, Barrie "conceived any discrepancy between his stories and the world as a shortcoming on the world's part and was only too happy to be able to rearrange matters in a pleasanter way".

It has been charged against Shaw that he talked too much:

and doubtless there were occasions when a guest did not get the chance of expounding himself as he would have liked; although, as Chesterton has pointed out, Socrates himself was nothing but a conversationalist. One day I was sitting at lunch between Lady Oxford and Augustus John. Augustus John told us that, when he was painting Montgomery's picture, Monty had said he would like to meet Shaw, and that the latter had agreed to go along to his studio. "I have no conversation," Augustus John remarked to us, "and Montgomery has little, but as we wanted Shaw to talk that was an advantage." "I once heard Arnold Bennett say that Shaw talked too much," I put in. "So he does," Lady Oxford agreed; "but I've no right to say so, I always talk too much myself." What Shaw said to Monty and Monty said to Shaw is known to those three and the Recording Angel. I expect that the two Irish worshippers of work would find themselves fundamentally in agreement. Shaw, I know, was pleased about the meeting. "I come up on Saturday to meet Gen. Monty at Augustus John's," he wrote to me from Ayot. "He is sending a car for me there and back."

In my day Shaw did not see very much of Chesterton though they frequently wrote to each other. G.B.S. reassured an admirer of them both who feared they were not the best of friends that their controversies were merely exhibition spars in which nothing could have induced either of them to hurt the other. Shaw's attention was first drawn to Chesterton by a review of Scott's *Ivanhoe* in the *Daily News*. Here, he thought, was a new star; so he wrote and inquired who he was and where he came from. Some time afterwards Chesterton and Belloc lunched with the Shaws but they did not meet very often. Shaw's set was the Fabian Society; Chesterton's, literary folk whom Shaw avoided, and who, Shaw declared, "loathed" him, although of Chesterton he testified, "I enjoyed him and admired him keenly: and nothing could have been more generous than his treatment of me".

When, towards the end of 1930, Maurice Chevalier came along to Whitehall Court, I could see that he was far from being at his ease: he was indeed exceedingly nervous. Things at once went more smoothly when Shaw, with a certain coyness, opened the conversation by remarking that, although he knew nothing of the making of films, he had written "several" plays. "A few have heard that, Mr. Shaw," Maurice replied, smiling. He had learnt English, he said, from a Durham miner when he was a prisoner in the 1914–1918 war, and he had taught the miner French. Shaw, remembering George Lee Vandaleur, and the "method" by which he had trained his mother's voice, inquired what Maurice's singing voice was like. "Vurry bad", said Maurice, not to be outdone in diffidence. I was afterwards told that, in describing the visit to a friend, Maurice had said that most of the time he had been in London it had been nothing but "Give, give, give"; with Monsieur Shaw it had been "Receive, receive". He meant that people were for ever pestering him for his autograph, his photograph, and to know all about his work, until he met G.B.S., when he had just to listen. He was touched when this spry old gentleman of seventy-four helped him on with his coat.

Once, when he was ninety-two, Shaw himself broke into a duet with a visitor; no other than Gertrude Lawrence. When I drove down to Ayot with her after lunch one Sunday we found G.B.S. still resting. Gertrude, peeping in upon the slumbering Sage, went into raptures over the pink and white of his cheeks and hair. He was now so ethereal that one would scarcely have been surprised to see him float off into the upper air; as he himself remarked to a spiritualist, "You are talking to a man who is three-quarters of a ghost". Presently G.B.S. woke up. Gertrude kissed him, and, although this was their first meeting, as she left he was crooning to her

> "Come little girl for a sail with me,
>   Up in my bonny balloon,
> Come little girl for a sail with me,
>   Round and round the moon!
> No one to see us behind the clouds:
>   Oh what a place to spoon!
> Up in the sky—ever so high,
>   Sailing in my balloon."

Then she joined in and they sang the next verse together. Few can have been audience to so astonishing a duet. A Sunday or two later, Gertrude and I motored down to Ayot once again, this time taking Lilli Palmer with us: Rex Harrison, Lilli Palmer's husband, was to have gone too but he was called away elsewhere. "What did you mean by saying that on the wireless last night?" Shaw greeted Lilli. On the Saturday she had mentioned in "In Town To-night" that she was going down to see him. Newspaper correspondents had not missed the remark, and the result was that five of them had been pestering him on the Sunday morning for permission to be present at the meeting. We were there for about an hour, and unfortunately one of his exasperating humours was upon him. Rex Harrison was then about to put on *Cæsar and Cleopatra* in New York with Lilli as Cleopatra and Cedric Hardwicke as Cæsar. They had a leading artist interested in doing the scenery, unusually important for this particular play; but he, naturally, would not definitely agree until Shaw had actually signed the licence. The artist was considering an alternative commission and a decision had to be given quickly. Shaw was all for the production, but, when asked to sign to that effect, he just dismissed the idea airily with a wave of his hand and a "That's all right!" In short he was being thoroughly and deliberately cantankerous. Over films in the same fashion he would repeatedly make Gabriel Pascal play mouse to his cat. Gabriel, putting it too strongly I thought, used to say it was a kind of sadism: whatever the cause, the effect was most irritating. And Shaw would not budge, yet Gertrude beamed tenderly on him as she twined an arm around him and kissed him once more on our departure.

Like Maurice Chevalier, Leslie Henson was one of the diffident ones. He was rather sad, his brother Bertram told me, because he had never met Shaw. I agreed to do what I could about it, and reported his condition to G.B.S. "Leslie will have to take his chance of finding me at home," said he. But one morning, when things were fairly slack, I rang up Bertram and told him that if he could collect Leslie and slip round they would have a good chance of seeing Shaw. Leslie was in the middle of an audition, but they were at Whitehall Court within half an hour, Leslie slightly nervous. "Mr. Shaw, I don't know what we are going to talk about," he said as he came into the study, "because I agree entirely with everything you have ever written or said." A sweeping announcement which impressed me. Shaw quickly put him at his ease with talk about the future of the theatre and how it would be affected by the cinema, just then ceasing to be silent. As Leslie prepared to go he remarked to G.B.S. that he was neither too blasé to want to meet celebrities nor too old to want their autographs. So Shaw asked me for one of our pink postcards informing collectors that he never gave one. This he ceremoniously signed. "Now let me have yours," said he, with his Irish courtesy, and asked me for a second card. "Agreed. Leslie Henson," the visitor wrote on it.

Among the writers who came to see us were Sean O'Casey and Lionel Britten, the latter a dramatist unusual outwardly and in mind. He had written a play, put on at the Arts Theatre, in which Shaw and other authors kept appearing. G.B.S. was interested in him and sent him to Russia where he was eager to study the art of the film. He came back bitterly disappointed: the Russia he had imagined was not the Russia which awaited him. Offering *Hunger and Love*, said to be his autobiography, to G.B.S., Lionel Britten wrote:

"This belongs to you, first because how much of you has gone to form my mind and what I am, and second because it was only your great and generous nature that helped me out of a world of shadows into the objective sunlight where work can become real among men. You may want to disown it but it is not discreditable to you, for its violence is only the turmoil in humanity which has burst its way up out of all the darkness that there is in the world." The book created some stir and was, I believe, translated into two or three languages.

Most of these callers might be described as casuals. The Shaws' circle of intimates were, in the early days, the Webbs and William Morris; and, latterly, Sir Barry Jackson, Lady Astor, Dean Inge, Lawrence of Arabia, soon to become Aircraftsman Shaw, and Mr. Apsley Cherry-Garrard, who lived at Lamer Park not far from the Shaws at Ayot. G.B.S. and Dean Inge held one another in mutual regard. To Shaw the Dean was "easily one of the first minds in England", and to the Dean G.B.S. was "one of the kindest friends I have ever had". After lunching one day at Whitehall Court, Dr. Inge and his wife left hurriedly in different directions. In five minutes, back came Mrs. Inge to borrow a few shillings. The Dean had gone off with her purse. G.B.S. and he went together on a cruise to Greece, and Shaw remarked of a photograph taken of the pair of them on board that it looked as if Dean Inge was saying to himself "Get thee behind me, Satan!" He gave me a copy of it inscribed "The Temptation". While they were in Athens, a proposal to demolish the little Byzantine church in the Athenian Piccadilly Circus, "almost", Shaw afterwards remarked, "provoked a revolution, though it was a serious obstruction to the city traffic, and though the citizens would have sold the

Erectheum to any American cheerfully for $100". The inference he drew was that the only excuse ever offered for the plunder of "the so-called Elgin marbles" was that the Greeks cared so little about the Acropolis that its fragments were far safer in foreign museums than at home. If, he thought, it could be established that the Acropolis was being carefully protected and that its fragments had been pieced together, the Government, or the municipality of Athens, should appeal to the League of Nations, through Professor Gilbert Murray's Committee, for the return of the Marbles.

The Shaws often stayed at Cliveden with the Astors, and Lady Astor was a frequent visitor to Whitehall Court. She was invariably kind to me, but she once, unintentionally I admit, upset my plans. I had two seats, the best in the Kingsway Hall, for G.B.S.'s Fabian lecture, and had asked a barrister friend to go with me. The day before the meeting, G.B.S. inquired if I would mind exchanging my seat for one on the platform because Lady Astor wished to be present, but could scarcely appear on Shaw's platform, where there was a vacant seat, as she was supposed to be speaking at the Albert Hall. The result was that I had to sit in a hateful position just behind the speaker and chairman.

We saw a lot of Sir Barry Jackson after he had surprised everybody, except himself, by making a success of the whole of *Back to Methuselah* at Birmingham Repertory Theatre. To me he was always generous with seats for shows. On one occasion he gave me three tickets for *Yellow Sands*, the Eden Phillpotts comedy which he nourished from near-flop to record-breaker. One of the two friends who was going with me could not join us, so I handed in the spare ticket at the box office. Just before the curtain went up, the commissionaire came to me with the price of the ticket, which had been sold. My friend and I debated what we should do with the money and she suggested that we should buy chocolates from the attendant. G.B.S., with his stricter sense of economic justice, said no; I should have given it back to the donor. As for Sir Barry, the next time he was putting on a show he rang me up and asked if I would like seats as he thought I might care to do another deal.

William Morris was, of course, before my time, as was Max Beerbohm, from whom G.B.S. gave me a letter with a pen-and-ink drawing of himself and "Where's Lily Elsie the noo?" in the corner, evidently a private joke between the pair of them.

It is written from the Grand Hotel, Venice, announcing the Beerbohms' return to Villino Chiaro, Rapallo, "our fixed abode", and promising that, on the first of their monthly visits to London, "I will write to warn you and Mrs. Shaw that we stand waiting hand in hand for an invitation to lunch with you". The Webbs in my day were the Shaws' oldest friends. Beatrice has told how, in 1899, she and Sidney began to meet "at Charlotte's attractive flat" on Thursdays, "to dine sumptuously between our respective lectures". As they got more and more involved in public affairs, they had less and less time left for visiting, although in later years they would go down to Ayot for the week-end. Despite Beatrice Webb's diary, which is rather waspish here and there to G.B.S., I know that she was very fond of him and had a high opinion of his judgment. When the Webbs wrote their book about Russia, and the other about trade unions, the proofs of both were read by G.B.S. before they were finally passed on to the printer.

Beatrice and Sidney Webb were, as I have said, inseparable. Shaw, on the other hand, would dash off to Russia, or to his Fabian Summer School, or to wherever his mood took him, while Charlotte remained tranquilly by her fireside waiting for him to come back. Lady Astor and she got on well together, and Charlotte saw them off on their trip to Moscow without the least wish to join them. So near a friend, in fact, was Lady Astor to both of them that she felt she ought to have been left in charge of G.B.S. when Charlotte died. She was inclined to think she had great influence with him. I am not so sure: probably he had learned not to contradict her. He seldom contradicted any of us: he let us have our say and placidly went his own way. As for Charlotte, she was happy to leave him dominating the stage while she remained stage manager in the background. "Just let us look at the lion in his den", I remember her whispering as she let Lady Lavery have a passing glance into the study. She called her husband "G.B.S.", as did everyone except his own family, to whom he was "George". Like Hilaire Belloc and Rudyard Kipling, who both had Joseph for a first name, and Arnold Bennett, who was christened Enoch Arnold, Shaw had an understandable æsthetic objection to his. In *Who's Who* he put the "George" in brackets. He would sign cheques and official documents "G. Bernard Shaw", but I never knew him use the full "George Bernard Shaw". All his books are by "Bernard Shaw" simply, and he requested people to refer to him as such.

Although Charlotte was a little stand-offish, she soon got to Christian names with people and I was Blanche to both of them soon after my arrival.

Whether she was always wholly in agreement with G.B.S. is unlikely. Generally speaking, their attitude would be the same because their approach to most questions was identical. I remember that they did differ when Mussolini invaded Abyssinia. G.B.S. admired what Mussolini had done in cleaning up Italy, and believed that the invasion was for the good of the Abyssinians, but, "I cannot agree with you", I remember Charlotte retorting with decision. She was a bit possessive, and she would have been no woman had she never been jealous of Shaw's attraction for other women. Although she never showed it outwardly, I sometimes felt that she was even jealous of the fact that I had to read and transcribe his shorthand. I knew the text of the latest play before she did. The Shaws had not the passion of the Webbs for one another, yet theirs was a tender affection too, and a strong one. A pretty incident at Whitehall Court comes to mind. Charlotte had kept very well until a few years before the war when she fell one day in Hanover Square, cracking a bone in her left arm and her pelvis bone. Indomitable as ever, she had got herself back to the flat before it was discovered that she had injured herself at all. For days the flat, with three nurses running round, was like a nursing-home. But Charlotte was good about illness, and very plucky, and she made a wonderful recovery. The first day she was allowed to get up, one of the nurses wheeled her in an invalid chair into the drawing-room. We were informed when she was installed and trooped in.

"Oh!" she cried. "I feel awful. I think I want to go back again." G.B.S. threw his arms around his wife and murmured a version of the ditty "O Mr. Porter", adapted impromptu for the occasion. The nurse and I stole quietly away.

The two Webbs lived as simply as the two Shaws; more simply in truth. Their aim was power, not possessions. They never had a car, preferring to hire one when necessary. Before the war they gave up 41 Grosvenor Road, where I first met Mrs. Shaw, and took a London flat, as well as their house in Liphook, where the Shaws visited them occasionally. In their later years they withdrew to Liphook altogether. For the last few years of her life, Beatrice Webb, who was about Shaw's age, was far from well, and got very little sleep. Some time before she died, Sidney had a stroke, and there was a nurse in the house for him all the time; but he never got properly about again. When Mrs. Webb died, Mrs. Shaw, who was devoted to her, remarked, much as Lady Astor was to say when she herself passed away, that she was surprised Beatrice had made no arrangements about who should look after Sidney: for myself, I cannot quite see what could have been done in that direction.

The Webbs were not great theatre-goers. They lived to time-table like a couple in a Swiss clock. I suppose they enjoyed it, but, as you read of them dashing off to William Morris to discuss Utopia, it will strike most of us as very dull. I think Beatrice had had a much merrier time in her early life. Only once do I remember the Webbs going gay. When Sidney had become Lord Passfield and was in the Cabinet, they gave a reception at Admiralty House, with a band playing in one room and an excellent tea in another. It was the last time I saw the Socialist Lady Warwick, who was looking charming in grey, with a Duchess of Devonshire hat and a bouquet of pink roses. G.B.S. was not there, of course; even a Government reception at Admiralty House would have been rather too jolly for him. The Youth in *As Far as Thought can Reach* thought it dreadful that the Ancient should go about "never dancing, never laughing, never singing, never getting anything out of life", and advised him to let himself go occasionally and have a good time. I often felt like that about G.B.S.; I don't believe he ever had a thoroughly frivolous afternoon. Like his Ancient, he would feel that these infant gambols would be painful to him, and request to be left alone to meditate.

CHAPTER VIII

WHAT GABBY DID

TWO GABRIELS CAME to us out of Hungary, Gabriel Wells and Gabriel Pascal. Gabriel Pascal was Gabby, concerning whom a legend has arisen about his irruption into the life of G.B.S. As I let him in, I ought to know. He arrived at Whitehall Court in a taxi, just after King George the Fifth's Jubilee celebrations in 1935. The story that Shaw paid for the taxi is a myth. Gabby paid for it himself out of the few shillings he had in his pocket, a circumstance which would not depress him. Money, as the film world was soon to be made aware, or the lack of it, never meant much to Gabriel Pascal. He had no appointment, and we knew nothing of this caller who was obviously a foreigner although he spoke English well. Perhaps his name made Shaw curious to have a ·look at its owner: anyhow, he agreed to see him, and I ushered Gabby into the study. He had come to convince G.B.S. that *Pygmalion* could be made into a film, and that he, and he alone, was the man to do it. G.B.S. never met a human being who entertained him more. Gabby had been an actor; but his height had always barred him from the parts he liked, a Puck who would Othello be. Latterly he had toured the Far East with puppet plays done in shadow on a white screen. He once told me over lunch, cooked by himself in his tiny Duke Street flat, of a prediction, made when he was a youth, by Cheiro who dabbled in the occult. In those days Cheiro, who was to him as a father to an adopted son, had foretold a string of events which Gabby maintained had duly occurred. Among these forecasts was a lucky date, the day, less than a week after their first meeting, on which Shaw had agreed to say whether or no he would agree to Gabby making the Pygmalion film. It was a Friday, and the thirteenth of the month at that, but Gabby was sure of himself. He told G.B.S. that if he had not received his contract by four o'clock in the afternoon he was off to China. As Big Ben struck four, the District Messenger whom we had sent round to Duke Street rang the bell and handed Gabby a large envelope.

Cheiro was right. Gabby, as yet unknown, had swept ahead of all established bidders for a licence to film *Pygmalion*. Not long before, Shaw had written from the *Llangibby Castle* asking me to tell one intermediary in Vienna that he would never consider the outright sale of his film rights in *Pygmalion* or in any other of his plays, and that any licence to produce would be on a royalty basis; to this ruling he always strictly adhered. Until Gabby appeared, all of them had insisted that to make a film of *Pygmalion* as it stood was not practicable: it had too many words. So, said they, the stage version would have to be cut for the picture. To Shaw his original text was Holy Writ. Just as he had always preached that an actor's job was to interpret the part which he, its creator, had imagined for him, and not to use it as the peg for a star turn, so for years he had refused to alter a line for air or screen. The B.B.C. must broadcast the whole of a play or let it be; and *Candida* was his only full-length play which would fit uncut into the ninety minutes or so alloted to plays on Saturday nights. It was not, as has been charged against his generation, that he failed to take the radio seriously. He took it very seriously indeed, vowing that if he were to begin his career again he would prefer cinema scripts and television to the platform. Over several years he did practical work for broadcasting as chairman and guide to the B.B.C. Committee for Spoken English. Experts in phonetics collected for the Committee facts about out-of-the-way words, words with more than one pronunciation, proper names, foreign words done into English; and the Committee decided the pronunciation to be recommended to B.B.C. announcers. Shaw discovered here that "no two speakers have the same vowels any more than they have the same finger-prints", and for once he was beaten when he tried to produce out of these conflicting sounds a standard pronunciation for Americans and British. Apart from the differences between Americans themselves, us ourselves, and the two groups of nationals, he found that young people of the age of thirty and downwards "simply refuse to follow the pronunciation of old gentlemen of fifty and upwards". On one occasion he recorded for the gramophone a set of records entitled "Spoken English and Broken English" in which he assured foreigners that if they spoke perfect English the natives would not understand them; but, he remarked to me, he found the gramophone rather a tricky medium because it was essential that the listener should run the record at the same speed as the speaker's voice.

Shaw himself, an ideal broadcaster, was as great a success on the air as any of the regulars: in 1932 he made the first broadcast to be relayed throughout the Union of South Africa. But if in delivery his talks were perfect, in effect they could be unfortunate. Once, when he had advised listeners always to be honest and tell their families the truth about themselves, a man complained that, taking him at his word, he had confessed to his wife that, some years before, he had been unfaithful to her, at which she had broken down entirely; his daughter had almost gone out of her mind; and his son had rushed at him with such violence that he had given him a double rupture. "You, sir," said the man, "just sit in your chair and laugh."

Before he broadcast, Shaw, like others, had to submit a script for approval. On one occasion the B.B.C. asked him to cut a passage from the script. He refused, so the talk was abandoned. For years he stood by his ultimatum that the plays must be broadcast exactly as written for the stage. At last he agreed to minor cuts, finally giving in when *Saint Joan* was done with Constance Cummings as the Maid. I myself have never listened to the complete broadcast of a Shaw play, but G.B.S. himself followed each with an attention so vigilant that he once invited a producer to borrow a revolver and use it on himself.

Shaw's flat objection to altering one word of a play for the screen was also mellowing before Gabby arrived. At first, in the days of the silent film, he would have no truck whatever with the cinema; for, he argued, the silent film killed a play stone dead, and should therefore be applied only to the corpses of plays which had had their run. "Mine," he remarked in his offhand way, "are immortal." Shaw did not think that the early talkies talked; to him they seemed to be just these same silent films with the sub-titles jerked from between the players' lips. He was interested in the talkies as in anything new; he himself was to anticipate by some years the next step forward, for *Back to Methuselah* has its "silvery screen nearly as large as a pair of folding doors" on which the colleagues of the President of the British Isles appear when he presses a button. Although here Shaw saw television on the way, he refused to see it when it did arrive. He would not have a television set at Ayot, and he declined one on loan when they put on *The Devil's Disciple* for his ninety-third birthday. "I'm afraid to look", said he, declaring that it was bad enough to hear the radio without seeing it too. In the early days of the talkies he was just as determined that they would have no play of his to maul about. It was George Arliss who changed the gabble of the first talkies into the conversation of living men and women, and, converting Hollywood, converted G.B.S. Both he and Mrs. Shaw knew their Hollywood, for they were film-goers like the rest of us, and often in the late afternoons between the wars they would go off to the pictures together. After Charlotte's death, when G.B.S. had withdrawn to Ayot, they put on for him at Welwyn a private show of *Les Enfants du Paradis*, the lengthy French film made during the Occupation. His comment was that he did not know when he had been so bored. My own film-going probably runs back as far as his, for the first film I remember seeing was of Queen Victoria's funeral. They were showing it when I was on holiday at Weston-super-Mare, and I remember how the pianist, thinking he ought to play a solemn tune, strummed a thing which I had heard at home and recognised, which I hope no one else did, as the "Funeral March of an Elephant". The Shaws never missed the film of a Shakespeare play, upon which G.B.S. had usually some caustic criticism. He came off second-best in one encounter with a film boss. Hollywood had driven a flock of sheep into *Romeo and Juliet*, and, a few weeks later, a second Shakespeare picture appeared, again with its flock of sheep. "You made good use of your sheep," remarked G.B.S. "Possibly, Mr. Shaw," the film man retorted, "but there happen to be 3,000 miles between the two studios."

G.B.S., quick to note the transformation in talkie technique begun by George Arliss, was convinced that England could better Hollywood's "casual gangs of American speculators". British International Pictures, first British company to make a talking picture, agreed to co-operate, and, ten years after I joined Shaw, *How He Lied to Her Husband* was made at Elstree with Edmund Gwenn, who had played Drinkwater in *Captain Brassbound's Conversion* and Straker in the first production of *Man and Superman* a quarter of a century earlier. At one Elstree rehearsal Shaw asked Gwenn to put more life into the scrap which enlivens the playlet. "I'll show you!" he, now aged seventy-four, cried to Gwenn; "come on!" And with this invitation Gwenn put him on his back. "You see," said Shaw, getting to his feet, "it's quite easy."

Within a space of twelve months Shaw's attitude to the talkies

notably widened. In 1931 he is proudly telling the Malvern fans
that there is no padding in *How He Lied to Her Husband*; that the
whole of the action takes place in one room; that it does not
jump "from New York to the Rocky Mountains, from Marseilles
to the Sahara, from Mayfair to Monte Carlo". Next year he is
telling Malvern just as proudly how the film version of *Arms and
the Man* has swept the physical and economic limitations of the
theatre out of sight. On the stage the battle of Slionitza has to
be described in a lady's bedroom; on the screen you see the
battle itself, and the flight of the fugitive sheltered by the
heroine; the characters can go anywhere, "upstairs and downstairs, into gardens and across mountain country" with a freedom "impossible in the room with three walls which, however
scene painters may disguise it, is always the same old stage".
Realism had carried the day. As he remarked on seeing
Matheson Lang in *The Wandering Jew*, "The only thing I liked
about it was that they could really burn him in the film". *Arms
and the Man* had been produced thirty-eight years before at the
old Avenue Theatre in London, the occasion of Shaw's well-
known repartee to the galleryite who booed. ("I quite agree
with you, my friend, but what can we two do against so many?")
Sir Bernard Partridge, the *Punch* cartoonist, and A. E. W. Mason,
the novelist, both at that time actors, were the Sergius and
Plechmanoff. When Shaw was at Stresa in 1926 I had a few
sharp words from him for "the Everyman people" from whom
I had sent suggestions for another production. I was asked to
impress upon them that it was no use offering him magnificent
casts before they were engaged and then bothering him, part by
part, "with the cold reality". Robert Loraine and Miss Casalis
would be "all right", and, if there was any question of a transfer
to the West End, "I shall not stand in my own light, but I will
not bind myself beforehand to sanction any foolish arrangement
that may be proposed". The screen version was first shown in
1932, three years before Gabby swooped upon Whitehall Court.
Shaw was as delighted with it as a boy with a toy train. It was,
nevertheless, a poor thing. He was still insisting that the play
must go on the screen as it left his pen; and for lack of backing
it had been shot in Wales instead of abroad where it belonged.
It is true that Shaw was impressed by what had been spent on
it, as many pounds, said he, as any manager could have afforded
to spend pence on the play. But Shaw had not yet met Gabby.
By now, somewhere in Europe, our Hungarian friend must

already have been pondering the plans which were to throw open an Aladdin's Cave.

These first ventures had educated him out of his flat refusal to have any play of his filmed at all, and up to the point of realising that the picture house was more useful to him than the theatre for his various messages to man. What Gabby did was to persuade Shaw to make the plays presentable in the new medium. It was the biggest concession Shaw ever made to anyone. "I went to G.B.S.," Gabby related to us afterwards, "and told him I needed several changes. He smiled and started his Irish fight; and I started my Hungarian fight; and I think the Hungarian is more effective than the Irish because I won. He sent me a wonderful scene which I consider a masterpiece of modern literature." Whether he was an authority on masterpieces of modern literature is neither here nor there. What carried the day was that Gabby believed in Shaw as passionately as he believed in Gabby, whereas Hollywood believed in nothing save its own slickness. Gabby may or may not have been right when he contended that any one of the Shaw plays was superior to anything that all Hollywood's playwrights and scenario writers could produce between them. He was manifestly wrong when he declared that not one of these scenario writers would have had the courage to write those supplementary scenes which he was now persuading G.B.S. to accept as essential: Hollywood would have gleefully fallen upon an entire play and turned it inside out. Shaw for his part regarded Hollywood with scorn and his own work as sacrosanct. Deadlock was complete. Gabby got his own way because his veneration for the plays was clearly sincere, probably higher than Shaw's own regard for all of them in his more pensive moments: for he once remarked that every time he saw a Chekhov play he wanted to go home and burn one of his own. So, although the original understanding was that *Pygmalion* should go on the screen exactly as it left the stage, G.B.S. wavered and at last agreed to write in one or two connecting scenes. It was the beginning of a new fame with the public, and it was to Gabriel Pascal that Shaw owed the fortune which it brought him; for at this particular point in the development of his attitude to the screen it is improbable that Hollywood and Shaw would ever have come to terms.

Gabby's simple aim was to fill up the gaps in the stage story of *Pygmalion*. Camera and microphone now followed Liza in the taxi from Covent Garden to her lodging in Angel Court, and off to bed; they are with her and Higgins' housekeeper while she is having her bath; they listen in to a lesson in phonetics; and they have a rollicking scene to themselves at the Embassy reception. G.B.S. and he discussed the new scenes and sequences together, but Shaw of course would allow no hand save his to touch the actual script which, as finished, was his alone. Each of them made his own contributions to the cast. G.B.S. had seen Wendy Hiller in *Love on the Dole* and stipulated that she should play Liza, while Gabby persuaded Leslie Howard to be Professor Higgins. Curiously, Leslie Howard did not see *Pygmalion* as a screen success; but, because it was Shaw, he agreed to play the part. They invited G.B.S. down to Pinewood studios to celebrate the birth of a real Shaw film. Mrs. Shaw, now eighty-two, felt that the outing would be too exhausting for her, so she stayed at home, asking me to go and see that G.B.S. did not take too much out of himself. I was glad to be there, although, if our octogenarian were to take it into his head to over-exert himself, nothing that she and I together might do would have restrained him; and on the way home he did, as it happened, give me the slip. Both of us expected that Pinewood would put up only a simple buffet lunch for perhaps a dozen people, and that we would then all go off together to have a look at the opening shots. But Pinewood did not accept the occasion any more tamely than Hollywood itself would have done. We found about one hundred guests assembled at three tables running the length of the room, with the notabilities, among them Lady Oxford, Anthony Asquith, and Leslie Howard, ranged upon a platform at one end. It was, in short, an occasion, rounded off by speeches, with reporters there in force to take them, and in particular Shaw's. G.B.S. was not to be cornered. He rose. "Ladies and gentlemen," said he, solemnly, "the toast is Shaw!" and sat down.

There was so much in the studios to whet his curiosity about how things worked that at last I had to remind him we had promised Mrs. Shaw to be home by four o'clock. He did not want to leave, and perhaps he was ruffled by us nagging women and by Pinewood trying to trap him into a speech. Anyhow, when we were well into London he asserted his independence and told the chauffeur to go to Bond Street. He had decided to call at Bertha Hammond's and have his hair seen to. For haircuts in those days he went to the barber in Whitehall Court, but Bertha had charge of his scalp which she massaged once a week with the yolk of eggs, saving the whites to make delicious meringues for her more favoured clients. While this rite was in progress I went off to a telephone box to put Charlotte's mind at ease.

Apart from those opening shots, Shaw did not see *Pygmalion* in the making. Any ideas for improving the original script would be sketched out by Gabby, and the pair of them would discuss the alterations amicably together. With the others who set out to make what seemed to them to be improvements on the film, Shaw, naturally, got most annoyed; and there has been more tinkering with *Pygmalion* than with any other work of his. Mrs. Patrick Campbell began it by having the last act of the play re-written with a love interest. "Absolutely forbid Campbell interpolation or any suggestion that the middle-aged bully and girl of eighteen are lovers", Shaw cabled to the Civic Theatre in Minneapolis when they proposed to put on her version of the play. In Germany and Holland, where the film was finished and on the screen some time before it appeared in England, they exasperated Shaw by departing from the dialogue. It may seem puzzling that in foreign countries a play which depends so strictly on how English is spoken should have proved as popular as it has done; but there would appear to be a general agreement among the nations that the accent in which a woman says something is much more important than what she says. Even in Russia *Pygmalion* ran for more than three hundred nights. Germany was as bold as Mrs. Patrick Campbell, adding a whole scene without consulting G.B.S. Professor Higgins and the Colonel take Eliza to a race meeting where from a grandstand she spies an old friend, an ice-cream seller, having a row with a man, at which she jumps up, clutching her parasol, and goes for him with spirit. In both Germany and Holland the actual photography was beautifully done. The Shaws and I went to see the two versions in private studios and all of us thought them good, although G.B.S. remained annoyed by the tricks they had played with the text. He was especially touchy about *Pygmalion* because there were such nice shades of accent to be studied, and his interest in the way people speak was almost a passion. Gertrude Lawrence once asked me whether I thought he would be likely to allow her to go on the air with a speech from *Pygmalion*, in which she had appeared in America. He was in a cantankerous mood at the time, for they had just done a broadcast of *Candida* which he declared would kill the play for five

years because, said he, the point of some of the dialogue had
been quite lost, and listeners would not want to see it on the
stage. So I told Gertrude that, as I had had enough snubs lately
and did not want to risk another, she herself had better approach
the ogre direct. She did, adding in her winning way that she had
been told he wore mittens and that she was knitting him a pair,
but that she was such a slow knitter she was afraid they would
not be finished much before Christmas. The mittens carried the
day. "Do what you like," said G.B.S. "The only condition is
that I must have the mittens by Christmas." But after the broadcast he sent her a two-page letter telling her that she did not
know anything about Cockney talk and that she had not the
slightest idea what she was trying to do. Gertrude was not at all
cross about it. I have never heard her utter one unfriendly
word about anybody. She was thrilled to have the letter, and
sent G.B.S. several threads from which to choose a colour for his
mittens. He returned one to her and the mittens duly arrived.
Shaw's own acquaintance with accents was not in fact nearly so
exact as one might infer from his Professor Higgins, nicely dis-
tinguishing Lisson Grove's from Hoxton's. His own secretary's
baffled him, perhaps because she has no accent worth noting.
He told me I was one of the few about whom he could not guess
which part of England they came from. Many say that my voice
has an echo of Shaw's Irish accent, and as far as I know I have
not a drop of Irish blood in me. It may be that I have acquired
the accent as in the old days a coachman's face was said to
grow like his master's.

When the Shaws and I went with several of the cast to the
press view of Gabby's *Pygmalion*, Leslie Howard was happy to
find himself mistaken. It was the beginning of a triumph which
went round the world; and from now onwards films of many of
the other plays were constantly being suggested and almost as
constantly abandoned. In these days the presentation of a new
film had not yet developed the elaborate technique of a Society
function, with one lesser Royalty at the least, and presentations
and bouquets and a mob of autograph hunters. I myself did
not see Gabby's next venture until it came to St. Albans while
I was living at Ayot during the war. When war broke out they
had just begun to turn *Major Barbara* into a film at Denham.
It was now thirty-four years since the play had been presented
at the Court Theatre before an audience of highbrows with a
leaven of Salvation Army officers. When in 1929 it was put on

again, with Sybil Thorndike, Lewis Casson and Baliol Holloway in the cast, we had to cope with a rumour that G.B.S. was on his deathbed. Throughout the February of that year he had been busy with rehearsals, and then both Mrs. Shaw and he caught influenza. Fleet Street decided that he was dying, until Shaw himself denied the allegation over the telephone from Whitehall Court. And off he went for the final rehearsals for the first night on March 5 which the pair of them saw with T. E. Lawrence, newly home from India, and Mr. Cherry-Garrard in their box with them. "Don't get him so near dying again," Charles Morgan said to me. "We were all waiting with our obituary notices ready."

When war came, I was in some doubt about whether my duty lay with the film or elsewhere. G.B.S. decided for me. Writing from Frinton, he referred me to "a furious letter" of his in *The Times* which he said would clear up my mind about my duty to my country. Theatres and films, he argued, and truly enough, would be "needed most desperately" for the soldiers on leave and for the evacuated children. I could not possibly be more usefully employed, he assured me, than in helping Gabriel and himself with the *Major Barbara* film to keep the cinemas going. And, as I would be "giving people pleasure instead of helping to kill them", I might give my conscience "a complete rest as to all that". Alerts held up the making of the picture at the least hint of enemy aircraft on the way, but it was practically completed when Shaw went out to Denham to see how the transformed play came out upon the screen. After wheedling three new sequences for *Pygmalion*, Gabby now had G.B.S. well under control. They shortened the play here, and added bits to it there, from no fewer than sixteen new sequences, of which, for lack of screen time, only six could be included, one of them the scene where Rex Harrison, playing Cusins the Oxford professor, is overcome by a glass of vodka. Those who are nearest to a play or a film are frequently furthest from the public. Leslie Howard did not see success in *Pygmalion*. Gabby thought *Major Barbara* the most "universal" play Shaw had ever written. The public agreed with neither of them; and on *Major Barbara* the American public in particular. In America they are not greatly interested in the Salvation Army, and there the film was less popular than the screen appearance of G.B.S., made by him in place of the customary "trailer" to announce the picture. He had already had a gay debut in the talkies; it was, indeed, I who, unknown to him, arranged it all. When Movietone launched out into the new medium they asked me whether I could persuade Mr. Shaw to give one of their short talks running to some seven minutes. I promised to see what could be done about it, at which a stranger 'phoned me up and we lunched like conspirators at Simpson's in the Strand. I then rang up G.B.S. and told him that Movietone were to be in Ayot neighbourhood and would be glad to show him how the new invention worked. He at once agreed; so they collected their equipment and went off to Hertfordshire. The day had opened with rain and I feared that we should have to begin all over again; but at noon the skies cleared, and when I rang the Movietone man up he reported that Shaw had been "wonderful" and that the film was now on its way to the United States whither in the early days talkie films had to go to be developed. G.B.S. had stipulated that he must approve of it before it began its round of the picture houses, and all of us went along to the New Gallery for a pre-view. It was great fun. Shaw began by remarking that, although his face and Mussolini's were somewhat alike, Mussolini could never remove his frown, whereas he was able to do so at will; which he promptly did, beaming out upon the audience. His smile swept the United States. The trailer announcing *Major Barbara's* advent was equally successful. I went with him to Denham when he made it, and although we had an appointment several days ahead they, in the manner of the film world, kept us waiting for more than an hour before they could bring together the correct lamps, the desk at which he should sit, and so on. A few days later half a dozen of us saw the result from the front row of the dress circle in a Watford cinema. As they announced that it was about to come on, G.B.S. whispered to me, "Now watch and you will see my teeth come down". But his denture remained steadfast and the performance was triumphant. The trailer was never shown in this country.

Three whole years of the war were next taken up in making a film of *Cæsar and Cleopatra*, a good picture, in my opinion, although the play is not regarded as one of the best. By now he had accepted the fact that the stiffness of the stage must give way to the flowing movement of the screen. He not only agreed to cuts in the play but he wrote in several scenes to knit the story together. While the film was being done at Denham, Vivien Leigh, the Cleopatra, was working alongside her

husband, Laurence Olivier, who was making his *Henry V* in
the studio next door. Gabby had wanted Sid Field as Britannus
so he brought him along to see Shaw at Whitehall Court. Why,
G.B.S. demanded, did he want to play in his film? "I don't,"
said Sid. "It's Gabriel Pascal who wants me." G.B.S. sent him
off with a copy of the play to read, but Sid could not fit in the
dates when they wanted him at Denham. Now and again Shaw
went over to watch them at work on the new picture: it did not
need to be done regularly for Gabby came to him once a week
with "stills" to show him the picture as it grew. He was elated
to see the limitations of the stage break away into the immensity
of the film. Gabby had certainly let himself go; sending his
people out to Egypt that they might be shown galloping across
an authentic desert with real palm trees all about; buying
£200 worth of sand for his own desert at Denham; building a
platform high beyond the park trees to take the flying leaps of
Cæsar and the others from the harbour wall into the sea. All
the camera equipment had to be lugged up to this platform by
a narrow ladder like a ship's gangway which G.B.S. and I one
day climbed together: when we got to the top it was as if we
were standing upon a flat roof far above the tree tops.

The finished film was shown to the trade at the Odeon,
Marble Arch, which I had remembered attending when it was
first opened as the Regal with all manner of variety turns and
waitresses darting among the guests with sandwiches and glasses
of wine. Our own trade show was followed this time by a
magnificent luncheon put up by Mr. Rank, a celebration which
Shaw missed by being out of town. For the première Queen
Mary herself arrived at the Odeon, creating such a traffic jam
that Gabby appeared too late to be presented. There was a good
deal of chatter about what the film cost to make, a subject on
which I have no exact knowledge, for it was no concern of
Shaw's. Gabby certainly never worried about what he spent
either personally or in business. We found him the most
generous of mortals, showering lovely gifts upon all and sundry
at Christmas or whenever there was the least pretext for giving
somebody something. Whenever he went abroad he would
bring back magnificent boxes of fruit and sweets. To G.B.S.
his usual gift was a fountain pen which was always welcome for
Shaw used a fountain pen regularly, and as regularly, for some
unaccountable reason, ruined it. He gave me a beautiful little
watch, which I still wear; and one afternoon he arrived at the

E

Ritz for tea, half an hour late, with a pair of beige open-work woollen stockings dangling from his arm for me. Such being the nature of the man, it is more than likely that he did spend a great deal more on *Cæsar and Cleopatra* than he need have done. Yet even if the popular estimate of £1,300,000 be correct, it must in justice be remembered that the responsibility was not wholly Gabby's. The war's delays meant time and money; and delays were frequent and various, from air-raid warnings to actors having to leave the set for Home Guard drill. Some of them were at it one afternoon as G.B.S. and I left the studios.

"Hail, Cæsar!" a voice called out from the ranks; and all of them stood to attention as the frail old man passed by.

CHAPTER IX

FOBBING THEM OFF

"Fob them off!" was Shaw's order of the day directed at the mob clamouring for autographs, for prefaces to books not otherwise distinguished, for permission to act the plays, for advice, for appointments, for cash, for promises to open bazaars, speak at dinners, address earnest societies: each greedy for a flicker from the flame. To most of them he was much too polite.

He told a newly married friend that his letters went into two classes. The first were "the ordinary ones" answered by me. The others were special ones reserved for his own hand "in the next moment of intimate leisure and friendship". It was, he said, an excellent plan in theory; the drawback was that, as he never had a moment of leisure "only an occasional pause from exhaustion", the ordinary correspondents got efficiently answered and the friends never got answered at all, even when they made such violent gestures to attract attention as getting married. Again, he calculated that he could have written about twenty additional plays in the time he had spent writing to correspondents; and "if these people had existed in Shakespeare's time, his literary output would have been very much reduced". But he could not answer all of them, and, as we did not possess the "large office and about thirty clerks" which he estimated would be needed to do so, the famous postcards were printed off by the hundred. There was the pink card (latterly it turned blue) for the autograph-hunters, in numbers our greatest pest. Many sent simple scrawls like:

I am an admirer of your plays and have the autographs of Sir M. Campbell and Sir H. J. Wood and would like your autograph. My brother says you would not sign but I says you would and I know you will. I hope you will give it for my present as I soon shall have my 9 birthday.

Your little friend,
XX.

PS. You will not have to pay the stamp money as I have put the stamp in the envellope.

Shaw's eyebrows would seem to shoot up at the autograph-hunters who lay in wait for him in person. I remember one of a party of schoolgirls struggling towards us across the stalls as we left a play at the New Theatre. "Please may I have your autograph?" said she, opening her album. "Certainly not!" snapped G.B.S., "and if you are going to collect autographs you will come to a bad end". "What a frightful nuisance", sighed the child, turning away.

When he was ninety-two he did give in to a woman in Cheshire to whom, eleven years earlier, he had answered, "No; I don't ask for yours"; he now conferred upon her not only his autograph but a birthday photograph of himself taken in the garden. Usually, however, the pink postcard carried a rebuke to the effect that he did not regard "unsportsmanlike requests by strangers to forge his own signature for their benefit as legitimate collecting", adding that he signed enough genuine documents every day to give collectors ample material "for the proper exercise of their peculiar industry", and that his secretary had instructions to return all albums and refuse all applications which ignored this distinction. "Unsportsmanlike" aroused the ire of schoolboys, many of whom protested; so, on my own authority, I altered the reproof to "requests by strangers for his signature". All was peace. Upon occasion, too, if the approach were especially skilful, I might add after "his secretary has instructions to return . . ." and so on, "but she sometimes obliges if she happens to have a spare signature by her", gumming on an autograph clipped from a returned cheque. Another trick with signatures was to cut from a letter a signature I could not decipher and paste it on the envelope carrying Shaw's reply; or, if I wanted to keep the original letter, I would cover the return envelope with a sheet of carbon paper and trace over the name lightly in pencil. That, I would tell myself, will make him ashamed of his writing; unless he were a bank manager. I have never been able to read the signature of any bank manager: perhaps the intention is that all correspondence must be addressed to the bank and not to individuals.

The economics of signing copies of the books were expounded on another printed postcard. Shaw was often requested by correspondents not personally known to him, he explained, to inscribe his name in copies of his books which they offered to send for that purpose. Many of the requests, made in good faith, were appreciated by him as such; but if he were to comply he would be immediately overwhelmed by applications from speculators anxious to get rich quickly by purchasing his books at shop prices and selling them at the fancy prices which autographed copies commanded. He was therefore obliged to reserve his autograph for volumes which were his spontaneous personal gift, and accordingly he begged to be excused.

A short head behind the autograph hunters, writers in search of a preface were our next affliction. Shaw was patient as ever. He told one of them not to waste time on other authors but to badger the publishers, and let his own light, and not other people's, so shine before men that the publishers would see his good works and put him among the best-sellers. A printed exposition of his point of view called attention to the fact that prefaces by him owed their value in the literary market to the established expectation of book purchasers that they would prove substantial and important works in themselves, and that a disappointment in a single instance of this expectation would destroy their value. A request for a preface by him was therefore, he pointed out, a request for a gift of some months of hard professional work; and when this was appreciated it would be seen that, even with the best disposition towards his correspondents, it was not possible for him to oblige them.

But if Shaw could thus sweep aside those who tried to poach on his reputation, he would go out of his way to help any young writer who might seem to show promise. He advised one of them, who naïvely inquired whether a man could "educate himself to be a writer", to turn over the leaves of a good encyclopædia until he found something that interested him, and then follow that up. It was no use, as Shaw wisely remarked, knowing how to write unless you had something to say; and, if you had, the words would come if you had any literary faculty; "if you have none, you must seek some other method of expression".

Quite a number of these aspirants wanted to know how to write verse. To one of them, very busy with manual work during the day, Shaw made the astonishing suggestion that he should cultivate the habit of talking in rhyme, such as "Molly, you sinner, where's my dinner?" or, "I'm going shopping, down High Street, Wapping". A father sent along some lines "My Irish Daddy" which his daughter had written about the Liffey. Shaw added a verse to it for him.

"At last I went to Ireland. 'Twas raining cats and dogs.
 I found no music in the glens, nor purple in the bogs;
 And as for angels' laughter in the smelly Liffey's tide!
 Well, my Irish daddy said it, but the dear old humbug lied!"

The Sage took a boy's delight in writing doggerel. There are the lines in which he introduces his *Sixteen Self Sketches*,

> "On Shakespeare's portrait
>   Morris ruled
> Ben Jonson was by it befooled. . . ."

and so on. Playing round a similar theme he gets just beyond doggerel with

> "This Bust thou seest here portrayed
> It was by Sigmund Strobl made:
> A master who in daily strife
> With Nature could outdo the life.
> Oh that I could express my wit
> As well in ink as he hath hit
> My face in marble, I'd outshine
> All who have ever penned a line;
> But since I cannot, reader, see
> The genius he has made of me",

which he wrote under a photograph of himself and pasted in the complete Shakespeare put up at Sotheby's auction of the belongings from Whitehall Court. Often he was just childish: as in a parody on "Who Killed Cock Robin"; and in these lines, dated 1880, which I found at the back of a drawer and which he gave to me:

> "In a lone old square a maiden fair
> Concealed rich gifts from fame
> She filled with love's consuming care
> The hearts of all who sought her there
> And Mary was her name.

"Her will controlled both young and old
None ventured to resist her
Her sisters oft she led a dance
And e'en her brother owned her sense
Although he seldom kissed her.

          "Much obliged to you.   Exit Poet".

To whom he wrote them I do not know. Again, he would
scribble rhyming couplets on photographs of Ayot and send
them to Ellen Terry who once lived near the village with
Godwin. One ran

          "Here Ellen, the Shakespearean
                    nailer
          Bought picture postcards from
                    Miss Taylor".

This the local weekly newspaper reprinted with the word
"Terry" after "Ellen". Shaw, then aged ninety-two, swooped
upon the editor, declaring that the surname had been added
because no fewer than three Ellens (Ellen Terry, Ellen
O'Malley and Ellen Pollock) had been eminent in his plays
and suggesting that if the paper wanted to be so informative,
it might, at some local Shakespeare festival, alter Ben Jonson's

          "Sweet Swan of Avon, that on
                    banks of Thames
          Did oft delight Eliza and our
                    James",

          "Sweet Swan of Stratford-upon-
                    Avon that on the bank of
                    the River Thames in London
          Did oft delight their Majesties
                    Elizabeth Tudor and James
                    Stewart."

But the editor shot back that he had quoted the distich just
as the Mutual Broadcasting Corporation had sent it over the
air to America; and for once Shaw was silenced.

He even essayed a clerihew for his Edinburgh printer,

"Mister William Maxwell
The typographical crack swell
Should not have associated
    himself with that old Beaver
By printing his silly play
        called Geneva".

Irresponsible nonsense had an attraction for Shaw which would lure him into correspondence of the most futile sort. He is invited, for example, to put Patricia, Countess of Cottenham, in her place because she stipulates "no Irish need apply" when advertising in the *Morning Post* for a cook and parlour-maid. "Nonsense!" he finds the time to answer. "Patricia C. of C. has just as much right to notify that she objects to Irish servants as I should have to notify a similar objection (if I entertained it) to English servants, or that a cook or housemaid advertising for a situation would have to add 'No Countesses need apply' ". Again, for some reason or other, a commercial firm once reported to him a reproof which they had got from a peer whom one of their clerks had addressed as "Mr. Lord . . ." The peer told the firm to remove his name from their lists "as he is not one of their customers and never will be as long as letters are addressed by them so incorrectly". The firm told the peer that the addressing clerk, "a lady of literary tastes and a particular student of Thackeray's works", had assured them that she was under the impression "that Mr. Lord was a menial in your Lordship's employ, possibly the head gardener or maybe the steward of your Lordship's estate"; with more facetiousness about the packer, "a fellow of lowly birth and of Labour tendencies" who had mistaken the peer's title for the name of a country public-house. The complete correspondence was sent to G.B.S. who took it quite seriously, pointing out that the Sanger brothers were christened Lord George and Lord John, adding, "You seem unfortunate in your clerical staff. My envelope was addressed 'Mr. G. B. Shaw, Playwrite, London' ". A postcard came to Whitehall Court two days later, "Have sacked the lot. Am attending night school."

But he would go to endless trouble in dispensing guidance of a practical sort. He had fifteen hundred words of advice for young playwrights set up in article form, a galley proof of which I posted off to all inquirers. They must not, he warned them, send their plays to anyone but a manager, and certainly not to their favourite playwright in the hope that he might place their work for them. There were six sound reasons against that proceeding: nobody but a manager could produce their play, whereas, if a playwright read it, he might, all unconsciously, absorb and eventually use for himself its main idea; moreover, another playwright knew no more than anyone else what the public could fancy; it was not the playwright's business to be bothered when the aspirant could easily find out for himself what should be done; a manager would be "infuriated" if an established playwright offered a beginner's work in place of his own; no stranger who could deliver the goods needed any introduction, the demand for promising plays being so much greater than the supply; an introduction robbed the manager of "such credit and gratitude as attached to the discovery of a new genius", and to brand himself as a nuisance was "not the best way to begin in a profession for which tact, knowledge of men (especially their weaknesses) and a sense of humour are among the elementary qualifications".

The beginner was advised to go off and join the Society of Authors; next, to have half a dozen copies of his play typed; register one of them; and then to sit down and choose his manager as carefully as he chose the title of his play. He must drop the puling artist asking for sympathy and become the man of business asking another man of business to risk several thousand pounds in a very uncertain speculation. No commercial traveller offered china to an ironmonger, boots to an oyster merchant, or brandy to a Bible warehouse, yet many young authors had been guilty of the folly of sending melodramas to West End comedy theatres, plays about funny fat men to young and beautiful actresses in management, and tragedies to famous comedians. The author ought to be a better judge of where to send his play than any actor-manager. Did not many a comedian among them long for a sentimental part and many a tragedian like to turn clown? Less delicacy, Shaw went on, was needed to approach the commercial manager of a theatre who, although he might hire a theatre for each production as he hired a taxi in the street, generally had some particular taste, delighting, for example, in revues and "unable to understand how any sane mortal can endure a play by Ibsen".

The impatient beginner was warned that there was not, and never had been, a ring of privileged playwrights blocking the way to all outsiders. G.B.S. then committed himself to the statement that "no commercial manager will produce a play by an unknown novice when he can get one by a playwright of established reputation, out of whose work large sums of money have been made repeatedly". It would, I should say, depend upon the established playwright's play. Shaw had a tendency, which did not weaken with the years, to regard as a winner anything from his pen. He was not always right: to take one example, after he had clamoured for a West End production of *Buoyant Billions*, it came off in five weeks. But, as he reminded his young playwrights, fortunately for them the number of eminent playwrights was so small that they could not keep the theatres continuously supplied with plays, and, whilst the managers were waiting, they must either take any plays they could get as stop-gaps or else close their theatres. So the young author could drive his bargain accordingly. Just as Shaw had no use for publishers, so he had none for literary agents: he accordingly advised the novice to leave the agents alone unless he lived in the country "or even in the Dominion backwoods". No agent, he affirmed, could do more for normally situated authors than they could do for themselves if they had intelligence enough to write a play and sense enough to take their business seriously.

He warned the beginner not to try to get his play produced by underselling his fellow authors. As a matter of business, he agreed, no manager would pay more than the author was willing to accept: and an ignorant or feeble-minded or too eager author might be willing to accept too little if he did not realise his obligations to his profession: but his sacrifice would be as unnecessary as dishonourable, because a manager who had resolved to produce a play would never be deterred by an item so insignificant, relatively to his other expenses, as standard fees to the author. A natural eagerness for production was the bane of young authors but "the experienced playwright who takes his profession seriously does not, when he finishes a play, wait idly, palpitating for its production. He writes another". I can vouch for it that one of them, at any rate, never failed to do so.

This manifesto of Shaw's to young playwrights is a fair example of the understanding with which he would survey a problem. The wit which made him famous was often nothing but an expression of this gift for seeing things as they are and not as others saw them. Thus he told a man who thought his talents

were wasted in the Army that the only solution for one of his
sort was "to find a woman willing and able to keep you as a
household pet on the chance of your proving a genius. It is a rash
speculation for the woman, but not an unhappy one compared
to the average woman's lot, provided she is clear in her mind as
to your being no use as a breadwinner or anything else that is
normal, useful and sensible." High in the scale of our time-
eaters were those who yearned to have their idol before them in
the flesh. "If you wish to preserve your ideals," G.B.S. warned
one of them, "never meet your favourite author face to face. The
poor old gentleman cannot possibly live up to your expectations.
Be wiser next time."

Relatives did not trouble us much; indeed the one of whom
we saw most was a considerable help, a cousin of Shaw's who
would take my place when I was away. She had married and
gone out to Egypt, returning to England when her husband
retired. Not many of the others visited G.B.S., in spite of the
throng of them scattered over the globe. In twenty-two years,
Shaw's grandparents on his father's side had fifteen children.
His cousin Charles calculated that, in Australia alone, descend-
ants of these aunts and uncles numbered two in Western Australia, two in Victoria, one in New South Wales and one in
Tasmania; in which States Charles counted twelve second
cousins and thirteen third cousins. Although G.B.S. possessed
an unexpected and completely detailed knowledge of his family
tree, he had no family feeling for its individual twigs, and
possibly the family were a trifle awed by the later Shaw whom
they had known as "Sonny". Charles tells how a young second
cousin, Freddie, being taken by his father to Adelphi Terrace,
clung desperately to a lamp-post and would not budge, however earnestly his parent might assure him that Shaw would not
eat him. Charles himself, on the other hand, records that his
wife and he "have just returned from lunching with Cousin
Bernard, the most charming and considerate of men". They had
come over from Australia to London for the Silver Jubilee of
King George V, rushing around so much that the excitement
was too great for the poor lady who had a stroke and died.

As the years advanced, those who wanted Shaw to go to them
had a special pink postcard warning them that G.B.S. was now
obliged to restrict his personal activities on the platform to
special and exceptional occasions, mostly of a political kind, and
that he therefore begged secretaries of societies to strike his name

from their lists of available speakers. So also, he requested his correspondents to excuse him from opening exhibitions or bazaars, taking the chair, speaking at public dinners, giving his name as vice-president or patron, making appeals for money on behalf of hospitals or good causes, however deserving, or doing any ceremonial public work. Words flew when this pink card arrived at the address of a literary society on Clydeside; Clydeside went seven times better than Cæsar's Romans who "thrice did offer him a kingly crown which he did thrice refuse". Its tenth summons to G.B.S. brought with it the lure of a forty-guinea fee: in forwarding the pink card, I had therefore to add a note assuring them that Shaw had quite made up his mind not to go to Glasgow, and passing on his suggestion that they ought to keep their forty guineas for a younger man who might need them. The douce president of the society was dumb-founded that G.B.S. should refuse their fee ("nearly £50", he muttered, awestruck) and rattled off the names of "the most famous novelists, scientists, philosophers, and politicians of our day", who had been getting the society's name into the newspapers for them, adding, with the innocent snobbery of that kind of Scot, that even "Edgar Wallace has promised to come on his return from America". He felt hurt that one who could "bask for hours, almost naked on a raft" on the Riviera, and "spend whole evenings with a famous Yankee pugilist" could refuse the more refined relaxation of talking to the Rev. H. S. McClelland and his cronies. He found Shaw's "curt reply" very rude and regretted that G.B.S. could not be "both a genius and a gentleman". Shaw sent off a second postcard, chaffing him in what he took to be the Scots vernacular, whereat the president went whimsy in the Barrie manner, ending with a practical, "Now what about a lecture date for next season?" But Shaw was not to be caught, and Clydeside had to make do with Edgar Wallace.

The foreign stamps from this correspondence of thirty years make a brave collection: for there were not many corners of the earth from which some inquirer had not something to ask. It might be how to find a wife; or would he permit a caricature of himself on the stage; or was Shakespeare a homosexual. Most of them had to be happy with a civil orange-coloured card telling them that though Mr. Bernard Shaw was always glad to receive interesting letters, he seldom had time to answer them, for his correspondence had increased to such an extent that he had either to give up writing private letters or give up writing anything else, under which circumstances he hoped that writers of unanswered letters would forgive him. As for the caricature, Shaw assured its sponsor that, while he was "accustomed to such jokes and quite insensitive to them, it is going too far to expect me to write letters authorising them". Many who were foiled by post tried their luck by telephone, which between the wars would buzz with pointless questions. In the Adelphi Terrace days our telephone number was never in the directory, but at Whitehall Court we all came under one number, and callers would try to get me to put them through to G.B.S. Latterly, when I was in London and he in the country, they would ring him direct at Ayot where he had "Codicote 218" printed on his notepaper. At one time he did not dislike the telephone, but, as he entered the nineties, he found it trying to listen: he would not put the receiver to his ear properly, and he was growing a little deaf, especially for calls from the United States which always came through indistinctly to Hertfordshire. So his housekeeper Mrs. Laden would answer the telephone for him. She knew that he did not care to be disturbed at his morning writing, from which she would only fetch him for anything important. Before he would speak he insisted upon knowing who was on the 'phone, and, "Tell them I have nothing to say", he would ask her to reply if she did not know who was there.

The oddest missives which the postman left for us were a series of badly written letters that did not make much sense, with dirty little packets addressed in the same hand and containing bits of coal and sprigs of ivy. I got in touch with the Chief Constable of the neighbourhood indicated by the postmarks and he traced the packages back to a poor woman who was rather feebleminded. She intended the coal to mean coals of fire and the ivy friendship. From Greek Street, Soho, came another strange communication addressed simply to Sir Bernard Show: "Pleace be kind anaf to see me a Russian Lady. I am you Great Admirer. Please be kind to sper me fife minits".

There was no indication of either town or street, yet the sorter, as with dozens of other unusual addresses, never faltered; indeed, only once can I recall a letter addressed to G.B.S., and not intended for him, coming our way; and that was not the sorter's fault. I opened the envelope automatically and could make nothing of the letter. Then I saw that this time "G.B.S." stood not for George Bernard Shaw but for "Greyhound

Breeding Society"; and that the writer was a man who wanted his dog entered in the stud-book. From Karachi (in an envelope "On Divine Service Only") "George Bernard Shaw Esquire, Philosopher and Writer, London (England)" was easy; and, from Vienna, "Mr. Bernard G. Shaw, Man of letters, Writer, Statesman, Politician, etc., London" was enough. Johannesburg sent a neat effort, "To", then a pen and ink drawing of G.B.S., then "England", a simple one to deliver to Whitehall Court. Many correspondents paid homage on their envelopes: "Grand old Author Playwright" (Denmark); "Greatest English Comedy Writer" (Buenos Aires); "Wit of the World" (The Gag Writers' Protective Association, New York); "Irishman, Care Anybody, Anywhere" (Michigan); "The One and Only: Please Find Him Mr. Postman" (New York); "Author (of all he surveys)" (Beverley Hills); "Critic of Things As They Are" (California). They came from China, Denmark, Germany, Austria, South Africa, Moscow, Brazil, Colombia, addressed to His Excellency Mr. Bernard Shaw, Dr. Bernard Shaw, Hon. Bernard Shaw, or Sir Bernard Schaw, at "Whereever He Lives"; "c/o the great newspaper *Times* (if you please)"; "c/o Hon. Mayor of London"; or "c/o Buckingham Palace". One from a U.S.A. Army lieutenant was for "Mr. George Bernard Shaw, Great Britain" and all the letter said was "Mr. Shaw, I like your plays". A Czech, writing to "His Majesty, Author King, George Bernard Shaw, London, Anglie", and "bowing to kiss his noble hand", remarked "I to be poor eighteen year old, alone learn your language in order i to be Sir Author to write", and requested him to sign "two smal picture".

Now and again some busybody judging himself (or herself) worthy of a response more elaborate than a printed postcard would protest. "A great many people", as Shaw told one of them, "having written once, write a second time to tell me that I might have had the common courtesy to reply to their nice letter. They don't seem to realise that writing is my profession, and that if I wrote to them all my own work would be impossible". Or they might scold me. "Dear Miss Cross Patch", began one such, an Englishwoman living in Germany before the war when she had been a fervid admirer of the Führer. She used to send me articles to lay before G.B.S., and at last I had to tell her that it was useless to bother him with them.

On another occasion a foolish person took up our time by inquiring what G.B.S. thought about lending books. Shaw told me to reply that "nothing suitable to the occasion occurs to him at the moment, and that he does not recommend the lending of books by private persons except as a means of getting rid of them". At this the inquirer conveyed to G.B.S. his belief that Shaw personally "would not have corresponded in such manner", and invited him to "take the time to run thru the letter written by glutton-headed Patch (and a patch job did that party make)". Then there was a commercial institute who regarded me "as one who wantonly veils the light from the eyes of youth," because G.B.S. would not go and speak to them; and there were others who just wouldn't believe that I existed, or anyhow that my name must be assumed. Charles Ricketts, who designed the dresses and stage settings for *Saint Joan*, writing to me on some trivial matter, ended his letter with "What a charming name you have! It suggests a vivacious person in a play by Sheridan." A somewhat different impression was made upon the brother of the Rev. Sylvester Horne, the famous preacher, who told me that if I should ever go to a fancy dress ball it ought to be as a medieval saint with a suspicion of horns and hoofs. Another artist went one further, suggesting that Blanche Patch was an alias for G.B.S. himself, and hoping Shaw would not mind if he used the name "signed on the message from you" for a nom de plume. "I am trying," said he winningly, "to develop a daintier type of illustration which I want to keep distinct from my other work and 'Blanche Patch' would be an ideal name to use as a signature." This artist had a wife "who kept a little mascot in her purse" and was interested in numerology. The lady had worked my name out "and finds it good $9+3$ — the number of artistic expression, so I sincerely hope you will not have any objection to my use of the name. Thanking you for the inspiration." Numerologists rattled Shaw. Another of them who claimed that he had detected a code in the newspapers was reminded that any correspondent who announced the discovery of a cipher was "at once classed as a lunatic and politely evaded or ignored", for he knew people, otherwise sane, who wasted their lives over ciphers, unaware that, as there are only twenty-six letters in the alphabet, the name George Bernard Shaw, or any other name, could be formed by taking the third letter in the titles of Shakespeare's plays, which considerably exceed twenty-six in number. A belief in any sort of cipher, added G.B.S., cut the believer out of his "experienced consideration".

Now and again, some correspondent like the Irish bus driver would write to chide G.B.S. himself. This bus driver was annoyed because he had not seen any comment or sympathy from Shaw on the death of King George the Fifth and "a small word from you would do more than a thousand from Mr. De Valera". Twice, he said, he had nearly run G.B.S. down, and "the next time I shall just pass over you and then get my name in the papers 'the Driver who killed Bernard Shaw'. You were not the only one. I missed Mr. Churchill at Westminster at Mr. Asquith's service. I did not know who he was." Another of the chiders was a solemn creature in whose opinion Shaw ought to be "ashamed to utter such contemptible conceited remarks", when, on being asked whether he had "even a little idea" of what was going to happen during the coming year, G.B.S. replied that he never had little ideas; all his ideas were big ones.

But Orientals were easily the most foolish of our letter-writers. Making every allowance for our irksome English tongue what could be nearer imbecility than:

"Oh, sweet grand Pa! . . . Let me tell you something about me. I am a lady, or, a girl, or, a child, whatever to you, I don't know of 20. We are 9 in number. I mean to say, that I have two more elder sisters and 2 elder brothers and 4 young brothers. My sisters are married. The eldest is the sweet mother of a good family. But poor my second sister! She is the most soft and good in our family. Four years ago she was married, but fate laughed at her. Her husband was a good and reverential man in the home died in the event of the rainy season. Now pa! hear about my poor brother. . . . Now shalln't I ask you anything? I must Grandpa, how is Grand ma? How old is she? I want to know in detail from your pen only. I have promised to my friends that I should show them your pen's signature. I have not to remind you that a promise breaker is a shoe maker. Reply sharp."

Then there was the "noble youthful poet" who wanted to marry into the Shaw family, "a very modest favour", he added. Addressing G.B.S. as "most respectable Mr. Poet" this young man explained that his own works were masterpieces. "I try", he said, "to live according to Goethe's words: 'Man be noble, helpful and good'. I wish to become acquainted to a poet's family. The motive of this wish is to become known to a daughter or a relative lady from whom I should be able to enter into correspondence with same with the aim to offer her a happy marriage. Oh! Would it not be wonderful, if Mr. Poet could indicate me a young lady of his family or relationship? Up to date I have not yet entered into relations with a lady in order that I can confer my undivided sentiments to that lady whom I should marry".

The World's Greatest Spiritual Healer ("cures all kinds of aches and pains on the spot") wrote to his "Respected Dear Precious Holy Soul" to say that "a foreign visitor passing by the land of pride you dwell upon has for a long time carried with him a keen desire to meet you personally before leaving your shores; provided the so established desire be not considered out of the reach of possibility", and he subscribed himself in "a longing hope". More hopeful still was the other native of India "in the direst need of £5,000" to marry off half a dozen daughters and "regain a footing in the world", begging to bring to Shaw's kind notice "that a daughter's marriage at the age of 12 or 13 is compulsory upon a father or guardian and it costs about £200 to £250 per marriage and I have to perform 2 or 3 marriages this year". Fewer of our pests than one would imagine asked for actual cash. G.B.S. had made it pretty generally known that he did not propose to give money away, and in the later years, when he saw his own income being levelled down, he issued a very reasonable protest to those who sought to level theirs up at his expense. But there were enough of them to justify sending out a new pink card after the others begging that Mr. Bernard Shaw should be excused from the appeals received daily "from charitable institutions, religious sects and Churches, inventors, Utopian writers desirous of establishing millennial leagues, parents unable to afford secondary education for their children: in short, everybody and every enterprise in financial straits of any sort". All these appeals, said the new card, were founded on the notion that Mr. Shaw was a multi-millionaire. The writers apparently did not know that all his income, except enough to meet his permanent engagements, was confiscated by the Exchequer and redistributed to those with smaller tax-free incomes, or applied to general purposes by which everyone benefited. Clearly Mr.

Shaw's correspondents could not have his income both ways: in cash from himself and in services from the State. "He does not complain of this system, having advocated it for more than half a century, and nationalised all his landed property; but now that it is in active and increasing operation it is useless to ask him for money: he has none to spare."

For years he had been dealing in a keen yet friendly trade union spirit with the amateur dramatic societies who appealed for leave to perform his plays, and I have already told how he advised them to turn themselves into continuing bodies aiming at a permanent series of performances each season to educate their neighbourhood in the drama. But now yet another postcard (white this time) went round stating that, while private domestic and school class performances of plays were privileged, "if numerous spectators are invited to witness them in large buildings they may damage the Author", and that "admission without payment is not a valid defence in such legal action as may ensue". Any mention of schools filled G.B.S. with dread. Thus, when Rugby invited him to see a cut version of *Captain Brassbound's Conversion*, he retorted that "To tell an author about an unauthorised performance, on a card headed with the emblem of piracy, is audacious. To allow him to witness a mutilated version of his play is to invite murder. I have sent on your invitation card to Mr. Galsworthy (I presume the card intended for me was sent to him) and shall endeavour to forget a transaction which has so many deplorable aspects". So with a proposal that there should be a school edition of the plays. He would have nothing to do with schools and colleges at any price: "no book of mine shall ever with my consent be that damnable thing, the schoolbook". Let them buy the cheap editions if they wanted them. By a school edition they meant, said he, an edition with notes and prefaces full of material for such questions as "Give the age of Bernard Shaw's great aunt when he wrote *You Never Can Tell* and state your reasons for believing that the inscription on her tombstone at Ballyhooly is incorrect". The experienced students read the notes and prefaces and not the plays, and "for ever after loathe my very name".

Yet Shaw's hard head did not always win. A Negro once wrote and told us how he had been in England for some years, how very unhappy he was, and how, as he rested his foot on a newspaper while blacking his boot, he saw in it a picture of

G.B.S. and thought he had a kind face. So would Mr. Shaw pay his passage back to wherever he came from?—Jamaica if I remember. G.B.S. thought it over for a day or two and then decided to send the money along. Then there was our friend the sailor. Every six months, for the first three or four years I was with Shaw, a letter would arrive from him, always starting off "Able-bodied Seaman . . ." and always alleging that he had the chance of quite a good job which he could not take because his jacket and vest or his medals were in pawn. With the letter he would enclose the pawn tickets, amounting to a little under ten shillings, for these items, together with a photograph of himself, taken, I imagine, many years earlier. It became a regular routine to post back to him his photograph, pawn tickets, and a ten shilling note.

CHAPTER X

FRIENDS, AND OTHERS, FROM U.S.A.

A PRETTY HULLABALOO would have arisen could Shaw have assembled the Americans whom he liked. Most of them did not acquiesce in things as they are, yet no two would have agreed on how they would prefer the world to be. Mark Twain was one, and Henry George; Lady Randolph Churchill and Upton Sinclair; Gene Tunney and Lady Astor; Charles Frohman and Pola Negri; Henry Wallace and William Randolph Hearst.

Mark Twain came first. "I, who am now in my eightieth year," G.B.S. told an American friend, "was a small boy when I first discovered him; and therefore I have no idea of how he strikes the Bob Sawyers and Huck Finns of to-day. I can only say that I have known great men who have delighted in him as much as I did; and if the younger generations do not agree with us, so much the worse for them."

One of the great men was William Morris, "a confirmed Mark Twainer who rated *Huckleberry Finn* as one of the world's great books and read it over and over again". Shaw himself put Mark as high as Washington and Lincoln, and, when a Mark Twain memorial was mooted, declared that the United States Government must offer it a site worthy of these other two. If it could be carried out (in marble "about ten feet high"), there would be no danger of future generations forgetting him, although, said G.B.S., his type had disappeared with the strange rapidity with which all American types disappeared. "I hope", he added, "his soul goes marching on, and that this old Mississippi pilot may still have a hand in steering America through the rapids."

The boy Shaw had become a youth of twenty-three when he encountered his first group of live American citizens. They were the Edison telephone pioneers; and when Shaw was twenty-three the telephone, for which his affection had grown definitely less cordial seventy years later, was a novelty, "in some sort," as he, with his forward look, remarked when applying for a job with the Edison people, "a tangible part of civilisation." He got the job, which was to persuade people, at half-a-crown for each consent secured, to have telephone poles set up on their property. When he put in his pocket that first half-dollar from the United States even he would have blinked if some crystal-gazer could have seen for him the cascade which was to follow it in the years to come. The half-crown was all he got for six weeks' canvassing, and although in a couple of months he found himself manager of the wayleave department, when Edison and Bell joined telephone forces he seized the chance to quit the business life.

Three years later an American turned Shaw to Communism. When he declared himself a Communist, Americans, and others, might tell themselves that it was only his fun. Shaw, who knew what he believed, had no doubts about it. "I am a Communist," he stated flatly, "converted to that faith by Karl Marx fourteen years before the same thing happened to Lenin." It says as much for the friendly tolerance of the American people as for Shaw's prestige among them that, in spite of opinions which would have kept anybody else loitering around Ellis Island, President Truman could have found it possible to pay tribute to G.B.S. when he died. "The extraordinary eloquence" of one American, Henry George, was what made Shaw, at the age of twenty-six, give up writing novels, divert his attention to economic science, and swept him "into militant Marxism for the next ten years". Henry George had seen, said Shaw, that the conversion of an American village to a city of millionaires was also "the conversion of a place where people could live and let live in tolerable comfort to an inferno of seething poverty and misery". So Henry George proposed that rent should be nationalised by a single tax on land, an idea which he had borrowed from the French reformers of a century before. He came to London to speak about it, and Shaw went to hear him in the Memorial Hall. The effect was similar to that of a revivalist meeting upon a sinner. He left with a copy of the orator's *Progress and Poverty*; and it was this which sent him off to the British Museum to read, as I have already mentioned, Karl Marx's *Das Kapital* in the French translation. Marx convinced Shaw that Henry George's Single Tax was not enough; that rents when confiscated must be used as capital in industry. So on went G.B.S. to socialism and the

Fabian Society. The Fabians also owed their beginnings to the United States, for the Society was born two years later from a split in the Fellowship of the New Life run by an American named Thomas Davidson. Not only Shaw and the Fabians, but, as G.B.S. disclosed when he came home from Moscow, Stalin himself was much in America's debt. The final success of his Five Year Plan, Shaw told an American friend, was the result of practical proposals from the United States. G.B.S. said that he could not answer for the accuracy of the statement that a Pittsburgh firm had actually outlined the Five Year Plan, which he described as "rather like the Salvation Army's Self-Denial Week stretched out to five years"; but he believed that the Plan had been based by the Soviet Government on the estimates of "their American consultants".

"The first general report made by these engineers," Shaw declared, "was submitted by them to London experts before it was delivered, and received some important additions from them. It was so terribly critical of the existing confusion that the London people concluded it would be suppressed; but the partner who handed it in at Moscow told me that within 48 hours the Soviet Government had 10,000 copies in general circulation, besides setting up a loud-speaker campaign to emphasise its lessons."

It is improbable that Shaw himself would have lived happily among his Communists. They would almost certainly have put him away for urging them to forge ahead to something new; for to Shaw Communism was but an incident in the panorama of man on the move. When twelve American Communists were charged with wanting to overthrow the Government, G.B.S. remarked that the Government would have accused St. Peter himself with sedition as well as murder were he not beyond their reach; yet he was backing the twelve for the identical reason that he backed Washington and Jefferson for having advocated the overthrow of the British Government and the march forward to a United States.

The bare bones of Communism were all that Shaw had in common with the Communists. Not one of them came within the circle of the Shaws' own friends, all of whom looked on life less bleakly than the comrades. Upton Sinclair was somewhere between the one group and the other. Mrs. Shaw liked his work, and he posted to her from America each new book as it came out. She sent them off straight away to be bound in two volumes because she found the whole too heavy to hold in her poor hands. Lady Astor was the Shaws' great American friend; indeed throughout Charlotte's later years they saw more of her than of anyone else. Often during the war she would arrive with two or three Americans in a large American car with a Service driver: wealthy though the Astors were, they could get no more petrol than anybody else. When she was leaving after tea one day Lady Astor introduced the woman chauffeur to G.B.S. as the Baroness of somewhere. "Why did you leave her out here?" demanded Shaw. "It is quite all right," the Baroness reassured him. "I had tea in the kitchen with the housekeeper and the maids." "Do you know," I asked one of the maids after the visitors had gone, "who you had to tea with you this afternoon?" "Indeed we do," said she, "and very nice she was too; much nicer than the lady we had the other week who felt it beneath her dignity to have tea in the kitchen."

It was Lady Astor who brought Charlie Chaplin, with his agent Mr. Barton, to luncheon at Whitehall Court. The Shaws had met them at the Astors where, round about the same time, G.B.S. had had the difficult experience of being introduced to an American who was blind, deaf and dumb, the famous Helen Keller. Charlie Chaplin had arrived in England at the beginning of 1931 for the première of *City Lights* which Shaw and he saw together: I was there, too, sitting behind the pair of them. The Shaws gave the luncheon a few days later, with Amy Johnson, Mr. Cherry-Garrard of the Scott Expedition, Mr. and Mrs. Ernest Thesiger and Lord Leitrim to meet the others. In private life Charlie Chaplin was often quiet and serious, although I was told that if a party was inclined to go flat he would suddenly rouse himself and help his host through the sticky period. Possibly the others bored him at Whitehall Court; anyhow he left them over their coffee and came wandering round the flat, looking at the books and the pictures and the view across the river. I took him into the study where he prowled about, scanning the dictionaries and the reference books and foreign versions of the plays. Then his eye lighted on a row of these in English, well worn, with red blotches on the binding, like the marks of a blood-stained thumb.

"Detective stories?" he asked, smiling.

"Rehearsal copies of the plays," I explained. G.B.S. had marked them on the cover with blotches of red ink so that he could pick them out easily, and the margins were covered with the notes he had made when producing and rehearsing the plays.

We had many other visitors from Hollywood, most of them on a skirmish over film rights. That was probably why Mary Pickford went down to Ayot one afternoon, convoyed, I think, by Gabriel Pascal. It was during the war; I was away on holiday at the time, and nothing came of the visit. They were for ever angling for one of the plays as a magnet for some film project or other, but G.B.S. had a clearer idea of what he was selling than did they of what they were eager to buy. In 1928, some years before Gabby whirled into our lives, he sent up rather a crude balloon to attract Hollywood's attention to the film possibilities of *Cæsar and Cleopatra*. It arose from the descent of Pola Negri on Whitehall Court, an event in which I was heavily implicated, for on the following Sunday a newspaper published my picture, declaring that here was a woman who in one day had achieved the distinction of casting fifty press photographers into outer darkness. The news had got around, as news about film stars will, that Pola was lunching with G.B.S. We were besieged. If there were not fifty camera-men, there seemed to be that and more, clamouring from early morning for a picture of the luncheon party as if it were a public festival. All day we mounted guard, and not one of them crossed the threshold. Shaw's schoolboy escapade was to write a report of the visit in newspaper English and offer it to an evening paper where it duly appeared as a gossip feature. The original version, transcribed from his careful shorthand, ran:

"It is an open secret that Pola Negri saw great screen possibilities in *Cæsar and Cleopatra* when it was produced by the Theatre Guild" (his shorthand for "Guild" is written with the hook on the wrong side) "in New York three years ago. It is equally well known that Mr. Shaw's plays have been dismissed so often by the critics as 'all talk' that he has confessed to an impish desire to let them have their way by showing them his plays with the talk omitted. On other grounds, too, Mr. Shaw is known to be a movie fan. Therefore, though the official report is that nothing has been settled, it seems not impossible that Pola Negri's hurried visit to London will not have been in vain. At all events, the conversation can hardly have been confined to the great film actress's famous orphanage in Poland after Sir Almroth left".

"Sir Almroth" was Sir Almroth Wright, the bacteriologist who advised G.B.S. on the details of *The Doctor's Dilemma*. He was also, as Shaw went on to note in his chit-chat, "the implacable Anti-Feminist who declared that the inferiority of women was capable of anatomical demonstration" and "quite the last man in the world any other host would have invited to meet the most famous enchantress in the film world". Sir Almroth left "with every air of having enjoyed himself thoroughly", and, concludes the amateur gossip writer, "Pola Negri followed later, looking triumphant". Only two words of Shaw's original were altered in the published version; and one of them was Pola Negri's married name (the Princess Mdivani) a correction which he himself had anticipated with a question mark. I would have cheerfully exchanged a picture of the gathering for a dictaphone record of their talk.

Several Americans sent G.B.S. presents of cameras and fountain pens. One of the latter was a present from Gene Tunney who retired from the ring as undefeated world heavyweight boxing champion after beating Jack Dempsey. Shaw, who had been going to boxing matches since he came to London as a youth, saw Gentleman Gene defeat Georges Carpentier, and promptly prophesied that he would beat Dempsey. "How do you figure that out?" asked Gene. Because, Shaw replied, of the way he could ride punches: at which Gene explained that he had learned the trick from *Cashel Byron's Profession* which G.B.S. had written after leaving the Edison people and just before the Henry George conversion. Nineteen years later he was to turn his early novel into blank verse as *The Admirable Bashville*, one of his merriest skylarks, with its Mellish, "trainer of heroes, builder up of brawn;" Paradise,

> "a bloke
> What gets his living honest by his fists;"

and Cashel himself, "this soulless mass of beef and brawn," willing to back Bashville "against the world at ten stone six". He had the jargon of the ring all pat. . . . "flush on the boko napped your footman's left . . .;" then the report of the prize fight—

> "The Dutchman let at once, and seemed to land
> On Byron's dicebox; but the seaman's reach,
> Too slow of execution at long shots,
> Did not get fairly home upon the ivory;
> And Byron had the best of the exchange; . . ."

Three years after the victory over Dempsey, the Shaws and the Tunneys brightened for one another a gloomy holiday which the four of them happened to be taking in Istria. "Tunney has just blown in," G.B.S. told me on a postcard announcing their arrival. "We are both very well and getting a real rest," added Charlotte. "The Island is dull, but that is good for us! Mrs. Tunney has been very ill and given us a great fright but we think she will be all right now." They both got bored with the cold and the rain; even G.B.S., now seventy-five, complained, which was unusual for him, of having to walk a mere eighth of a mile, in the teeth of "the bitter bora", from their quarters to the dining-room. "There is nobody here that we know," he told me, "except Gene Tunney. A settled melancholy, peculiar to the place perhaps, devours us." There seemed to be nothing for it but to dash off another play; but Gene came to the rescue. "Mr. Tunney is a most wonderful help," Mrs. Shaw commented, gratefully. "He takes Mr. Shaw off to the polo ground, or the golf course, or sailing, or something, and so keeps him from writing, which is splendid." Through the years they remained in touch with one another: on the day after Shaw's ninety-third birthday Gene went down to Ayot and told him round by round of Mills' fight against Lesnevich the night before. He was astonished that the old gentleman knew as much about each of them as he did, astonished too to find him so hale, "as clear as a bell", in his nineties. Ayot looked like becoming a Mecca for boxing men: Joe Louis too was eager, perhaps not unaccompanied by a press photographer, to make the pilgrimage.

There is something fascinating about the determination with which an American sets out on the trail of a social lion: the only flaw in the technique is a failure to appreciate the quarry's point of view. Long before I joined him, G.B.S. was offered £300, and, as he afterwards put it, "a private fee of £500 from a leader of New York Society on condition that the first words I breathed with American air should be uttered in her drawing-room". He was as little interested in the woman's dollar roll as in the bait laid for him on behalf of William Randolph Hearst. A friend of Mr. Hearst's invited Shaw to "a small and entirely private dinner to Marion Davies in one of the private rooms at the Savoy", adding that, if Mr. Hearst were in England in time, he too would be there. "Say," G.B.S. scribbled on the invitation, "I never heard of Marion Davies, and would not go to a little dinner at the Savoy if she were all the 11,000 virgins of St. Ursula rolled into one. I am no good for games of that sort." Then, "I have now ascertained," he wrote to the intending host, "that Miss M. D. is a film star. Do you seriously believe that these young and beautiful ladies want to meet old gentle-men of 65 and 72, or to be made an excuse for their meeting one another? If so, you must be more innocent than the woolliest lamb in Hamleys' toyshop. I just wont go. Mr. Hearst and I, old as we are, have still gumption enough left to be able to meet without making Miss Davies yawn and spoiling your festivities." The man was genuinely surprised by this aloofness, for, he assured Shaw, Mr. Hearst had "expressed more interest in your work than that of any living writer". In the end victory went to America, for the Shaws met him five years later, when, in a pause of their world tour, they went ashore to look at Holly-wood, and Mr. Hearst sent a plane to pick them up. The plane carried in large lettering an advertisement for one of the Hearst papers, which seemed to his guests, coming from their less dynamic civilisation, a little unusual; and the plane had to make a forced landing, which did not disconcert them, for they knew nothing about it until it was all over. Mrs. Shaw had written to me that she had felt "a little nervy" about the visit itself but she came away as happy as G.B.S. who enjoyed Mr. Hearst as a social phenomenon and liked him as a man. They brought back with them photographs of the Hearst home and of Marion Davies, hostess during their stay. "Marion", he told me, "is by far the most attractive of the stars who are not really eighteen."

It was the only time that Shaw consented to sleep on Ameri-can soil. The *Empress of Britain* picked them up at Los Angeles and took them down the coast, through the Panama Canal and on to New York where G.B.S. was booked for a lecture at the Metropolitan Opera House, but he refused to spend the night ashore. He was playing hide-and-seek with the newspapermen, and when the moment for landing arrived he dodged them down one gangway as they swarmed up another. The lecture gave more pleasure to Shaw than to his audience, a gathering of the prosperous Rotarian type of citizen who had come along for a frolicsome evening. Shaw let them have a sermon on Civics which must have been disappointing to those of them who were expecting antics.

Three years later he paused at Miami on his way to Panama aboard the *Arandora Star*. I have a photograph of him, seated on the tennis deck between two bay trees in tubs. A covey of news reel men are "shooting" him in languid conversation with a visitor who displays a length of elegant white sock. "My reception in Miami", Shaw has written on the print, followed by some of that chatter about the weather to which, as I have already remarked, both he and Charlotte were so oddly addicted. "I am afraid you are having a miserable cold time in London whilst we are being roasted in the Caribbean: we both feel rather guilty about it. But the news from New York suggests that the ice cap is spreading again. . . ." A week before they had "a most infernal storm" and "to my great disgust I was violently sick for the first time since my Jamaica trip—was it 1911?"

Shaw's reluctance to step ashore into the United States was not due to any dislike of the inhabitants. He was, as I have said, essentially a shy being who shrank from people; yet he was attracted by the friendliness of Americans and their greater sense of equality. His trick of occasional over-statement is an American trick; his gift for monologue, an American gift. He admired the American passion for trying something new, such as their reform of spelling which, as I have recorded, he himself adopted. He was all for Americans when they were breaking barriers down, and rude to them when they were setting barriers up. Thus he would explain that the hundred per cent. American was ninety-nine per cent. idiot. Thus, when an American proposed a Shavian Society as an asylum for the sane, he told me to reply that an asylum for the sane would be empty in America. The only American from whom G.B.S. ever got as good as he gave was Lady Randolph Churchill, Winston Churchill's mother, with that sharp repartee of hers, when, Shaw having described an invitation to luncheon as an attack on his well-known habits, she retorted, "Know nothing of your habits; hope they are not as bad as your manners". It happened long before my day; but after I went to Shaw I found that he had let a spate of three hundred or so words loose in his defence, ending with a meek, "If I can be of any real service at any time, that is what I exist for; so you may command me."

Years before the dollars began to trickle from the United States, Shaw took the long view of the American market. He even welcomed, with utter amiability, pirated versions of his work. The shilling edition of his fourth novel, *Cashel Byron's Profession*, had already been pirated in America when Annie Besant decided to run its predecessor, *Love Among the Artists*, in her magazine, *Our Corner*, and so, as in later years he asked me to point out, "made it accessible to the American publishers and threw it into the public domain in the U.S.A." As that was so, the fact that a firm already happened to be publishing for him in America did not, he readily agreed, prevent them from availing themselves of their right to publish his non-copyright works, "as I never objected to the practice, and actually preferred publishers who had been keen enough about my books to 'pirate' them". In my time we always published simultaneously in America and England, save on some special occasion, as when he wrote for a Dickens Society in the United States a preface for a *de luxe* edition of *Great Expectations* which was being done for them. Like boxing, Charles Dickens was another of those unexpected subjects for which Shaw's enthusiasm is accepted by the Shavians with an air of apology. But nearly everybody read Dickens when Shaw was a boy. Charlotte was one of the few exceptions. When she was laid up in her last year she would read Priestley or Wells but she would never take a volume of Dickens from the set at Ayot. We had two sets of all the works at Winchelsea, but as children we were not allowed to remove the handsomely bound and illustrated edition from the Rectory drawing-room where I read several novels before I went off to boarding school at the age of eleven. Shaw himself had met Charles Dickens, and that caused a flutter when the American preface came to be written, for Dickens had shown him a different ending to *Great Expectations*, dropped on Bulwer Lytton's advice, and now there was a great scurry to find whether any of the Dickens family possessed the original. Thanks to William Maxwell, who joined in the hunt, it was discovered, and each ending is duly detailed in the preface, with Shaw's comment that Dickens had "made a mess of both".

I never felt that Shaw's books got the circulation they deserved among the huge reading public of the United States, and in Shaw's own opinion they were never sufficiently advertised. But from the moment that the police released the company doing *Mrs. Warren's Profession* at New York's Garrick Theatre appreciation of his plays so grew with the years that Broadway saluted his death with lowered lights. The year before the episode of *Mrs. Warren's Profession* Shaw had already written specially for Arnold Daly *How He Lied to Her Husband*, one of nine of the plays to have its first world production

in the United States. *The Devil's Disciple*, with Richard
Mansfield as Dick Dudgeon, two years ahead of London, was
followed by *Cæsar and Cleopatra*, then *How He Lied*, *Heartbreak House*, *Back to Methuselah*, *Saint Joan*, *Too True to Be Good*,
Village Wooing, and the *Simpleton of the Unexpected Isles*.

As I have said, I do not believe that when Shaw wrote *Back
to Methuselah* he had any idea that the play would reach the
stage. He wrote it because he felt that it was there to be written,
much as the New York Theatre Guild felt that it had got to be
played. I hope that the Guild's enterprise did not leave them
out of pocket: as tickets for the five *Methuselah* plays were offered
in batches to a membership audience I do not suppose that they
would in fact lose on the run. Shaw and the British Treasury
owe much to those American pioneers. By the time of the war he
had become an established British export, the Treasury making
over to him in sterling payments involving thousands of dollars
a year. He got £20,000 the year New York revived *The Doctor's
Dilemma* and *Candida*; and when the war ended not less than
that came to him from *Man and Superman*, and still later a handsome amount from *The Devil's Disciple* and *Cæsar and Cleopatra*.
It is true that when G.B.S. had paid toll on this substantial
income the balance was not much more than might keep a
vegetarian in life. Nevertheless, America, almost alone among
foreign countries in acclaiming him after the war, brought
consolation to the spirit if not to the pocket.

Once we had a payment in kind, not cash. The Baxter
Theatre, Virginia, who were using farm produce as money,
sent G.B.S. a ham in settlement of his royalty. He returned the
offering with a "Dont you know I am a vegetarian?" The
Shaw vogue brought us many queer communications from
Americans. The neatest had a postage stamp photograph of
G.B.S. in the bottom left-hand corner of the envelope; above it,
a postage stamp cancelled "George" (in Texas) on New
Year's Day; in the next corner one cancelled "Bernard"
(Iowa) on May 24 (Empire Day); below it, a third cancelled
"Shaw" (Virginia) on July 26, his birthday. How the Post
Office people of these three States were coaxed into collabora-
tion is mystifying to an Englishwoman used to sterner treat-
ment. The United States has, I believe, four towns named
George, two Bernards, and four Shaws; so another admirer
went to the trouble of repeating the tribute, this time from
Iowa and Mississippi. America also played its part in the

autograph menace. G.B.S. walked innocently into a trap set by
one collector who inquired whether he had any objection to
his naming a pill he was about to put on the market the G.B.S.
Pill. Off went a postcard "If you dare to do it, I shall sue you".
And back came a confession that the man had never manufactured a pill in his life, and did not intend to do so. He had
made a bet with a friend that he would get Shaw's autograph,
and he thanked him for letting him win. But G.B.S. ignored the
letter of an American woman who alleged that she wanted to
name a soap after him. He was blunter with American women
than the chivalrous demeanour of their own menfolk would
have led them to expect. He requested one group of them never
to write to him again "on that eminently pretentious paper".
They were the Women's Action Committee for Lasting Peace
and they had asked him to autograph a book for an auction to
further the idea. He told them crisply not to mix up Votes for
Women with "the useless and irrelevant Lasting Peace
business"; and anyhow that in England Votes for Women
had kept them out of their fifty-fifty share of government more
effectually than their former disfranchisement, the first general
election in England after that event having resulted in first-
rate women candidates being defeated "by male nobodies".
Reproved but not abashed, the Lasting Peace ladies auctioned
the letter for more than they would have got for the book.
He told another American woman that he would like to say to
her "Dont be an idiot", or something of that sort, "but it
would not be polite; so I mustnt". She was pestering him to
attend her husband's concert or to "grant him an audience in
order to listen to one of his compositions". It was odd, in her
opinion, that "an American woman who belongs, as you once
remarked, to a barbarous country should remind you that it
matters not how illustrious you may be as a writer, you have yet
to learn to be a man". Shaw asked her what she would say to
his wife if she were to write to the lady's husband and tell him
that he had yet to learn to be a man because he had not gone
to a Shaw play. "Why the deuce," he inquired, "should I go
to your husband's concert if I don't choose, or have something
else to do?" In like fashion, an American woman pianist was
furious when he declined to attend a recital she was giving at
the Æolian Hall. He told me to tell her that it was a delusion
on the part of American artists to persuade themselves that his
influence and presence at their concerts could help them, for he

was now "completely superannuated in that respect and many others". She flared out with the names of Gluck, Handel, Beethoven, Strauss, Tchaikovsky, Glinka, Dargomizhsky, Rachmaninoff, "and others", who were all on the programme, which she felt might be of some service to G.B.S. As for her, she had no need of the services of "even a Bernard Shaw". In the field of music, "according to the world's best critics", she had arrived without his aid. And so on.

Among American men, too, we had our oddities. There was one, rather like G.B.S. in appearance, who carried a singing kettle around with him. There was the other who passed on to Shaw a fantastic plan for the marriage of Mrs. Simpson to King Edward VIII on the deck of the U.S. battle-cruiser *Indianapolis*, attended by two other cruisers and a division of destroyers at anchor off Southampton. "If," he added graciously, "the Archbishop of Canterbury were present, he could perform the ceremony." Then there was the adventure of the climbing American. Across the landing on the stair leading to the flat at Adelphi Terrace stood what Shaw described as "a strongly fortified obstacle giving my flat the appearance of a private madhouse". Even Lawrence of Arabia was intimidated: "the barbed wire gate", he called it. They had it put up after a thief, sneaking in during a luncheon party, had gone off with a guest's overcoat and Charlotte's best table silver crammed into the pockets. Alice, the maid, daughter of Mrs. Bilton, the Shaws' Norwegian housekeeper of those days, had strict orders not to admit beyond the gate anyone who did not have an appointment. Leon de Swarte, our American invader, did not wait for one. We first heard of him when he wrote to G.B.S. from the United States, informing him, as so many did, that he would like to be a journalist, and adding that he particularly wanted to see him. Next he announced his arrival in London and demanded an appointment. When Shaw refused, he began writing a series of ridiculous letters, some of which he repeated in the personal column of *The Times*. "Would Shumble meet Swumble for a wumble and a good tumble?" was one; which I translated "Would Shaw meet Swarte for a walk and a good talk?" We ignored the nonsense. Then, one Saturday morning, when the Shaws were out of town, I opened a package containing twenty £1 notes and a letter from de Swarte thanking G.B.S. for the operation which he had "so successfully performed" on him. At this I wrote to

Shaw suggesting that the affair was becoming something more than a silly joke. Shaw was succinct as always. Would I take the numbers of the notes; put them in an envelope; go round with them to Scotland Yard; explain that the reference to an operation was unintelligible, but that I recognised the handwriting as that of a man who sometimes wrote crazy letters; and say that he ought to be looked after? "How nice," they remarked at the Yard, "to get a big sum of money like that on a Saturday morning!" The detective flattered himself when he had run de Swarte to earth that he had talked him into good behaviour; but he was soon at it once more, this time inviting Shaw to meet him by the Marble Arch. The plain-clothes man who went there in Shaw's place was again congratulating himself that he had stopped the fellow's nonsense when G.B.S. came home one evening to find the flat in an uproar. Helen Wills had invited him to watch the tennis at Wimbledon, and while he was there de Swarte had clambered over our spiked gate to look round the flat for his interview. He bolted when the maid appeared, but was held in conversation by the workers in an office downstairs while she telephoned Scotland Yard. They took him off to Brixton prison where they kept him for six weeks as an alien without a passport: he had destroyed his own, for another of his eccentricities was a craving to be taken for an Englishman. He was shipped off to the United States and we heard of him no more.

Leon was one of very few Americans with whom I ever found myself at variance. Another was a lieutenant in the American Navy who wrote an article about Shaw for an American magazine in which he made G.B.S. say, upon being asked whether he felt he had influenced the world, that he hoped so, but that he had not made the slightest impression upon "Patch", as he could see by the mistakes in her work. I regarded this as libellous on my professional skill. Shaw agreed with me, especially as he was certain that he had never used the words put into his mouth; and would never have called me "Patch" to a stranger. I insisted that the libel should come out of the article when it went into book form and the publishers at once agreed, remarking somewhat petulantly that they thought I would have understood that the writer had a great affection for Mr. Shaw. I said I could understand that; but what I failed to appreciate was his lack of affection for me. Later the author sent me a copy of the book inscribed "To Blanche Patch with

F

profuse apologies and depending upon her forgiving nature",
followed by a food parcel. And more recently when he was in
London we met and had a good laugh over my pretended
irascibility.

A mutual interest in tracing our ancestors back through the
centuries was a more friendly bond between Americans and
me, though I never succeeded in connecting with my family the
many American Patches who wrote to me. While trying to find
the origin of the name I discovered in the records of the
Huguenot Society that a John Patch, who had come to London
in the reign of Henry VIII, was, as an alien, taxed in the large
sum of fourpence a year. As these French Protestant refugees
had to change their names I suggested that this John Patch was
none other than the Huguenot refugee, Giovanni Pazzio, at
that time making quite a name for himself as an artist. My
brother John, then engaged on a history of the Patches, remarked that my theory was ingenious and like that of a claim
posted on a church porch near him that St. Paul had preached
there. When visitors asked the incumbent if it was true, he
replied, "You can't deny it".

My mother's family had a slight connection with the Navy,
for her mother, Mrs. David Blaiklock, was the daughter of one
of Nelson's commanders, a Captain Parkinson, of whom we
have a portrait. What might have been an heirloom was
unfortunately destroyed by a too patriotic member of the
family. This was a letter from Nelson to Captain Parkinson
saying, "If you will be ready at 11 to-morrow morning I will
call for you in my coach and we will go and call on old
pudding-face", "old pudding-face" being none other than the
son of one whom Americans might well regard as the creator
of their United States, our George IV. Incidentally my
Christian name arose from a whimsy of Captain Parkinson who
gave all his daughters the names of the Nelson ships on which
he had served: thus I have a sister called Hero, as were my
mother and also my grandmother.

One of the American Patches wrote from Ohio to tell me that
his ancestor Nicholas Patch had crossed the Atlantic from
Somerset for Salem, Massachusetts, as far back as 1636. Another West Country Patch was the Samuel Patch to whom Mr.
Cherry-Garrard introduced Gertrude Lawrence and me at the
sale of the books from Whitehall Court. Among these was a set
of the green American edition of the complete works named

Ayot St. Lawrence, in regard to which a curious incident arose when they came up at the auction. As the titles on their paper wrappers had faded, I had at one time inked the lettering in, and, by a misunderstanding, the catalogue now declared that this was Shaw's own handiwork. The slip was corrected before bids were invited, for, unbelievable as it may seem, it was felt that even so slender a link with the great man would have given additional value to the set. The books in fact fetched £30, no extravagant figure for thirty volumes, and possibly the bids would have gone higher had Shaw and not I inked the titles in. For the man was becoming almost a legend, and the older he grew, and the more remote from the world of men, the more insistent were the demands for a sign, however trivial, from the oracle; and the more resolute had we who watched over him to be in shielding him from those who clamoured for a glimpse or a whisper. Our firmness must have ruffled many of them, although one, an American business-man, Mr. F. Darius Benham, produced an unexpected halo. Concluding, for some reason which remains obscure, that he owed his prosperity to other people's secretaries, he decided to acknowledge the quality of some of us; so one morning there arrived for me at Whitehall Court an ornate certificate announcing

BENHAM AWARD OF MERIT

Order of the Seraphic Secretaries

for unfailing courtesy, tact, thoughtfulness, charm, urbanity, gentleness, civility, amiability, good temper and sweetness,

Blanche Patch, secretary of George Bernard Shaw, is awarded the degree of Impeccable Amanuensis.

F. DARIUS BENHAM.

In one corner is a seal with the letters 'SS'; in the other my number in this distinguished company. I regret that it is as far down as 379. But all of us were women.

CHAPTER XI

COMRADE SHAW

WHEN G.B.S. WAS WELL past his ninetieth birthday his housekeeper, Mrs. Laden, suggested to him that he ought to have a man in the house. There had been some thieving in the village and she was nervous. She herself locked up at night except for the door from the dining-room to the garden which G.B.S. would see to himself after going out to have a look at the sky before going up to bed. In more than forty years nothing had ever been stolen from Shaw's Corner, although one night it was thought that someone had tampered with the kitchen window, and once during the war, as I have said, the garden gate was lifted from its hinges by some sportive young hobble-dehoys who left it some yards up the road. Now, after a small burglary or two in the neighbourhood (later believed to be the work of an escaped prisoner), the housekeeper thought that it would be well to have a stronger defence than she and Shaw and Maggie, the housemaid, could put up.

"A man!" exclaimed Shaw. "I would feel more afraid of a man than of you!"

G.B.S. was shy of the ordinary run of men and women. With the dwindling group of his own intimates he was completely sincere and quite at ease; for the large general body of devotees he had ready a public performance of himself which was a kind of shell to protect his natural diffidence; but the mass of people intimidated him. He did not, like Horace, hate the vulgar throng and keep them at a distance: it was rather they who kept him at a distance, and he was somewhat envious of the way that his secretary seemed to get on with them. He always appeared to be astonished that I knew much more about the working classes than he did.

If the aim of the better Communists is to have people dwelling in friendliness together, I would be surprised to find Moscow to-day much ahead of what Winchelsea was in my childhood. Among our friends were the resident policeman; Mrs. Bragg who washed my father's surplices (the choir had

none); the blacksmith who let us play with his bellows; and
Charles Barling, the village grocer, who was also the church
organist. One day he gave "The Vicar of Bray" as a voluntary
because he thought it was connected with the clergy, and he
liked the tune. My mother hinted that it was not quite suitable,
but she might have been even more astonished if, in later years,
she had heard my youngest brother offering "The Policeman's
Holiday" as a voluntary at a service in a church in a small
town in Kent where his regiment was quartered. He told me
that, played *andante*, it was very effective, and several members
of the congregation asked him where he had learnt it; or was it
his own composition? My mother was the grocer's deputy in
his absence, and when she played we were all nervous lest she
should break down—all save one simple-minded old lady who
attended the services with her sister. She preferred Mother's
execution, saying she could hardly hear her, and frequently
ejaculated "Oh dear! Oh dear!" not only during the hymns, but
at the end of the prayers. When my father became a little bent
in the back she declared that he reminded her of Punch.

John Carey, the church clerk and gravedigger, was very
popular with us, and we were delighted when we could in-
veigle him into playing cricket with us in the Rectory garden.
As well as cleaning our shoes and knives, he worked the pump
which supplied the house with water and helped Stivvie at
times. Stivvie was our gardener. He had been with the previous
Rector who had only one grown-up daughter, so, very naturally, he disliked the idea of our large family invading his
domain. He particularly resented our habit of jumping over the
flower-beds instead of going round by the paths as his late
employers had done. To keep us at bay he would carefully lock
up all outhouses when he left the premises, and he went as far
as to suggest that a cottage might be built for him in the grounds
to allow him to keep a continual watch over us, and so protect
the fruit and flowers which he was always growing for local
flower shows. Nevertheless he put up with us very well and
encouraged us to visit him in the greenhouse where we sometimes tried to give him lessons in speaking French after our own
lessons were over.

Carey was our star turn at the village concerts, which, with
bazaars, Sunday and Day School treats, were the big occasions
for meeting people. Sunday School was held in the ordinary
day school, with a short service in the morning before going on

to church and a full length session in the afternoon. For a short time I helped at the morning service, but, as I have already remarked, I have no gift for teaching. It alarms me to be confronted with a row of children awaiting instruction, though normally I get along with them very well. I once had such an exhilarating effect upon a two-year-old boy, with whom I was walking ahead of his mother, that he suddenly loosed hold of my hand and began shouting and chasing some harmless cows all over a field, so causing his mother considerable consternation, for until then he had been afraid of the creatures.

Although Mother managed the afternoon sessions at the Sunday School, I am not sure that her efforts could be called religious teachings. She would take along books of adventure stories to read to the children, and my sister Hero declared that Mother and her fellow teacher, who held a class at the opposite end of the room, each read as loudly as they could so as to outdo the other. The coastguards' children were always prime favourites with my mother. This may have been because they had to walk a matter of one and a half miles from the coast and were very regular in their attendance. Anyhow they usually received the best presents at our annual Christmas party.

Although Winchelsea is usually spoken of as a village, it is really a small town and has, I believe, the only unreformed Corporation in England, the Mayor being elected each Easter Monday. As one of the lesser Cinque Ports, Winchelsea was summoned to Parliament in 1264-65, and returned two members from 1366 to 1832, when it was disfranchised. There are vaults under some of the smaller houses, said to have been used by smugglers and others storing contraband goods. The church of St. Thomas à Becket stands in the centre of the town, with the streets laid out by Edward I surrounding it. Winchelsea had some eight coastguards and the wife of one of them looked after our bathing suits and tents in our absence. At that time one of the Martello towers, built to defy Napoleon, stood on the beach, but when the sea began to encroach and undermine it, it had to be blown up. The coastguards sometimes allowed us to go inside this tower and on one occasion, when we were running round the top of it, one of our playmates, Harry Martindale, who in later years became a famous chemist, fell, and had to retire in some confusion while his breeches were stitched up by the coastguard's wife.

When we first went to Winchelsea, the Town Hall was used

as a gaol, or lock-up, and the Court Room was overhead, but soon after our arrival the lower room was converted to a library and reading-room, and the upper room was used as a concert room. In the course of the restoration a painting on wood was discovered up the chimney, and the figure painted on it is said to be St. Leonard blessing the fruits of the earth. The concerts held in this upper room were great fun; the time when one of my brothers sat on the chairman's hat all the evening being a special occasion. During the winter we had Social Evenings once a month, and the admission charge was twopence. The village postman, the coachman from The Friars, and two charwomen were among the artistes. Occasionally, I would contribute a banjo solo—in these days of brilliant banjoists I should have been considered, quite rightly, a very bad performer on an instrument which had a disconcerting habit of snapping a string at the wrong moment. The coachman knew but one song which he sang without accompaniment, the refrain being "Under the trees, with her bowl on her knees, Maria sat silently shedding green peas". He unconsciously added to his success by putting a penultimate "e" into the word bowl! Our postman, comparatively young, would ask when delivering the letters at the Rectory if Miss Blanche could come round to the Town Hall, where there was a piano, to run through a song he was proposing to sing, and if I did not play for him Mother would. She was a good reader at sight and loved accompanying singers. The older ladies who attended these Social Evenings considered that there ought to be some censorship of what was to be sung, regarding me as much too young to decide what was a suitable comic song and what not. One evening my father came along because Mother was not well and I could see that he was not very pleased with one of the songs given by the railway porter. However he restrained himself and it was not until we were leaving the hall that he was overheard saying to the offender, "I hope I shall never hear such a song again".

Now and again G.B.S. would take a sudden interest in my family and observe how strange it was that he knew so little about us, adding, with a lift of the eyebrow, that it was surprising to find the daughter of one who must have been an old-fashioned Tory secretary to George Bernard Shaw. I imagine that my father always voted Conservative; I know that I grew up among those who regarded Liberals as a different species.

Winchelsea was in the Rye Parliamentary Division and at election times the village would be decorated in the party colours, purple and orange for the Conservatives, red and blue for the Liberals. Mother was very annoyed when our nurse, at one election, put the Liberal colours on the perambulator and flaunted them herself while we walked at her side decked in our purple-and-orange rosettes. Harvey du Cros was nursing the Hastings seat when we moved to St. Leonards, and soon after our arrival he defeated the Liberal, Freeman Thomas, who later became Lord Willingdon. My father, who was then an old man, said he would not bother to vote because it was too far to walk to the polling booth. My brother Tom and I must have been keen young politicians for we arranged with the local Conservative offices to send a car for him. But when it arrived he went out to tell the driver that he refused to be driven to the polling booth, and anyhow he had been out in the early morning and had already registered his vote!

I am no politician, and even at election times G.B.S. never attempted to discuss politics with me. He once told an American that he had never been able to convert me to his views. He may have discussed politics with Charlotte, in fact he is certain to have done so, but when I was living at Ayot the subject never cropped up at meal-times. If Shaw ever voted at any Parliamentary or local election it was not to my knowledge, nor in my day did he ever speak in an election campaign. He was often asked to do so, but he always replied that his electioneering days were over, sometimes adding a crisp note to the effect that, in the days when he did speak, "all my candidates failed to get in".

Who were his candidates? He would back anyone whom he might describe as a Communist, and, as far as I could gather, to him anybody was a Communist who believed in a common supply of gas and water: he even told his Chief Constables at Harrogate that they could not object to Communism as such "because our police organisation, which is the measure of our civilisation, is flat Communism". Utterly deflated, Communists might comment. He himself went all the way: he was the complete extremist. I feel sure that he was perfectly sincere when he startled a group of simple Lancashire chapel-goers with his remedy for idlers.

"I would like to take everyone before a tribunal," he said, "and, if it were found that they were not doing as much for the community as the community was doing for them, I would give them a few days to make their peace and then put them in the lethal chamber. I would have no Weary Willies and Tired Tims." The rumour of his ruthlessness must have got around, for, in the days before the Welfare State swallowed up the last of them, I do not remember having seen one tramp come to the door at Shaw's Corner. His old suits went to the men working about the place, and they had to be very old before they were allowed to go. Shaw knew what he wanted, and it was not philanthropy. In his opinion, an ideal society is not one in which everyone is helping everyone else, but one in which nobody needs to be helped "except by way of the co-operation which raises no question of charity". All the energy he could spare for public work was devoted to stopping the making of messes, "not to mopping them up whilst other people are making them without restraint". He was too sound a realist to believe in the brotherhood of man; he held that what people needed to be taught was that, though they had plenty of good reasons for hating one another and "the better they understand one another the less they will like one another", that did not justify them in injuring one another. "If I like my neighbour there is no need to preach 'mutual appreciation' to me," he told a sentimental supporter of the Cause. "If I detest and despise him as he probably deserves, then it is folly to invite me to love and esteem him; but it is highly important to warn me that my detestation and contempt give me not the slightest excuse for shooting him at sight, or throwing dead cats over the wall into his garden." To another disciple of the brotherhood of man who wanted to name their aim the Neighbourly Society, he retorted that the suggested title would not suit him as he was tired of pointing out the "folly of advising unlovable people to love another".

The more nervous members of the community were not quite correct when, upon hearing G.B.S. declare himself a Communist, they concluded that he must be a terrible fellow like one of the men in the Kremlin. A maid at Whitehall Court was sure of it. "I don't know what Mr. Shaw will think of me", she remarked one morning. I inquired why, fearing that she had perhaps burned something of value. She explained that she had written to him to say that she was sorry to notice that he had declared himself a Communist. "How can you work for a Communist?" the other maids had asked her.

The truth is that G.B.S. was much more thorough-going than

Moscow, even in his nineties when surtax had cooled down the ardours of his middle years. In the early days at Adelphi Terrace I remember he passed on to me for transcription a clear declaration that he was "in favour of dividing up the income of the country equally between everybody, making no distinction between lords and labourers, babes in arms and able-bodied adults, drunkards and teetotallers, archbishops and sextons, sinners and saints". To a reader in Mexico who asked for something more explicit he replied that he did not suggest that Socialism would cure what this man vaguely termed "the evils of humanity", but that he had traced certain specified evils to inequality of income and inferred that they would not occur under equality of income. "No sane person," he added, "refuses to wear spectacles because they do not cure toothache."

Moscow had a mere ripple of Communism as practical as that, whereas G.B.S. remained its apostle right into the middle of the second World War when he was still convinced of the "need for equality of income, involving a standard income to which all incomes must be levelled". He thought so much of *Everybody's Political What's What*, where he repeats his belief in absolute equality of incomes, that he surrendered to it his war allocation of paper, refraining, for the time, from having his plays reprinted. We were working on the book during most of the war, and its chapter on medicine was sent to Sir Almroth Wright for revision. He told Shaw that he was sorry to see such a big engine going so completely off the rails. The book had a good sale, although it did seem to me at the time that I had already transcribed much of it for *The Intelligent Woman's Guide to Socialism*, including his unequivocal declaration in favour of equal incomes. On this in 1948 he wobbled. He was now ninety-two, and in a recurring panic about his bank balance, on which subject he could have readily reassured himself by glancing at his pass-book. So he decided that it would be "crude" to divide up; that it did not matter if "one in a hundred thousand or so has ten times as much to play with"; that the test was if everybody had enough to marry anybody, and that anyhow the directors of proletarian culture needed handsome houses with pictures, books and pianos. He had forgotten his earlier boast that, as a young man, he had seen communally at the National Gallery all the pictures he wanted to see and read, communally all the books at the British Museum. He was, moreover, I thought, generalising rather wildly when he argued that, although five pounds a week will not condescend to marry three-pound-ten, fifty thousand a year will marry five thousand: income snobbery, it seems to me, flourishes as strongly at the higher level as at the lower.

When Shaw thus advocates superior incomes for superior citizens, I fear that the sensitive proletarian may be shaken by the suspicion that G.B.S. himself was rather the superior person. One must face the fact that he was a superior person. He was not the Superman, nor did he ever believe that he was; but in most of the attributes of a civilised human being he was clearly superior to the multitude past whom he used to stride along the Strand. I cannot find any evidence much later than 1889 that Shaw regarded the mass of people as capable of governing themselves, and the 1889 reference is a guarded one in his introduction to the *Fabian Essays*, where he affirms his "conviction of the necessity of vesting the organization of industry and the material of production in a State identified with the whole people by complete Democracy". A year or two later he did draft for a General Election a leaflet "Vote! Vote!! Vote!!!" in which he argued that it was "the selfish, the indifferent, the short-sighted, the lazy man who could not see why he should trouble himself to do so". But in his postscript to the Diamond Jubilee edition of the *Essays* he declared that governing is a highly-skilled craft and "should be left in the hands of the five per cent. naturally qualified for it". What was needed, he would argue, was a qualification for candidates, not for voters. "Everyone who is capable of suffering from bad institutions and silly legislation should have a vote and a choice of representatives; but that choice should be between qualified persons; and the real problem of democracy is to devise a test which cannot be passed by windbags, cranks, adventurers, trade agents, popular generals or actors or preachers without political capacity." And he granted that to take away the vote from citizens under thirty would not only leave a large class politically defenceless but "would be defeated by the vote of that class". Let them all have votes therefore, so long as they used them under his direction.

He would relate with glee how, when the democratic councils in Jamaica opposed his old friend, Sydney Olivier, who was Governor there, Olivier refused to consult them and just went ahead; and how, in eighteen months or so, they would see that he was right "and stop howling about it". What G.B.S. and Olivier each wanted was his own way, whatever the majority felt about it. His own political philosophy was that of "the Czar and the Grand Dukes," said Shaw, long before the 1914 war, although he happened to differ from them as to the most desirable form of government.

He was only forty-nine then; and his determination to get what he wanted did not weaken with the years. Thus, after backing the suffragettes and finding that the electors did not rush to vote for women, he proposed what he called the Coupled Vote, meaning that we should all be compelled to vote for a woman at the same time as we voted for a man; and he coolly defined this system of compelling us to vote for somebody we did not want as setting up "the true democratic political unit".

What he consistently declined to acknowledge was the right of people to govern themselves. When he talked about liberty, he tended to be confusing until you perceived that at one moment he meant liberty for other people, and at another liberty for himself. Thus it was the ABC of Socialism that private property was incompatible with liberty or with personal property; a landlord could "not only make his tenant his slave but seize his toothbrush if he refuses tribute". Then liberty is scorned because it produced Hitler who "owed his existence and his vogue solely to the futility of Liberal parliamentarism on the English model". The remedy? What we needed, he proclaimed before the war gave it to us, was positive and efficient State control and enterprise and initiative everywhere; and what we got was "resistance to the State, obstruction, and endless talk about Liberty, 200 years out of date".

By democracy, he declared, he meant a social order aiming at the greatest available welfare for the whole population and not for a class; and there is no doubt at all that he sincerely believed what he said. It is equally beyond doubt that he had no intention whatever of allowing the whole population to decide what form that social order was to take. He would write off to a window-cleaner in the north of England and assure him that, as the British Parliamentary system was far too slow for modern requirements, "a British adaptation of the Soviet system was indispensable". Then someone would artlessly inquire whether dictatorships make people happier than democracies. Happiness, forsooth! "About happiness I know nothing," he would snort in reply. "An able dictator can effect reforms in six months that parliament would wrangle about for 60 years." He accepted the dictators because of their reforms: it was the reforms that won him always. He approved of Hitler when he ended unemployment. He approved of Mussolini when he drained the Pontine Marshes. He could not begin to appreciate their venom for Jews and coloured people. He himself had no feeling whatever against Jews, among whom were many of his own friends.

Stupid Russians, stupid Germans, and stupid Englishmen have all on occasion charged G.B.S. with being something or other of which they happened to disapprove. He was nobody's disciple but his own, which may be why the official Labour Party and he have never contemplated one another with very great affection. Shaw, it must be remembered, had been quite an effective Labour Party of one before the others made their appearance at Westminster. From the age of fifty he was for six years a vestryman and borough councillor in St. Pancras, and during that time he never voted otherwise than on the merits of the question on the agenda, and was for the most part "a party all to myself with complete impunity". He gave me, for a student of local government, an amusing account of what it was like. In 1898, he explained, before the old London vestries became borough councils, the vestrymen used to job one another's boys into posts in the office without any question of qualification, until at last it was discovered that one of them could neither read nor write, whereupon, "in spite of horrified resistance", Shaw managed to get a committee to investigate. The vestry of those days habitually struck rates which fell short of the estimates by 2d. in the £1 and, when Shaw remonstrated, old vestrymen wept and said he had "no bowels of compassion for the poor". When the Local Government Board auditor came in with the borough councils he found "a monstrous overdraft" at the bank.

The Vestry jobbery was all traditional, explained G.B.S. There was no scientific organised graft as in America and other places where local governing bodies were new things. For instance, a contractor with one of the big jobs was always expected to present the chairman of the committee in whose department the job lay with a service of silver plate; and the cost of this was borne by the ratepayers, appearing in the accounts in disguise. "But the acceptance of this," Shaw informed our student of local government, "ranked with attending a City dinner, or going to church, as a sacred usage. The old vestrymen whose houses were gleaming with plate acquired in this way would have been shocked if the contractor had tipped them a £50 note." It was to the credit of these vestrymen, he added, that though they had each other intimidated to an almost incredible degree, they used to come and tell him about it, knowing that he could afford to snap his fingers at their terrors.

Shaw was also in at the birth of the Independent Labour Party, and, thus early, the "most mistrusted" delegate at its first meeting in Bradford. Robert Blatchford was "terrifically applauded" when he proposed that all other political parties should be kept outside. Dead silence greeted G.B.S. when he opposed him; but, on the vote being taken, it was Shaw who won. He never forgot to tell the Labour Party when they were wrong; and the Labour Party never forgot that he had told them. Even his enthusiasm for Moscow had its limits, and there were times when it seemed to me to be uncommonly generous. Russia has never accepted the Copyright Act, and not a rouble ever reached G.B.S. for plays performed and books read by Soviet citizens. Although it is true that in Russia the foreign author is entitled to a fixed royalty on the sales of his book if he spends it in Russia, he may not take a kopek of it out of Russia, and I often thought that G.B.S. might have directed towards Stalin a trickle from the flood of wrath let loose upon others detected in giving performances of his plays without sending him the expected royalty. He could be obstinate in his devotion to the Soviet. Thus, he would admit to an unfriendly critic that, in the complete suppression of intoxicants, it had been beaten by the ease with which, "in a vast agricultural country, the peasantry can distil spirits for themselves out of almost anything"; and that "the stuff they make is so bad that it is better to supply them with comparatively drinkable spirit than to leave them to poison themselves". But, "meanwhile the Soviet is working for the root remedy which is to make life bearable for everybody without anæsthetics". Nobody except Shaw ever pretended that the Soviet was wending towards a teetotal Utopia; on the contrary, the Kremlin's carousals have given the Soviet a touch of our common humanity which it seemed to lack.

It was the Soviet mania for work which hypnotised Shaw: and here for once he refused to be an extremist. He did not believe that industry should be controlled by the workers. Although a younger G.B.S. had regarded the Guild Socialists with a cautious amiability, he protested in his later years that the workers could not manage a baked-potato stall. Whatever he may have thought of Communism, his enthusiasm for Communists was restrained. As he told his Chief Constables, though Communism is not itself seditious, "Communists occasionally talk intolerable sedition", and, he owned, "there are just as great fools among Communists as among other bodies". He was inclined to be rather off-hand with Karl Marx himself. He claimed *An Unsocial Socialist* to be socially interesting as "the first English novel written under the influence of Karl Marx, with a hero whose character and opinions forecast those of Lenin"; and he once contemplated a novel of much greater length and larger scope but found himself "too young for the job", so *An Unsocial Socialist* was published as a complete novel and novel-writing "given up for ever".

This to one inquirer: to an American Negro he said that his atmosphere was full of Darwin ten years before he was aware of the existence of Karl Marx. He was twenty-six when he read *Das Kapital*. At sixteen he was "up to his neck in Darwin". Marx made a Socialist of Shaw, but he had no other influence on his culture. The famous dialectic, he declared, had no effect on him; and the *Fabian Essays*, which he edited in 1887, were "completely Marxless". As for Marx the man, although he did change the mind of the world "more extensively than Jesus or Mahomet", he abused everyone who was not "his abject disciple" so fiercely that he kept only one friend, without whom he would have starved. While many ordinary men, Shaw explained, cannot bear contradiction, especially if they have no sisters, "geniuses cannot bear agreement, perhaps because it is an assertion of equality".

On the class war itself, he was a heretic, for, he argued, the cleavage cut right through the classes, not between them. It was not only a cleavage between Lord Londonderry and the Durham miners, but between Lord Londonderry's servants and tradesmen and the men of their class who hewed the coal. Yet, although Shaw might mock the mass of men and women when it was proposed that they should govern themselves or run their own industry, he scorned a nationalisation which just meant "boards of directors with your most popular mob-orators in the chair", and the proletariat still "getting nothing but its keep". Moreover, an early Fabian, Bertrand Russell's first wife, has put it on record that, while Shaw had less factual knowledge than other Fabians, "there was always his burning sympathy for the underdog". Here his courage was defiant and unwavering. No one could imagine Stalin, or even Lenin, leaping up, as time and again did Shaw, in defence of a human being who needed defending. I have mentioned how he pleaded the cause of the Chicago anarchists and Wilde and Roger Casement.

When the anarchists were condemned, it was Shaw who prepared a petition for their release; and Wilde's was the only signature. When Wilde made a fool of himself, Shaw was one of those who met him at the Café Royal and urged him to bolt for it. When Wilde refused and went to Reading gaol it was again Shaw who got up a petition for his release. When two of the Irish Republican Army were sentenced to death for assassinating Sir Henry Wilson, it was Shaw who protested against the Court's refusal to allow their justification to be read in public. When Willie Gallacher, Communist M.P., was charged with sedition it was G.B.S. who stood bail for him ("Are you worth £200?" the magistrate asked. "No," said Shaw, "I would hardly like to say that; but I've got £200, if that's what you mean"). When a German film actor was hauled before a de-nazification Court for having appeared in *Jew Süss*, it was Shaw who wrote and told the Court that the proceedings were "not only stupid but actually a criminal undertaking". So to the last, when it was a group of human beings who needed a spokesman. He would appeal to the Government for the dockers on strike, or to the United Nations for State-less refugees, or to anyone in authority for any victim of injustice. Here he appears to be in the direct line of the revolution of 1789 and the *Rights of Man*. But it was Man the individual whom he championed; from man in the mass he shrank. In a general way he may have commended the proposition that the workers of the world should unite; for practical purposes he did not believe that even the Socialists among them ought to do so. As he once assured one Socialist, to shove all of them into the same committee room in the names of equality and fratern-ity and unity was "like trying to make sugar candy out of sulphur, saltpetre and charcoal". He liked the early Fabians, he told me, because they were all more or less of the same class and age, "no illiterate working men, no born rich, no born poor, and not five years' difference between the oldest and the youngest".

Such being his fastidious nature, it is not surprising that, with all his humaneness on questions of abstract justice, Bernard Shaw never seemed to get to know anything about the people around him. One day an elderly man came to repair the door bell at Whitehall Court. Before he had been there half an hour, he had given me his life story: how, after the 1914 war, he had married a French girl, lived in France for twenty-five years; escaped to England the day before Dunkirk and now wanted to get back to France. Shaw would never have drawn out the account of these adventures. At Ayot during the war I used to attend a weekly working party for the troops where I met people who had lived in the neighbourhood for many years. If, on returning home, I mentioned their names to Shaw, he would express surprise that he had never heard of them; and in the village they were only less nervous of him than he was of them.

He was not stand-offish because he felt important. In London he would swing along not noticing anyone unless somebody touched him, when he would stop and be most affable. In the days when there were cigarette cards, although he himself, not being a smoker, never had any, he would be quite pleasant to little boys who asked him for one, while his neighbour, Sir James Barrie, a reputed child-lover, would glower at them and hurry on his way. He was always ready to be friendly. In the barber's shop at Welwyn Garden City, where he used to get his hair cut, one of the assistants had a friend who said he could tell the character of a man from the texture of his hair, and apparently the assistant had been sending off clippings from the scalps of his more eminent clients, Shaw's among them. He wrote and told G.B.S. what he had done, adding that he was disappointed because in his case his friend had no reactions at all. Shaw was hugely tickled. "Anyone picking up my hair cuttings to-day?" he inquired on his next visit.

Shaw would always cover short journeys on foot, preferring the Underground to a bus or taxi (he never kept his car in London) for a distance of any length, because, hoarding as always the precious minutes, he maintained that it was quicker. If I chanced to be travelling on the same train I would see him peering around like a lively bird. He was the most observant of men; with all his shyness, he had got to know enough to create Mr. Burgess, Eliza Doolittle, 'Enry Straker and Felix Drinkwater from the Waterloo Road. While he missed rounded relationships, he would amass a heap of little facts, remarking one morning, for example, that I must have been very well brought up as he noticed that, no matter how dry the day, I always wiped my shoes on the door mat before going into the house! On the other hand, he could be unobservant at times, and thoughtless. I might be away for a week or so with influenza and he would receive me when I returned to work as if I had been there all the time.

Although G.B.S. could produce surprising bits of information about all sorts of people he was quite without interest in the gossip of the village. Nevertheless, although there was not even this slender bond of gossip between him and those who served him, they must have liked him, for not one ever left his service. His chauffeur, Frederick Day, normally not a talkative individual, once remarked to me that he "would do anything for Mr. Shaw": and he was devoted to Charlotte too. She, like G.B.S., definitely disliked gossip and would have nothing to do with the villagers at Ayot. She was a lonely type of person, quite unresponsive to those who claimed to be distant relatives, and there were a number of them, but those who were fortunate enough to be admitted to her friendship found her both generous and warmhearted. She was extremely well read and educated and before her marriage, and before the days of world cruises, had travelled extensively. Like all Victorian ladies with ample means for plenty of servants, Mrs. Shaw was never interested in the actual running of a house, but, having a most capable housekeeper who conferred with her every morning, she had no need to worry herself with such matters. This housekeeper was Mrs. Clara Higgs to whom G.B.S. had a tombstone set up in the churchyard at Windlesham in Surrey, to which country she and her husband went to live when they retired.

"Would you," he asked the mason when he ordered it, "like the money in advance as I am 92 and may not live long?" The tribute paid to Mrs. Higgs in the epitaph disclosed a warmth of appreciation which many found surprising:—

"Bernard Shaw, writer of many plays, raised this stone in grateful memory of his faithful friends and helpers, Clara Rebecca Higgs, who passed away on 4th August, 1948, in her 74th year, and of Henry Bachelor Higgs, who followed her on the   in his   year. For many years they kept his home and garden at Ayot St. Lawrence, in the County of Hertfordshire, thereby setting him free to do the work he was fitted for. No playwright was ever better served".

Clara Higgs deserved her tombstone. She saved Charlotte any amount of worry, controlling things at Ayot while the Shaws were abroad, and managing the entire household for them while they were at home. G.B.S. owed her, and all of us, to the discernment of Charlotte, and I consider that he was extremely lucky in his staff. They too were lucky in him, apart from the fact that at Shaw's Corner they were in contact with more interesting people than they would have seen elsewhere.

Mr. and Mrs. Higgs were followed by Mrs. Laden who proved to be a treasure from the moment she came to us down to the difficult days of Shaw's last accident and illness; an intelligent woman who swooped down upon the house-work, including all the odd jobs once done by a between-maid, removed during the war by the Ministry of Labour. She was a first-rate cook, and as her husband had been a vegetarian she was able to supply G.B.S. with the sort of dishes he preferred; and she knew too how to bake the bread he liked. Charlotte could never have found anyone more able to look after him and run his house as well. When Mrs. Higgs was at Ayot she had Charlotte to direct her. Mrs. Laden did everything: Shaw's only job was, at her request, to check the household books from time to time. His first attempts were such a failure that he eventually provided himself with a small portable adding machine which, once he had mastered its intricacies, gave him enormous pleasure. Mrs. Laden had travelled abroad with her husband and had also had experience in hospital nursing. She had seen several of Shaw's plays acted, but, like myself, she never aired her opinion of them to him. Of her department she was queen. Outside it she remained in the background. Keeping to her own province, she expected others, including newspaper men, whom she firmly controlled, to do the same.

Shaw accepted her rule with docility. All he asked for was a quiet retreat from which to launch his wit upon the world: and so, his poise undisturbed, he could look out from Ayot with detachment upon mankind. He did not rate us highly; yet he would not have had us put upon. His verdict on Charles Dickens neatly expresses his own political attitude towards the human beings among whom he lived. He had "a complete disbelief in government by the people and an equally complete hostility to government in any other interest than theirs".

CHAPTER XII

THE MYSTIC

I POSSESS A COPY of an early manifesto by G.B.S. which he refrained, for some reason or other, from including in his collected works.

"My own faith is clear," it declares: "I am a resolute Protestant; I believe in the Holy Catholic Church; in the Holy Trinity of Father, Son (or Mother, Daughter) and Spirit; in the Communion of Saints, the Life to Come, the Immaculate Conception, and the everyday reality of Godhead and the Kingdom of Heaven."

On Going to Church, the pamphlet in which he makes this declaration of faith, evidently achieved some sort of circulation in the United States. It is undated, but it was probably written round about the meeting of the two centuries, for, says Shaw, "if you should chance to see, in a country churchyard, a bicycle leaning against a tombstone, you are not unlikely to find me inside the church if it is old enough or new enough to be fit for its purpose". He had stopped riding a bicycle long before I knew him; and I should have said that he had stopped believing in the Holy Catholic Church long before that, if indeed, as commonly accepted, he ever did believe in it. Shaw who, at the age of ninety-two, wrote to *The Times* complaining that he found it impossible to make himself understood because nobody using the same words meant the same thing by them, was as responsible as anyone for that general misapprehension. He would frequently imagine a meaning of his own for somebody else's idea and then demonstrate how wrong it all was.

The only association with the Church which he actually shared with the rest of us was baptism. He was baptised into the Established Church of Ireland by the Vicar of St. Bride's, Dublin, the Rev. William George Carroll, husband of his father's younger sister Emily. Their eldest daughter, also Emily, and "Tah" to the family, lived latterly in Eastbourne. Shaw's father used to say, G.B.S. told one of our correspondents, that this Vicar would have been a bishop if only he had been able to keep his temper. A considerable scholar, he taught G.B.S. his Latin grammar, and was "the first Protestant clergyman in Ireland," his nephew testified, "to go on the platform and support the Home Rule movement, then in its infancy. . . . I have even heard that in his scholarly way he was a Republican." The Vicar duly recorded the christening of his infant nephew, but after that a kind of mystery descends upon Shaw's admission to the Church. The parish of St. Bride's, originally prosperous, became, said Shaw, "hopelessly poor and Catholic", and was abolished. What happened to the record of the christening? One story is that the registers went to Trinity, Co. Dublin. Shaw's own view was emphatic. "The register recording my christening, among other historical events," he told another inquirer, "went to the Four Courts and perished in the famous siege of that building during the post-treaty troubles. I," he added dramatically, "am an Irishman without a birth certificate."

The early pamphlet relates how, as a child, he was compelled to go to church in his best suit on Sunday mornings with his two sisters, and how, though he escaped from that "intolerable bondage" before he was ten, it prejudiced him so violently against churchgoing that twenty years elapsed before, in foreign lands and in pursuit of works of art, he became once more a churchgoer. His flesh crept, he declared, at the recollection of the genteel, suburban Irish Protestant church and "the unnaturally motionless figures of the congregation in their Sunday clothes and bonnets, and their set faces, pale with the malignant rigidity produced by the suppression of all expression". Then comes a curious confession. He was sure, he said, that if he had been turned loose in a real church, and allowed to wander and stare about, or hear noble music there, instead of "that most accursed *Te Deum* of Jackson's and a senseless droning of the Old Hundredth", he would never have seized the opportunity of a great evangelical revival to begin his literary career with a letter to the press announcing "with inflexible materialistic logic, and to the extreme horror of my respectable connections, that I was an atheist". Subsequent denunciations by the faithful were surprisingly few. A pious journalist in the Bahamas once called him an old goat who was "bound to catch hell" for selling a copy of the Breeches Bible. G.B.S. had found it lying about and thought it an unattractive piece of book production. Some pages were missing and it would not have fetched much had not Shaw scribbled on the flyleaf, "I can't bear to have this ugly old thing in the house", which put the price up to £40. Shaw's comment upon this critic was that the silly fellow need not be anxious about him. If, he argued, he ought to be hanged for selling one ugly Bible, what should be done to the Bible Society which sold thousands of much handsomer ones every day? He added that he had half a dozen Bibles left and that he never travelled without one, a disclosure which may perplex his friends the Freethinkers. Freethinkers and Christians were each eager to capture him: he eluded both groups, leaving the one as puzzled as the other. Bradlaugh, he said, could not have "thrown the most bigoted audience of Plymouth Brethren into such transports of rage" as he threw the Freethinkers on one occasion at the Hall of Science when he "dealt with the whole mass of superstition which they called free thought and showed that it did not account even for bare consciousness". On the other hand, he was just as emphatic that "what is called God by the people who threw Charles Bradlaugh out of the House of Commons does not exist, never did, and never will". Yet an unexpected tribute to the Bible Society bobbed up in a reply to someone who wanted his advice about spending money on radium for the hospitals. By all means; buy a pound or two, Shaw agreed, but (a note of caution) do it out of income from sound investments and not capital. Radium treatment, he hastened to point out, was not discovered by "the Research people" whose activities had had "the effect of distracting attention and diverting funds from fruitful and essentially noble work in physics to useless enquiries and the pseudo-bacteriology which assumes that God made typhoid and tetanus bacilli, and duly let them loose in the Garden of Eden to be named by Adam along with the other animals. The silly people don't even know their own silly business. I assure you the Bible Society is a far worthier market for spare cash than the Research Societies. Bible science, such as it is, is sounder than the science of Pasteur and Lister, and is now much less blindly believed in".

Shaw's letter embracing atheism may have been his first writing to be published; but against that one can set the statement by Frank Harris (and Shaw revised the manuscript in which it was made) that his first literary composition was "a prayer in three movements ending with the Lord's Prayer".

These later heresies of his, he told a man in Devon who was

conducting an argument with him about the Resurrection, would have made him liable to prosecution as an apostate were it not for the fortunate circumstance that, though he was duly baptised as a member of the Episcopal Church of Ireland, he was never confirmed, and the responsible parties were his god-parents, long since dead. His next attendance at an ordinary church service was more than seventy years later, when I looked up the hymns for him. I did not very often go to the services at Ayot, for, as a girl at home, we were by no means a typical Rectory family in the matter of churchgoing. As long as we turned up at the morning service on Sundays, Papa was quite satisfied, at least I suppose he was. Anyhow he never mentioned churchgoing to us, nor can I remember his ever saying a single word to me about religion. He left all such instruction to our nurses and governesses. He did once reprove me for singing "God Save the Queen" in a ribald manner, saying that *hymns* should not be sung like that. Until then I had not realised that the National Anthem was a hymn, possibly because our nurse said a friend of hers had a bustle which played "God Save the Queen" as its wearer rose and sank gently to her seat. On Sundays at Winchelsea we children sat and, in the winter, shivered in old box pews. These pews were high, and when we knelt down, facing the expanse of dividing wall, we would some-times insinuate the edges of a hymn-book through the cracks in the wood. On the other side knelt a family of grown-up sons, and if one of them gave the hymn-book cover a tug we children would call that catching a fish. Occasionally they would slip sweets over to us, usually sugared almonds. When the pews came to be dismantled, I was told that the books in the Rectory pew had to be put to one side as some of the messages written in them were not intended for general circulation. The only heat-ing in the very lofty building was a hideous stove in the middle aisle with a black pipe to carry off the smoke, and probably the heat with it. Our pew had a quite useless oil stove, but, as we grew older, we added to our comfort by carrying hot-water bottles and rugs to church. Probably others in the congregation were doing the same thing. Anyway an objection from either of my parents would have been unlikely, both of them being of quiet and practical tempers. I remember once when my father was ill, and a clergyman came over from Bexhill to take his service for him, how he went to church with a sermon of his own in his pocket as he had no great faith in his deputy. Another

visiting clergyman was so absentminded that when he had
finished one sermon he just turned over a page and went
straight on with the next. He did not realise what he had done
until he remarked to my mother at lunch that the service
seemed to have run a little late.

It would seem to be my destiny to flit through rectories.
Our own at Winchelsea was older than the one in which the
Shaws found themselves at Ayot, and it had about it an atmosphere which the latter lacked. It was built over the vaults of an
ancient church which the sons of a predecessor of my father's
discovered by chance and promptly opened up, admitting the
public at so much a head; but, as this was consecrated ground,
the Crown came down on the enterprise and had the vaults
bricked up again. One afternoon, my brothers and I tapped the
walls all the way round but failed to find the secret cellars.
Our garden had been the churchyard and in my day it had a
large garden with fruit trees and a tennis court in an adjoining
small meadow. Sometimes on a spring evening I can picture
our garden at home. It was very different from the
one at Ayot. In the Shaws' garden there was no place where
you would like to go and sit. To G.B.S. his garden meant
nothing at all. He thought much more of its statues than of its
flower beds: there was one of a lamb by Prince Troubestkoy;
another was the life-sized figure of St. Joan to which Shaw
was most attached. He said it was the only one he could live
with because it showed her as a peasant woman, and not
dressed in armour like a film star. But of flowers he knew little;
he was not interested, so the gardener was left to do what he
liked, which meant that he kept bees and bred canaries and
fantail pigeons.

To serve a hamlet of fewer than one hundred souls, Ayot St.
Lawrence church is an elaborate edifice with its portico and
colonnades running out in the Grecian manner to a mausoleum
at each end. One holds the bones of Sir Lionel Lyde, who was
responsible for the structure, and at the other end are those of
his wife, Dame Rachel. The village story runs that, as the pair
were unhappily married, Sir Lionel determined that he would
use the church, which kept them together in this world, to
separate them when they had left it. The ruins of this church's
predecessor stood by the roadside a couple of minutes from
Shaw's Corner, and further on was the house which was the
Rectory when I went to Ayot: it had been a day school before

the war, and G.B.S. then had its windows glazed with vitaglass, as he did his own sitting-room. Now and again I went to church at Ayot. I never knew either G.B.S. or Mrs. Shaw do so, but Shaw, finding where I had been, would begin to take a sort of interest in the proceedings and kept quizzing me about how many were there and what went on at the services. At first I told him, but after a bit I refused to say anything more. Then, during the war, he proposed that he should go with me to see the installation of a new Rector. He had never seen an installation before, and as Michael Furse, Bishop of St. Albans, who officiated, was an old acquaintance, he thought he would go to church again and see what was to be seen.

"I would like to know how they stage-manage the affair," said he. As I left the luncheon table early to be in time for the induction I asked him whether he was coming along and he replied that he did not think he would; so off I went by myself. As I sat waiting for the service to begin, I heard a slight commotion behind me, and, turning round, saw G.B.S. sitting there in a back seat. I waved and beckoned him to a vacant place beside me. As he came forward I noticed that he had changed quickly from the tweed suit which he had been wearing at luncheon into a darker one. He could respect the conventions as neatly as the next man.

He turned an appraising eye upon the Bishop in his splendid robes as he conducted the new Rector round to the various points before he came to sit on a chair in the chancel where he promised to observe the Thirty-nine Articles. I steered G.B.S. through the Prayer Book and looked up the hymns for him. He joined in the singing: it is odd how those hymns of childhood linger in the memory. As we left, the Bishop came out and shook hands with Shaw, and then with the whole congregation who had meantime blocked his way of retreat. Shaw's comment was terse.

"A great farce," he remarked, as we walked back to Shaw's Corner. "No man would agree to those Thirty-nine Articles with an easy conscience. It shows he has not read them."

He would never have any patience with dogma in any form; as I ought to know, for in my time I imagine I have answered as many inquiries about theology as about politics. It was the dogma he loathed, not the Church saddled with it. One Palm Sunday, a year or two after the war, he might have been Bishop Furse himself, all but consecrating a new wrought-iron gate at the entrance to Ayot's demolished Abbey. Shaw told them that the village was still in the 14th century; that the people in that century believed in God, and, being domestically minded, had to give God a home and a habitation. So they built the Abbey. A Bishop with an eye for beauty had stopped its complete destruction; otherwise, he added modestly, there would have been nothing in Ayot St. Lawrence to attract visitors.

"There are no stained-glass windows," he said, "in fact there are no windows at all; there is no room. It is exposed to wind and rain, but it is still the House of God. It is most fitting therefore that on this day, we, the inhabitants of this old village, should be gathered here on the Green to accept the gate which will open to the Abbey. To-day is Palm Sunday and all of us will be singing till Easter Day:

> "Lift up your heads O ye gates
> And be ye lift up ye everlasting doors. . . .

"It is most fitting that this beautiful gate should be added, not as a barrier, but as an invitation. It is in keeping with the spirit of the Abbey." G.B.S. then pronounced a kind of benediction, "This is His way, and this is His Gate", and, pointing to it, passed through, followed by the Rector. Small wonder that somebody rang him up from Dublin round about this time to check a rumour that he had become a Catholic. "In the Church of Rome," he retorted, ready as ever, "there is only room for one Pope."

And indeed, if he were to be canonised anywhere it would be among the worthies of the Ethical Church. Already, in a stained-glass window of the West London Ethical Church, he appears with Anatole France on the other side and St. Joan between them.

"I am not a Roman Catholic," he told another sectarian who might have had more sense than to ask. "If I had to be fitted into any religious denomination, the Society of Friends, who are at the opposite pole to the Roman Catholics, would have the best chance. But in the face of my very explicit writings on the subject there is no excuse for describing me as a member of any of the Churches or sects, unless the believers in Creative Evolution can be described as a sect." To another he added the Jains to the Quakers as having been nearest to his own creed; "but when I went to India and visited a Jain temple I found it full of the crudest horse-headed idols." He did not believe in miracles; in the Resurrection; in the millennium, or in the immortality of G.B.S. Hilaire Belloc might very well have had his old friend in mind when he wrote:

> "He didn't believe
> In Adam or Eve;
> He put no Faith therein.
> His doubts began
> With the Fall of Man
> And he laughed at Original Sin."

The idea of personal immortality scared G.B.S. "Horror" is, again and again, his word for it. "The horror of it would drive you mad".... "An unimaginable horror".... "Only a child incapable of comprehending eternity could face such a horror".... "I abhor it". In one of his last prefaces he mocks the "senseless activity" of the spiritualists in trying to get into touch with the departed. Once, I remember, we were clearing up a drawerful of litter when we came upon a pen-and-ink sketch of trees and grasses. It had been done by his mother, who had never drawn anything before, while her hand, or so she insisted, had been guided by a spirit. "I said to her," G.B.S. told me, " 'If the spirit is guiding your hand, I suppose you could do it with your eyes closed?' 'George,' said she, 'I wish you wouldn't speak like. a fool at times'." I myself loathe this trance business; and Shaw scoffed at all claims for personal survival, either as a disembodied spirit or as one reincarnate. A newspaper man once asked him if he did not believe that he would "happen" again.

"God forbid," said Shaw, "unless it is a much more pleasant life than this one." And in his preface to *Buoyant Billions* he calls his mother's planchette "screeds" "wishful writings (like wishful thinkings) so clearly were they as much her own storytelling inventions as the Waverley novels were Scott's". She amused herself with spiritualism in her old age, he told Frank Harris, "to be able to play at communicating with her favourite daughter who had died". It may be that the preference for his sister rankled. This planchette of his mother's was the first to reach Ireland. As a child G.B.S. had attended séances since before the age of ten, and once, for the Society of Psychic Research, he slept in a house believed to be haunted. He accepted telepathy: a letter, he would admit, might arrive one morning from someone he had not heard of for years whom he had been thinking of the day before. But mediums made him impatient and he brusquely declined to attend a séance. This annoyed Hannen Swaffer the spiritualist, a faithful admirer of his: Hannen said he might refrain from going to a sitting without being rude about it.

"Meeting my old friends in an eternal other world does not tempt me," said Shaw. "Swaffer and I are pretty good old friends, but after a few thousand years of me he might exhaust my conversation and get a bit tired of me. I can bear to die but not to live for ever; and I am not in the least sad about it." He believed that the Life Force abandoned our bodies at the moment of death, which, he said, religion ought to nerve us to face "as a necessary and beneficent means of getting rid of worn-out incarnations instead of stuffing us with fairy tales in which we are all deathless Wandering Jews".

Shaw brushed aside John's vision of the Second Coming and the Great Judgment as "ravings", pointing out that John begins by declaring that these events will occur "shortly". Whether the thousand years were to expire in A.D. 1000 or (dating from shortly after the vision) in A.D. 1001 was hardly worth arguing about, said Shaw: it was a historical fact that the Christian world understood A.D. 1000 was the date prophesied, and the devout "prepared themselves accordingly". He suggested that John was a drug addict in thus imagining the passage of a thousand years in a moment, and the fact that he did so seemed to Shaw the same as the powers described by De Quincey in his *Confessions of an Opium Eater*. As for the Resurrection, acceptance of it put the believer "beyond the pale". It meant believing in the Ascension, "an astronomical absurdity involving the belief that the sky is the ceiling of the earth and the floor of heaven". He found it most unfortunate that in the Apostles' Creed the Resurrection should be professed as the resurrection of the body and personal immortality, thus giving "a pseudo-religious sanctity to the hideous custom of earth burial which if I had my way would be prohibited by law".

Although Christian dogma annoyed Shaw, he had none of the atheist's intolerance for the Christian ethic, for Christians as individuals, or indeed for their church. At Ayot he subscribed liberally to the repairing of the church organ and the installation of its electric engine. "I am not a Baptist but I enclose a cheque," he wrote, sending one in answer to an appeal from Welwyn for another organ; with all reverence he even put together for Elgar a new version of the lines in the National Anthem, beginning "Scatter his enemies". Shaw's ran

"O Lord our God arise!
All our salvation lies
In Thy great hands.
Centre his thoughts on Thee,
Let him God's captain be,
Thine to Eternity,
God save the King."

As he did not believe in Eternity, the suggestion can, at the least, be regarded as displaying breadth of mind.

It was those whom he dubbed the "Cross-tians" who ruffled Shaw with their "quite hopeless attempts to whitewash the Roman gibbet". What did they expect him to say, he asked one of them, "to such a mad remark as that 'In the cross we see God's love in action'? . . . Don't insult Jesus by saying that the whole value of His life would have been destroyed if He had not been hideously tortured and slaughtered."

The idea that anyone should atone for the sins of others incensed G.B.S. To him Methodism was "quite the most abhorrent and debasing form of religion that exists—the sort of Christianity that centres round the abominable doctrine of the atonement as preached by the followers of Wesley. This doctrine," he added scornfully, "spread tremendously amongst dishonest small tradesmen." To one correspondent after another he would denounce the more emotional interpretations of the Christian faith. "God is love" he dismissed as "a lot of charming flapdoodle". Another inquirer is assured that "the sentimental, 'Love one another' and 'Our Father' of Jesus do not fit into a world of thinly veneered unlovable savages. To love them would be unnatural vice". He asks another to tell him why, if Jesus had only to lift His finger to make the whole Roman army of occupation fall flat on the ground, He did not do so and give the world an overwhelming demonstration of His powers instead of exposing Himself to the mockery of the Jews. Nevertheless, the essence of the Christian faith had so strong an attraction for Shaw that Dean Inge had no doubt that "He who knew the hearts of men" would say of him "thou art not far from the Kingdom of God". From the first, William Temple was also one of the most discerning admirers of G.B.S.; and a kind of official blessing descended upon him from the War Office itself with a request for 4,000 copies of *Androcles and the Lion* to lend out to the troops during the war. Shaw gave them for nothing. Dick Sheppard, of St. Martin's and radio fame, even invited G.B.S. to revise the Prayer Book. On the whole, then, he may be said to have been on the side of the angels; nor had he any patience with the quibbles of agnostics. One of them asked whether it was indeed possible to apply in business, "Whatsoever ye would that men should do to you, do ye even so to them". Shaw replied that the text was not to be taken quite literally, for, "though a man might like his uncle to die and leave him a million he could hardly set him the example"; yet he urged every business man to remember that even under capitalism a bargain was not a good one unless it was good for both parties. Again, during the war, a man wrote to me saying he would be grateful if I would ask G.B.S. to employ his "powerful pen" in the case of a Grenadier Guardsman who had been court-martialled for refusing, because he "had no religion", to enter a church when on church parade, a denial, said my correspondent, to a soldier, fighting for freedom of conscience, of that very freedom "in what is perhaps one of the fundamentals of his mental life—a religious belief or unbelief". "Say," Shaw directed me, "that I have read the case; but as a man with no religion cannot reasonably object to entering a church, which is the same to him as any other building, and as, if he carries his point, he will only be given some much more tiresome fatigue, I should advise him to stick to his self-classification as Church of England. What would be said if a Republican soldier refused to take his turn on Buck, that is, on sentry-go at Buckingham Palace?"

G.B.S. considered quite seriously Dick Sheppard's proposal that he should revise the Prayer Book. His objections to certain passages in it dated back to the early pamphlet *On Going to Church* where he demanded why, if a man desires to follow a good old custom (which, incidentally, he did not follow himself) by pledging his love to his wife in the church of their parish, she must submit "to have a moment of deep feeling made ridiculous by the reading aloud of the naïve impertinence of St. Peter, who, on the subject of Woman, was neither Catholic nor Christian but a boorish Syrian fisherman". An age of strength and faith and noble activity, he felt, could have nothing to do with the Prayer Book as it has come down to us, "in spite of the stolen jewels with which it is studded"; but, after thinking over Dick Sheppard's suggestion, he decided that the job was too big a one for him to tackle. The Christian faith attracted

Shaw as a moralist, an æsthete and a mystic. For all his criticism of the Prayer Book, he finds it not only "studded with
jewels" but "once or twice beautifully touched with the
religious spirit". He thought that children ought to be taught
the Bible at school for the beauty of its language.

Before I knew him, he had been to Oberammergau to see the
Passion Play; and he had an unexpected liking for beautiful
churches: St. George's, in "a polite suburb of Newcastle"; San
Lorenzo, Florence, "a really noble church, Brunelleschi's
masterpiece"; and "who would guess from the repulsive
exterior of Westminster Abbey that there are beautiful chapels
and a noble nave within?" Milan, on the other hand, has a
"petrified christening cake of a cathedral". He found, however, that the services disturbed "the truly religious visitor":
he would have them "decently and intelligently conducted by
genuine mystics to whom the Mass was no mere rite or miracle,
but a real communion". Was G.B.S. himself a mystic? It seems
to me that there can be no doubt about it. For a time there was
a kind of ikon in the Shaw home, which G.B.S. eventually gave
to me. It was a tiny giraffe in pottery. Mrs. Shaw had a cheetah
in the same ware which also came to me because it looked so
lifelike that G.B.S. did not care for it. The giraffe and its long
neck was the central fact in the evolution rumpus. There was,
as Shaw said, "no getting away from him". Darwin maintained
that giraffes have long necks because they are the survivors of
the others who, unable to reach the tender tree tops, have died
of starvation. Shaw denounced this as "the universal struggle
for hogwash", and he was never more eloquent than in his
contempt for what he regarded as this "way of hunger, death,
stupidity, delusion, chance and bare survival". Moreover, the
theory of the survival of the fittest was disturbing to Shaw's
entire economic argument; for, he asked, did it not transform
the competitive system itself into something "positively
scientific"? The giraffe, G.B.S. argued, got its long neck by
stretching it towards the tender tree tops and wishing it into
existence. He went further: there was, he maintained, a power
outside the giraffe which caused it so to wish, and this same
power produced man when the monkey was "not up to the
mark" and could "produce a higher creature than man if man
is not up to the mark". That is the message which Shaw adapted
from Lamarck and proclaimed in one play after another.

He believed, then, that from the beginning a strange driving force had been doing the work of an omnipotent power, bringing on to higher forms of life down the ages the specks of protoplasm from which we all began, and creating eyes, nose, and ears to achieve its purpose. Nor did he accept these higher forms of life as altogether the result of qualities inherited from generation to generation and developed by the successive circumstances in which the individual found himself. There was, he held, a power outside the individual and his surroundings, superintending the destinies of human beings without actively controlling them. He expounded in another letter a theory of his own that the peculiar vitality which had enabled him to produce his works was apparently the result of some creative balance struck between characteristics inherited from both his parents. All sexual unions struck such balances, said he. In no case was the individual a mere bundle of inherited traits: every combination resulted in a creation on which the history of the parents threw no light.

The person whom Shaw regarded as religious was one who conceived himself or herself to be the instrument of a purpose in the universe which was a high purpose and the motive power of "a continual ascent in organisation and power and life and extension of life". Ultimately, he did expect some Being to emerge, "some Person if you like", I find him, in a forgotten pamphlet, telling the New Reform Club, "who will be strong and wise, with a mind capable of comprehending the whole universe and with powers capable of executing its entire will: in other words, an omnipotent and benevolent God". He believed, then, in a "mysterious power", as the doctor puts it in *Too True to Be Good*, "that gives us our life, and none of us knows anything about". In short, he accepted by instinct a truth which he could not reach by reason, and that, I should say, is the essence of mysticism. Thinking along these lines, Shaw was as nettled by dogmatic scientists as by dogmatic theologians. Their sincerity had nothing to do with the case they put up. The validity of a belief, as he assured one of them, somewhat tritely, was neither proved by the sincerity, nor disproved by the insincerity, of those who professed it. "St. Augustine sincerely believed that the earth is flat, and it is easy to imagine one of his contemporaries pulling his leg by pretending to believe that it is round. The jester would have been right and the sincere man wrong." Shaw was impatient with fixed beliefs, except, naturally, his own, and these were as fixed as anyone's.

He derided the lesser scientists: to him all save eight were less than great. He named the eight when he proposed Einstein's health at the Savoy dinner—Pythagoras, Aristotle, Ptolemy, Copernicus, Galileo, Kepler, Newton, and Einstein himself. The occasion was an appeal for the Jews of Eastern Europe, and Shaw, seventy-four at the time, took it so seriously that I got his speech to type out for him beforehand, an unusual request, for generally he spoke without notes. Of his eight great natural philosophers, said his notes, only three had made complete universes: Ptolemy, Newton and Einstein. The others had merely repaired them. These great men had been leaders of a movement of humanity which had two sides, one called religion and the other science.

"Religion," G.B.S. declared, "is always right. Religion solves every problem and thereby abolishes problems from the Universe. Religion gives us certainty, stability, peace, and the absolutes. It protects us against that progress which we all dread. Science is the very opposite. Science is always wrong. It never solves a problem without raising ten more problems."

All those great men had been trying to solve those problems. Copernicus proved that Ptolemy was wrong: Kepler proved that Copernicus was wrong: Galileo proved that Aristotle was wrong. But at that point "the sequence broke down, because science then came up for the first time against that incalculable natural phenomenon, an Englishman". As an Englishman, Newton was able to combine prodigious mental faculty with credulities and delusions that would disgrace a rabbit. As an Englishman, he postulated a rectilinear universe because the English always used the word "square" to denote honesty, truthfulness: in short, rectitude. Newton knew that the universe consisted of bodies in motion, and that none of them moved in straight lines, nor ever could. But an Englishman was not daunted by facts. To explain why all the lines in his rectilinear universe were bent he invented a force called gravitation, and thus created a complete British universe and established it as a religion which was devoutly believed in for 300 years.

"The book of this Newtonian religion," his notes went on, "was not that oriental magic thing, a Bible. It is that British and matter-of-fact thing, a Bradshaw. It gives the stations of all the heavenly bodies, their distances, the rates at which they are travelling, and the hour at which they reach eclipsing points or crash into the earth like Sirius. Every item is precise, ascertained, absolute and English.

G

"Three hundred years after its establishment, a young professor rises calmly in the middle of Europe and says to our astronomers, 'Gentlemen: if you will observe the next eclipse of the sun carefully, you will be able to explain what is wrong with the perihelion of Mercury'. The civilised Newtonian world replies that, if the dreadful thing is true, if the eclipse makes good the blasphemy, the next thing the young professor will do is to question the existence of gravitation. The young professor smiles and says that gravitation is a very useful hypothesis and gives fairly close results in most cases, but that personally he can do without it. He is asked to explain how, if there is no gravitation, the heavenly bodies do not move in straight lines and run away clear out of the universe. He replies that no explanation is needed because the universe is not rectilinear and exclusively British: it is curvilinear. The New-tonian universe thereupon drops dead and is supplanted by an Einsteinian universe. Einstein has not challenged the facts of science but the axioms of science, and science has surrendered to the challenge."

I do not know, for I was not there, whether Shaw delivered himself of all these remarks. The impromptu additions to them have a technical interest. He began, I find in the brief published report of the function, with the joke, expected even in 1930, about the transference of London, as a great centre, to the United States. Then, confronted by the greatest man of his time, he put the others into correct perspective.

"In London," said he, "great men are six-a-penny and are a very mixed lot. When we drink their health and make speeches about them we have to be guilty of scandalous suppressions and disgraceful hypocrisies. Suppose I had to rise to-night to propose the toast of Napoleon. The one thing which I should not possibly be able to say would be perhaps the most important—that it would have been better for the human race if he had never been born. To-night, at least, we have no need to be guilty of sup-pression. There are great men who are great men among small men. There are great men who are great among great men, and that is the sort of man that we are honouring to-night. Napoleon and other great men of his type were makers of Empire. But there is an order of man who gets beyond that. They are makers of universes, and as makers of universes their hands are unstained by the blood of any human being."

Einstein's opinion of Shaw is too interesting to lie lost in a newspaper file. "We are glad, and happy," he said, speaking in German, "that we have with us men from the non-Jewish world. Mr. G. B. Shaw has succeeded in gaining the love and joyful admiration of mankind by a path which to others led to martyrdom. He even dares to mock at what to others appears unapproachable. What Mr. Shaw has done could be done only by the born artist. From his box of tricks he has taken countless puppets which, while resembling men, are not of flesh and blood but consist entirely of spirit, wit and grace. By holding the mirror before us, Mr. Shaw has been able, as no other contemporary, to liberate us and to take from us something of the heaviness of living."

Asking Einstein to forgive them for having broken his "august solitude" in order to help "the poorest of the poor throughout the world", Shaw remarked that all of them had their little solitudes "even though, instead of exploring them for great discoveries, we can only cower in them like children crying in the dark. It is from these little solitudes that we send him our admiration, our good wishes and our prayers. Health and length of days to our greatest contemporary, Einstein!" From offering up prayers for Einstein, it was a short step to suggesting that a personal Deity directly inspired George Bernard Shaw. He happened to be having a dispute with a Catholic over *Adventures of a Black Girl in Search for God* in which he reviews the different ideas of God appearing in the Bible: Noah's, then Job's, then Micah's. As I have already mentioned, he wrote the *Adventures* in South Africa to fill up the five weeks during which Mrs. Shaw was recovering at Knysna from the effects of his erratic car-driving. It came to me early in 1932 and it had a sweeping success as a Christmas gift book when it appeared at five shillings in December, with five reprints before the end of the year, thanks in part to the beautiful engravings done for it by John Farleigh. A Catholic protested and wanted Shaw to withdraw the *Black Girl* from circulation and to make a public recantation. Shaw replied, reasonably enough, that 100,000 copies of the book had been sold and read and that the mischief, if any, was therefore done. He added that he had a more exalted notion of divinity than to believe in "an anti-vegetarian deity who, after trying to exterminate the human race by drowning it, was coaxed out of finishing the job by a gorgeous smell of roast meat". The reference is to the ebbing of the Flood: "And Noah builded an altar unto the Lord; and took of every clean beast, and of every clean fowl, and offered burnt offerings on the altar. And the Lord smelled a sweet savour"—repugnant, naturally, to the nostrils of G.B.S. who did not "as a matter of fact believe that Noah's deity ever existed or ever could exist". He felt that this controversial friend must agree heartily with Micah's "What doth the Lord require of thee, but to do justly, and to love mercy, and to walk humbly with thy God?"

"If you caught a priest offering rams and calves and his first-born (if he had one) as a sacrifice to Jehovah," he tells him, "you would throw him into the nearest lunatic asylum before he could say Hail, Mary. You think you are a better Catholic than I; but my view of the Bible is the view of the Fathers of the Church, and yours is that of a Belfast Protestant to whom the Bible is a fetish and religion entirely irrational". There follows as odd an utterance as ever left Shaw's fountain pen. "You think you believe," he wrote, "that God did not know what he was about when he made me and inspired me to write the *Black Girl*. For what happened was that when my wife was ill in Africa God came to me and said 'There are women plaguing me night and day with their prayers for you. What are you good for anyhow?' So I said I could write a bit but was good for nothing else. God said then 'Take your pen and write what I shall put into your silly head'—and that was how it happened."

Elsewhere Shaw has declared his belief that when he took his pen, or sat down at his typewriter, he was "as much a medium as Douglas Home"; that when he wrote a play he did not foresee or intend a page of it from one end to the other; that the play wrote itself. Many writers, without seeing anything supernatural in it, will explain the growth of a novel or a play in much the same way. But Shaw went much further in his claims for the *Black Girl*; and I would say that he was quite serious in his belief that God heard the praying women and thereafter directed his pen at Knysna. His attitude to prayer was a variant of the normal utilitarian one.

"If you pray that the horse you have backed may win," he told somebody, "you will not increase his chances of winning, but, if it makes you more hopeful until the race is over, it may be worth your while." His praying women were the Little Sisters of the Assumption at their home in Battersea, and the Mother Superior at Stanton Abbey. All of them prayed for G.B.S. daily. "Please go on praying for me," he said, in one of his last letters to the Mother Superior; and again, when they put up a plaque to him in Dublin, he wanted no ceremony, but only "the prayers of the Irish people, which are unpurchasable".

He was all for each of us having our own beliefs. I know the Mother Superior was disappointed when he published the *Black Girl* after she had begged him not to; but Shaw expected her to be as tolerant of his beliefs as he was of hers. He himself was near to prayer at the cremation of Charlotte. Mrs. Shaw, who had been an invalid from the beginning of the war, died quite suddenly, as I have recorded, at Whitehall Court in September 1943. She was six months younger than G.B.S., born in the January following his appearance in July 1856. On the Friday she had been well enough to be up and sitting in the drawing-room for the best part of the day, and in the evening G.B.S. helped her back to her bedroom. All next day she was practically unconscious, dying in the early hours of the Sunday morning. The service at Golders Green resembled the one held, when his time came, for G.B.S. himself. Neither was conducted by a clergyman. For G.B.S. the organ played, at his request, Elgar's "We are the Music Makers" and "Libera Me" from Verdi's Requiem, Sir Sydney Cockerell reading from *The Pilgrim's Progress* the description at the end of Mr. Valiant-For-Truth's pilgrimage. For Charlotte the ceremony lasted but four minutes and only Lady Astor and I were there with G.B.S. During the cremation Handel's Largo was played on the organ, followed by "I know that my Redeemer liveth". As the anthem neared its close, Shaw, standing with hands slightly out-stretched, sang the words softly, as though to himself.

"If Charlotte could only have known, how happy she would be," whispered Lady Astor. His acknowledgment of the sympathy with which he was overwhelmed was so cheerful that before sending it to the papers he asked me rather anxiously whether it might be regarded as frivolous. It said:

"Mr. Bernard Shaw has received such a prodigious mass of letters on the occasion of his wife's death that, though he has read and values them all, any attempt to acknowledge them individually is beyond his powers. He therefore begs his friends and hers to be content with this omnibus reply, and to assure them that a very happy ending to a long life has left him awaiting his own in perfect serenity."

It was their wish that her ashes should await his at Golders Green to be scattered over the garden at Ayot.

CHAPTER XIII

MAN OF BUSINESS

A MAN OF BUSINESS may be a perfect fool with figures: Shaw was that, once he had added them up. If in later years he even got a little shaky over the adding, as a lad he could cast with the best of them. It ran in the family, skipping his father who was as hopeless with figures as with the money they represented. George Carr Shaw excepted, the Shaws were more at home in the counting house than among the poets. An ancestor, Robert, founded the Royal Bank in Dublin, and with it the Dublin offshoot of the Shaw clan in that metropolis. "Old people still called it Shaw's Bank when I was a boy," G.B.S. told his cousin Charles from Australia. "I am a shy person, particularly so, for a bank manager," said this Charles, whose father before him had been a senior clerk in Melbourne Audit Office.

Shaw himself, it will be remembered, was promoted at the age of sixteen from office boy to cashier when the man who held that post in his Dublin estate agency borrowed from the cash the amount of a legacy he had been left, and was found out before he could pay it back. They forbore calling in the police, and, after supporting himself for a time as a church organist, the cashier became one elsewhere, thanks to a testimonial as flattering, G.B.S. afterwards declared, as the one which was to come to him. The defaulter's successor handled the accounts with such exactitude that the salary of Shaw the office boy shot up from £18 to £48 a year. "I, who never knew how much I had of my own," he told one of our correspondents, "proved a model of accuracy as to the money of others." He went on to £72 a year before fleeing to London. The famous testimonial, secured, with the best intentions but much to Shaw's own annoyance, by his father, followed him two years later. Shaw's wrath had long died down by my time, and, with much else, he let me have a copy of the original tribute. It runs:

15 Molesworth Street,
Dublin.
9th August 1878.

Mr. George Shaw served in our office from 1st Nov. 1871 to 31st Mar. 1876 when he left at his own desire.

He entered as a youth and left us having attained to the position of Cashier.

He is a young man of great business capacity, strict accuracy, and was thoroughly reliable and trustworthy.

Anything given him to do was always accurately and well done. We parted from him with regrets and shall always be glad to hear of his welfare.

C. UNIACKE TOWNSHEND & CO.
Land Agents.

In later years Shaw gave the National Union of Clerks his own version of his career at a desk.

"Although all my main clerking experience was over before I was twenty," he said, "I had, through an accident, been put into a position of trust and activity always previously given to a man of mature years; and my employer afterwards testified that I was a treasure (for which I was so ungrateful as to damn his impertinence in the secrecy of my soul); yet the highest salary I touched was either £72 or £84 a year: I forget which. And I began at £18.

"What is more, I was considered very well placed, and not at all without good reason; for the office was crushingly genteel; and if I had had any serious business intentions I could have made it the jumping-off plank for a lucrative and socially respected career in the business I was supposed to be learning, and would have learnt if it had interested me in the smallest degree."

Business, in the sense of making money, did not, in truth, interest G.B.S. He would never, for example, have dreamt of gambling on the Stock Exchange: he did accidentally pick up a few thousand pounds when Welwyn Garden City was acquired by the Development Trust, but there it was the idea he had backed, not the luck of the market. He looked upon money as an irrelevance so out of place in a civilised community that for long enough he wanted us all to have equal shares of it. The meaning to the ordinary worker of the increased cost of living never reached his conscious mind. Although he lived very quietly, spending much less than most men in his position, his outlay was considerable for one of his meagre needs, and I am sure that he was never aware of how it had risen after the war. When he wrote out the cheques for his monthly bills, there might be a vague impression that they were a little larger than they used to be, but he never realised what that must mean to us others who did not pay surtax. He flatly declined to face the fact that salaries earned before the war were quite insufficient in the succeeding years of peace. In his own mind, Shaw priced everything at pre-war standards, and he really believed that we were all on velvet. Even his accountant could not bring him to understand that, if he paid us more, he could include much of the outlay in expenses against income tax.

He would make the wildest statements about money. When Frank Harris offered him £600 for co-operating in an Oscar Wilde film, he assured Harris that, by lifting up his finger, he could get £10,000 for his name in the advertisement. When somebody asked him for a plan for post-war Britain he replied that, if he could be persuaded to write it, the answer would cost £25,000. He informed an American that if he had an income of about 150,000,000 dollars he might perhaps be able to advance all the money people demanded from him. "People don't think what it costs me to write letters", he complained. "I am asked questions that would require an elaborate reply which would be worth fifteen hundred dollars for the first serial rights. But they expect to get replies for nothing, forgetting that I have to live."

I once told him that someone had offered £50 for the Dolmetsch spinet at Whitehall Court. "Fifty pounds!" he exclaimed. "It's worth five hundred!" In the end it went for considerably less than that when he sold much of the Whitehall Court furniture. However skilled he may have been at totting up the land agents' ledger, large totals left him bewildered. When, between the wars, the chain letter stupidity was at its height I tore up one invitation after another asking Shaw to send it to nine persons to whom he wished luck, each of whom was to send it to nine others, and so on. It made G.B.S. quite giddy. "If this silly idea were carried out," said he, "it would break the backs of all the postmen and bankrupt all the Postmasters-General in the world."

Except that it would evidently have made fortunes for the

world's Post Offices, he may not have been so far out here; but he had no head for numbers. He could never, for instance, remember how many brothers and sisters I had. There, I should say, he was not interested; nor were they particularly interested in my famous employer, for my family never pestered me, as others did, to bring them to the notice of G.B.S. Numbers were beyond the range of those things which he could comprehend. When the idea of equal incomes went out of favour with him he declared that it was impossible because, if the national income were divided up, it would only yield each of us four shillings a week. When it was pointed out to him that his four shillings had no arithmetical validity, he readily agreed, adding that perhaps the figure should be forty!

His new alphabet was another sad case of how zeal, coupled with this lack of comprehension, whirled him quite off his feet. The proposals, first mooted in a letter to *The Times*, went out, finely printed on deckle-edged foolscap paper, to all our legislators; for he saw clearly that here was a job not for individuals but for collective action on the grand scale. So he himself wrote round to the British Council, the Statistical Society, the National Service Department of the Ministry of Labour, the Privy Council, the Royal Society of Arts, and one or two other public bodies, announcing that he was making his will and that he intended leaving to the nation, for a specific purpose, his property, "including certain copyrights, the value of which may run into six figures". It was to be a phonetic alphabet of forty-four letters, each representing a sound because "to spell English phonetically within the limits of a twenty-six letter alphabet is impossible". He calculated that, in writing and printing superfluous letters, our "ancient Phœnician alphabet" cost us the price of a fleet of battleships every year. Copying the same text for a minute in "Johnsonese and in phonetic, the time saved by phonetic will come out round about twenty per cent." But that, he argued, left out the time factor. "We are used to read per cent. as per cent. per year; but, in the test, per cent. is per cent. per minute. Now there are 525,000 minutes in a year, consequently the saving of twenty per cent. per minute means a labour saving of two months' working days per scribe every year. Multiply this figure by an estimate of the number of persons who at every moment of the twenty-four hours are writing the English language in the

British Commonwealth and in American and the total is astronomical."

The total would certainly be considerable; but Shaw's two months' working days are calculated at one-fifth of 525,000 minutes for a year of 24-hour days. Even given a full year, with no allowance for the five-day week, at eight hours a day, instead of his twenty-four, who among us is using the alphabet for more than one-third of the eight hours? The time saved would be nearer one week than two months a year per person; and against the saving would have to be set the cost of changing one alphabet over to another on all the printing presses and typewriters of the English-speaking world, to say nothing of the task of teaching a few million children a completely new alphabet and completely new spelling. But G.B.S. just swept merrily on, leaving the figures to take care of themselves. He was prepared to hand over for twenty years part of the income of his residuary estate to any Government department, trust, college, or society of private individuals willing to take on the responsibility of designing and producing a new alphabet; publishing a few English classics in it, and seeing that the leading libraries had copies of them, alongside those in our existing alphabet, "to let the fittest survive". If within twenty years nobody wanted his alphabet, then the money was to go "to other public purposes". It remains to be seen if any responsible body will be brave enough to take up this new alphabet. Shaw's conviction that somebody would is a perfect example of his remoteness from ordinary human kind.

He got Isaac Newton himself into a tangle. When Newton checks up the Duchess of Cleveland's allegation that the Good King Charles has been unfaithful to her with Nell Gwynn 100,000 times, Shaw sets him calculating:

"For each unfaithfulness allow a day—or shall I say a night? Now one hundred thousand nights are almost two hundred and seventy-four years. To be precise, 273 years 355 days. The additional day for Leap Year every four years adds 68 years 180 days. Total: 342 years 170 days. Now Mr. Rowley is only fifty, from which you must deduct at least fifteen years for his childhood. . . ."

A mathematician pounced on the calculation, pointing out with arid glee that, as there were 68 leap years in the 273 years, the 100,000 days became 68 days more, and that this number should therefore be deducted from Shaw's 273 years, 355 days;

instead of which he had blithely added 68 years, 180 days to the total. Shaw worked it out again and had to agree with his critic; so in the next edition Newton's calculation becomes:

"For each unfaithfulness allow a day—or shall I say a night? Now one hundred thousand nights are almost two hundred and seventy-four years. To be precise, 273 years 287 days, allowing 68 days for Leap Year every four years. Now Mr. Rowley is not 300 years old: he is only 50, from which you must deduct at least fifteen years for childhood. . . ."

Shaw was a stickler for getting his facts exactly right. When we were at work on *Saint Joan* he carefully checked up all details about the Church. In *Everybody's Political What's What* his exposition of betting on horse races was run through by William Maxwell, and altered at his suggestion. It was again William Maxwell who in another chapter lighted on Shaw's slip when he says that "to keep up the price of codfish, many were thrown into the sea". Cod, William pointed out, were never thrown back; they were cured and dried. So "codfish" became "fish", G.B.S., inclining to self-pity, remarking that he was becoming incapable of writing ten words without making some blunder.

Pounds, shillings and pence were in truth as remote from his active comprehension as the meaning of figures ranged in their thousands. I had to enter every royalty in our day book so that, in making his income tax return, he could set down clearly, to the last cent and pfennig, what each country sent him for his books, his plays and his films; before the war, America brought in most money from overseas, with Germany runner-up. The youth who had been complimented by the Dublin estate agents on his "strict accuracy" was now, as a man, complimented by his Inspector of Taxes upon the exactitude with which he completed his income tax returns. After a time I told Shaw I could not guarantee that the total was accurate, so for £60 we bought an adding machine, a heavy implement which I alone used. During the war, when things were getting more difficult, we decided it would ease the situation to have the books done by an accountant; the machine was therefore sold to a business man who could not get one. Meanwhile G.B.S. found himself going slower on figures. Before we had the machine, the working of which he never grasped, he was quite quick when we used to sit together adding up the columns. But with advancing years he was growing less sure of himself,

and after Mrs. Shaw's death, when Mrs. Laden asked him
to check the household books, he wanted this cumbersome
contrivance sent down to Ayot, forgetting that it had been sold.
It was then that he bought a small portable machine on which
he happily tapped out and added up the monthly housekeeping
bills, his interest held by the mechanical performance rather
than by any interest in the bills themselves. Always a lover of
detail, he once, when they were on Lake Maggiore, sent me a
little sketch of how a registered envelope, "but not an insured
letter with the value declared", ought to be sealed and forwarded to Stresa with traveller's cheques for £200.

Although he was as big a platform draw as Lloyd George,
Horatio Bottomley or Winston Churchill in their heyday, the
only fee Shaw ever took for public speaking out of London was
his third-class return ticket; and this only in his younger days.
When he became more affluent he paid his own expenses,
remarking that this was his contribution to the funds of the
party or society for whom he was speaking. "What are the
damages, Mr. Shaw?" an organiser of one of his meetings
recalled, thirty years afterwards, asking him in the ante-room.
"Boy," replied G.B.S., putting his hand on the man's shoulder,
"I've three hobbies in life: motoring, swimming and public
speaking. I never make money out of these hobbies." Yet,
although he might be a fool with figures, he was no fool with
people. He had the most clear-sighted objection to others,
apart from these societies to whom his speeches were a gift,
coining his name into cash. Perhaps he was too captious. He
would not permit the industrious compilers of anthologies to
use him as the decoy for lesser fry; and, if one of his household
monthly bills was under £1, he would instruct whoever was
paying it to get a postal order, partly because he did not want
to trouble his bank with entries for small amounts, but mainly
because he reckoned that, if a cheque was for more than £1,
nobody would think it worth selling for the signature, as some
sold cheques for lesser sums. I once suggested to him that, to
save troubling him with cheques, he should sign up a book of
them and send them on to me at Whitehall Court to be filled
in by me as the bills arrived. The idea horrified him, and for
the oddest reason. Both of us, he argued, might die simultaneously, and then someone might discover the blank cheques and
raid his bank balance.

Then there was the tortuous affair of *The Chocolate Soldier*.

But for his fortunate inability to state anything save the exact truth, I am sure that Shaw could have won renown at the Bar. His mind marshalled details in a flash, and in the case of *The Chocolate Soldier* he briefed counsel so effectively that, against odds, we snatched a brilliant, if Pyrrhic, victory. I say "we", for I was the only witness for the defence. It happened when we were at Adelphi Terrace and it began with a man turning up there from the United States to say that he had bought the film rights of *The Chocolate Soldier*, the musical comedy which borrows the plot of Shaw's *Arms and the Man*. *The Chocolate Soldier* had been shown to G.B.S. when it was first produced in London and he had then agreed that he would not object to it, provided they took out some of the material which in his opinion made a travesty of the play. G.B.S. did not go to see *The Chocolate Soldier*, but he heard afterwards that the passage in question had not been cut as stipulated. When films came along, it was obviously going to be a race to the screen between *Arms and the Man* and *The Chocolate Soldier*. Our American visitor wanted to talk the situation over with G.B.S. who at the time was out of town. I therefore told him that I would see whether I could give him an appointment. As that could not be arranged, I outlined for him Shaw's point of view: that *The Chocolate Soldier* and *Arms and the Man* were two distinct plays; that they were both written around the same battle, with the same incident of the soldier breaking into the lady's bedroom and that, if *The Chocolate Soldier* were to be filmed, care must be taken that nothing was to be quoted from the letterpress of Mr. Shaw's play, *Arms and the Man*, nor must his name appear in connection with it, as he would immediately prosecute should there be any suggestion that he had anything to do with the writing of *The Chocolate Soldier*. When the American went home he found that he could not begin his film without stating that it was "based on *Arms and the Man* by Bernard Shaw". So he came back to England and announced that he intended to bring an action against G.B.S. for stopping the film after he had bought up the rights of *The Chocolate Soldier*. Shaw ignored him until one day when he received a summons; and, as the other side were strongly represented, we had now to get to work. For months we were collecting evidence, and after many a consultation with our solicitors and in counsel's chambers I was instructed to give evidence. Our case was based on my letter, as only I had seen the man.

Mr. J. M. Gover, K.C., who, with Mr. Henn-Collins (later
he was the Hon. Sir Stephen Henn-Collins), represented us,
said that Shaw would not stand a chance, as the case was
coming before Mr. Justice Eve. G.B.S. kept buoyant and
instructed them, point by point, how to put the case for him.
As for me, I was very nervous: I was the only witness for the
defence and they told me that I must state for certain what
I had said to the plaintiff almost a year before. "Then she'll
perjure herself at once," said Shaw helpfully. "This is a comedy
written by Bernard Shaw," Mr. Justice Eve was told when
the case opened. "Well," said he, "I am glad to hear that
we are at last having some comedy in this Court. It is usually
quite the opposite." Almost immediately my spirits soared.
The plaintiff made a bad slip. He said that when I called
I had given him an appointment for two o'clock the next
day. Never while at Adelphi Terrace had I given an appointment for the afternoon; and in any case G.B.S. would probably not have finished lunch by then. Proceedings went on
all day, and, on the second day, when we had only been a short
time in Court, the judge sprang a surprise. "You have no case,"
said he to the plaintiff. "The letter says that *if* your film
mentions the name of Bernard Shaw you will be prosecuted.
But, until your film is made, there can be no case." The action
was dismissed, and I, to my relief, had never been called. Shaw
was awarded £800 damages and we went home to lunch. After
lunch came a ring at the front door. Could the ex-plaintiff see
either Mr. Shaw or Miss Patch? "I am not going to see him,"
said I. Shaw went into the drawing-room to find out why he
had called. It seems that he had come round because, although
it was he who had brought the action against Shaw, G.B.S. was
the only one who had been kind to him. When the man had
been pointed out to Shaw in Court, G.B.S. had gone over and
shaken hands with him. It was a maxim of Shaw's that you
should always make friends with your enemy while he is in the
way. And now the man told G.B.S. about his mother and his
laryngitis and almost cried on his shoulder. I do not think there
was any talk of money. Anyhow I was the one who got any
that was going: they paid me two guineas for my visits to
counsel's chambers and Shaw never worried about the £800
which the case had cost him.

He was the ideal creditor. A man once got a cheque from him
on the pretext that he was leaving London in such a hurry that

there was no time to get a reference from his own bank to a London branch. In return, Shaw accepted a cheque for the amount on the fellow's bank, an act which the bank itself failed to reciprocate. There was nothing there, reported the bank manager, adding that he presumed G.B.S. would prosecute. "I certainly won't," said Shaw. "I don't want everyone to know how easily I have been duped."

I can recall only one example of G.B.S. permitting others to cash in on his name; and that I imagine was to tease Gabriel Wells. This Gabriel was born a Hungarian, probably with a more Eastern ancestor. I vaguely recollect his telling me that, with neither money nor a word of English, he somehow got away to the United States after angering his father by fighting a duel. He became an American citizen, and, while mastering our language, he grew interested in English literature. By 1928, when he came to London, he had acquired great fame as a book collector, and, now a well-known figure at all the big auctions, he began to make a corner in Shaw first editions and manuscripts. Soon there was a positive Shaw boom: for two years fantastic prices were paid at the auctions.

Shaw never realised that the prices were fantastic. The conviction took root that his name was a kind of talisman; that if he wrote a foreword to a book, the book would inevitably sell like hot chestnuts in winter. When the booksellers sent in their orders for the six-guinea *de luxe* edition of *Buoyant Billions* he thought it was going so well that he suggested the price ought to be increased for the remaining copies. And "Why not sell the letters you have of mine," he wrote to his old friend Henry Salt, "and live in comfort for the rest of your life?" Salt took the tip and did in fact spend his remaining years in Shaw Lodge at Brighton. G.B.S., immensely tickled by the craze for autographed copies of his works, joined in the fun. He would not only autograph copies of his books but write messages in them and tell the owners to run round to Mr. Wells and demand £50 or £100 for each. Gabriel, with whom I became very friendly, assured me that Shaw was ruining the market with his inscriptions on the piles of books brought to him by complete strangers. I fancy G.B.S. did it all out of sheer mischief; anyhow Gabriel had to call a halt to his trading in Shaw's name, and I know that one or two manuscripts, for which he must have given about £200 at Sotheby's, fetched only about £25 when put up there some years later. Before the war Gabriel went back to the United States where he died in 1946 at the age of eighty. He paid £2,000 for the manuscript of Carlyle's *Past and Present* and gave it to the British Museum. My only mementos of him are a gramophone and several Christmas cards designed by himself and consisting mainly of disquisitions on moral behaviour.

The great days for Shaw manuscripts and first editions passed with Gabriel Wells, which is regrettable, for there must be a lot, of the latter at least, scattered about the globe, although G.B.S. went the length of having rough proofs of many of the later plays destroyed to keep them out of the hands of the collectors. He always had forty or fifty of these rough proofs of each play printed for rehearsal purposes, and this because in nearly every case his plays were performed before they were published in book form. They did not carry his name: they were "By a Fellow of the Royal Society of Literature", and most of them went to the producer to hand out to his cast. When we left Adelphi Terrace for Whitehall Court a dealer in second-hand books bought up a whole stack of these proofs and sold them separately, so that there are probably numbers of them all over the world. One of my regrets is that I did not pay sufficient attention to Shaw's invitation to take as many of them as I cared to have. I doubt if many of the rough proofs printed in recent years are of any great value, but in 1945 a copy of *Annajanska, the Bolshevik Empress* was auctioned at Sotheby's and fetched something over £30. When I sold my copy two or three years later, it brought me a mere £13. According to its author, this playlet, written for Lillah McCarthy and put on at the Coliseum in 1918, is "a revolutionary pamphlet". Originally it was called *Annajanska, the Wild Duchess*. "She told me," wrote Shaw on my copy of it (thus helping to raise its value to the £13), "that a few pages from the end she lost her hold on the audience. Thereupon I changed the ending; and the Wild Duchess became the Bolshevik Empress".

Despite the comparative slump in the value of Shaw MSS., there is, perhaps, one still lying about in some musty Birmingham cupboard which would be worth a lot to a collector, if to nobody else. It is a lost, unpublished story, *The Brand of Cain*, written when G.B.S. was twenty-eight. Among the papers which he generously passed on to me before he died was the shorthand of a letter he wrote asking for its return. It reads:

Hawkes & Phelps,   36 Osnaburgh Street, N.W.
    Shut Lane,   5/1/85
        Birmingham.
Gentlemen,
    Have you been able to make use of my story "The Brand
of Cain"? If not, I should be glad to have the MS back, as
I have an opening for it elsewhere.
                        I am,
                            Gentlemen,
                                Yours faithfully,
                                    GEORGE BERNARD SHAW.

The "opening for it elsewhere" was probably a young man's
effort at salesmanship; anyhow the letter was never answered;
the manuscript never returned; and he had kept no copy of it.
All that survived was his own recollection of the plot. The story
he told me, was about a woman who had committed a murder
of which she was never suspected. An amateur photographer
took her photograph and in the negative "the brand of Cain"
appeared on her forehead. G.B.S. was unable to remember
how the story ended. He explained to me that, although it was
purely imaginary, he had heard of things not visible to the
naked eye coming out in photographs. His mind was already,
in 1885, tending to roam beyond the rigidly material, a
tendency which was about to cause his revolt against Darwin.
Three years later he evidently embarked upon another adventure into fiction for, in 1928, he informed someone that I
had "just unearthed a beginning of a novel in 1888, which,
were not my own handwriting against me, I would swear I
never wrote, saw, conceived, nor heard of in my life".
    Among these relics of almost seventy years ago is the original
shorthand, now brown with age, of Shaw's efforts to sell *An
Unsocial Socialist*. On one side of a slip of stout pink paper he
has written:

David Douglas, Esq.,   36 Osnaburgh Street, N.W.
    Castle Street,   20/12/84
        Edinburgh.
Dear Sir,
    A novel of mine called an Unsocial Socialist has just
finished its course as a serial through the pages of a magazine
called *To-Day*. I am anxious to see it reprinted in a cheap

form. Will you allow me to send you the book to read? If you should find it worth a place in your 1/– series, I shall be very well pleased indeed to have my book so well introduced.

I am, dear Sir,
Yours faithfully,
G. B. SHAW.

On the other side of the pink slip is a letter, dated six days later, to "Chatto and Windus, Piccadilly".

Gentlemen,
Will you oblige me by reading a novel of mine entitled "The Unsocial Socialist"? It is in print, having already run through a magazine as a serial.

I am,
Gentlemen,
Yours faithfully,
GEORGE BERNARD SHAW.

Below he has written "The same *verb. et lit.* to Macmillan & Co. 30/12/84". In later days G.B.S. was "appalled" to think that George Meredith and John Morley were among those who had the job of reading those early efforts of his for the publishers. Meredith would have none of him. Morley, regarding him as a young man "whose head was turned by Ruskin", wrote about him "at such length that George Macmillan softened his firm's refusal by sending me a copy of John's report". Shaw often wondered afterwards how much Macmillan and Chatto paid these eminent gentlemen for reading his "jejune fictions". The usual fee was believed to be a guinea, but he had heard of "a lady with quite a respectable talent" who in those days read books at half a crown a time.

The Unsocial Socialist was the last of five novels written by G.B.S. Macmillan, and fifty or so other publishers, sent them all back to Osnaburgh Street; and by 1889 the royalties collected on them amounted to two shillings and tenpence. The man of business was not yet making money; but the rules on which he was prepared to do business were beginning to emerge. He would never pay to have anything published; he would never back a play with cash; he would never allow a penny of his earnings to go to a literary agent. It may be suggested that, when he had just enough cash to bring back his latest novel, he was making a virtue of necessity in refraining from giving a reluctant publisher money which he did not possess; and that, as he became famous, a subsidy was unnecessary. But cash was not the motive.

"If there is a principle to which I have clung as the first article of artistic virtue," he once told an aspirant, "it is that we should never pay for the publication of our own works, even if we were never to see a page of them in print. But for this iron rule I should now be a pauper." So with putting money in plays: "I owe my present fairly secure financial position to my iron determination never to invest in any form of public entertainment under any provocation whatever."

And he was his own literary agent, himself handling all his contracts, overseas as well as home. He would select his translator in each country and leave it to him to find a publisher there. The arrangement which I have already mentioned by which he himself paid his printer and his binder, his publisher taking the royalties due, was I think, unique in the publishing trade, and all the more acceptable to printer and binder as G.B.S. sent out his cheques promptly, by return of post: nor, like my own father, did he ever leave a tradesman waiting for his money, a considerateness which earned both of them the respect of the shopkeeping community. I remember once getting a frantic note from Shaw because he thought he had lost our P.A.Y.E. card, which in any event would have baffled him completely, and in real distress because the inspector had called for a cheque.

He denounced charities, and usually he succeeded in refraining from subscribing to them, although once, when a Lord Mayor of London appealed on behalf of 460,000,000 children all over the world, he received a cheque with, "For the kids. No acknowledgment expected. G.B.S." On another occasion he was caught for £100 at a Hammersmith meeting where he and Gerald du Maurier and others were appealing on behalf of Mrs. Cecil Chesterton's Cecil Houses for homeless women. When Shaw heard that Mrs. Chesterton had gone on the streets to find out for herself what a homeless woman had to put up with, he commented that if she had only stayed there a little longer "she would not have gone back home, she would have found what a pleasant life it is". From the Hammersmith platform he declared, "Not a penny do I give"; then, carried away, he announced that if they collected one hundred pounds he would add a second. They rushed around and found the money and Shaw had to send his cheque along. Charlotte and he had their retinue of private pensioners but, "Go away," he wrote to one of them who wanted to come and talk to him. "I have not time for broken-down old women." And he flatly refused to support the hospitals when they were voluntary. In the preface to *The Apple Cart* a denunciation of them brought a protest and the usual sharp rejoinder. It was precisely the element called 'soul' in our charitable institutions that he loathed, said he. In a properly organised community there should be no room for benevolence and gratitude in such necessary services as the care of the sick and of children. There should be no such horrors as philanthropists and beggars; like other people he sometimes had to give money and others had to ask him for it, and, "it taxes all my self-control to avoid hating them as heartily as they hate me".

His scorn for money extended to the things which money buys: his indifference to material possessions was complete. When he handed over his Irish property to Carlow Urban Council, the probable motive was a lack of interest in the idea of owning it. The property was a tiny Parish Hall with a few cottages, which, as he informed the Council with a certain family pride, he had "inherited as the great-grandson of the Thomas Gurly whose monument is in one of your chief churches". When the cottages came into Shaw's possession he "received nothing but the legal ownership, a bundle of mortgages and several dependent relatives". He cleared off the mortgages, "provided otherwise for the surviving relatives", and found himself left with a net revenue of £150 a year, "confiscated by the British Government to defray the expense of military operations". So he invited the Council, and they acclaimed the offer, to accept the property as the nucleus of a trust, not associated in any way with himself, to which citizens of public spirit might make future contributions. It is true that, as he said, he would not "eat a mouthful or drink a spoonful or buy a suit of clothes the less", because of this surrender, but many a one would have held on to the property in empty pride of possession. Possessions he regarded as lumber; although he had been an art critic (or it may have been because of that fact), he never bought a picture for the sake of possessing it. He might acquire one as an excuse for being kind to somebody, never as a man making an attractive investment. He looked on picture prices as a racket, and in the late nineteen-twenties he told Chelsea why.

His friend Harriet Cohen, the pianist, friend also of Arnold Bennett, offered her house for a show of clever flower pictures by Gertrude Harvey at five pounds apiece, and G.B.S. wrote a note about it. All his life, he declared, he had been confronted in picture galleries "with price lists conceived in hundreds of guineas for which no sane person, even of the millionaire class, could be expected to sacrifice more than five pounds". Outside the galleries were "seedy artists, starving artists, borrowing artists, begging artists, stealing artists, drinking and drugging artists, despairing artists and dying artists; whilst on the pavement sat the screevers to whom they snobbishly denied the name of artist with pennies enough pouring into their caps to save them quite comfortably from the razor, the pistol and the gas stove".

Recognising the quality of the woman artist's work which he was introducing, he "called her attention to that great American genius Mr. Woolworth, who has given us wonderful shops in which you can buy any article for sixpence. No shop windows detain me in my walks as his do". He reminded her that he, Bernard Shaw, had been glad to receive five pounds for many of the best criticisms he ever wrote, and that George Russel the painter supported Æ. the poet by editing a paper on week-days, and on Sundays painting an Irish (or Tir nan Ogge) landscape of extraordinary quality for which he easily found a purchaser at five pounds. He exhorted her to become the first Woolworth artist, and give London the first one-woman show of five pound pictures. Both Charlotte and G.B.S. often went to Harriet Cohen's recitals, and Shaw stayed for two hours at a party in this same flat, sitting on the floor talking, or singing to his own accompaniment on a piano which a bomb was soon to leave in smithereens. But Chelsea did not at all relish Shaw's views on picture prices, and C. R. W. Nevinson, artist son of his old friend Henry, retorted with an invitation to Shaw to reduce the prices of his theatre seats below cost, when even he "would be prepared to sacrifice sixpence for a stall".

In his later years any such suggestion would almost have sent Shaw into a frenzy. Until he entered his last decade he was never unduly perturbed about money. When he was ninety he accepted philosophically the modest royalty on the 2,000,000 Penguin copies of the plays published to celebrate his birthday. Then a phobia about surtax took hold of him. On the one hand he would contend that, in spite of the rise in the cost of living, his royalties had not gone up for fifty years, which was manifestly absurd because the price of theatre seats, on which the royalties were paid, had certainly not remained stationary for half a century. In the same breath, he would protest that he did not want any more income, for he had persuaded himself that he was now paying the Exchequer £147 for every £100 he earned. It was the last of the long run of illusions about figures. Useless to assure him that this applied to invested money only. No. "I am sticking to my figure of £147 as the easiest to remember." So Flora Robson must not come to the West End lest *Captain Brassbound* should draw the town and leave him bankrupt. And he will not help Maurice Evans with *Man and Superman* in New York. His American earnings are "taxed and surtaxed by the United States Government and the residue taxed and surtaxed by the British Government. . . . I am longing for it to flop, before I am quite penniless, cursing the day you were born."

He toys with little economies. He cannot afford heavier winter curtains for the drawing-room (perhaps because he himself seldom sat there). He finds a good country tailor to make his suits, which, incidentally, were always unlined, more cheaply than in London. He writes to the National Health Service authorities inquiring how he stands for registration under the Act. They have appointed a doctor who is in private attendance on him; "and I wish to retain him in this capacity. He informs me that he must not act in both capacities. All the same I wish to have a National doctor in case the war taxation should leave me unable to afford a private one, and as a social example. Must I have either two doctors or no doctor? The matter is not pressing, as I am in no immediate need of medical service. Still, as I am in my 93rd year, I may presently need a death certificate."

The levelling down of incomes, which had seemed a pretty dream when I typed it out for him in Adelphi Terrace thirty years before, was beginning to leave him rather restive.

CHAPTER XIV

ASPIRING METHUSELAH

"How do you keep fit?" somebody once asked G.B.S.

"There is no 'how'," he replied. "You do or you don't: that is all." Already these memoirs have recorded mishaps which might have happened to Samson: the germ picked up in the Pekin theatre; how he was stung by an insect on the way to Geneva; the motor accident on the Port Elizabeth road; how he slipped and hurt his leg in China. Then he is violently seasick: and that presumably might have happened to Samson too. But not his rheumatism or the lumbago which overtook him in mid-Pacific. He knew what lumbago meant. "I am sorry for the lumbago!" he wrote to me from Gleneagles, "but holidays always leave one a wreck and I hope you have now paid the penalty in full." And, again, "I am in bed with colic, but shall be well before this reaches you." From Stresa Mrs. Shaw reports that he is "getting stronger". Influenza attacked him as it did any other mortal, and it was to smallpox that he owed what to the world at large was probably his most distinctive feature. He could not shave, and the famous beard was born, "so like a tuft of blanched grass," said he, "that pet animals would nibble at it." He wore it slightly shorter in his later years: his hair, cut every three months, went thinnish, but he would not allow his Welwyn barber to trim his eyebrows which to the end bristled in playful ferocity. Once, I remember, when he was recovering from a bout of influenza, Dr. David, Bishop of Liverpool, called for information on something he was writing. Shaw was not well enough to see him, but next day I took the Bishop in to the invalid, reclining on the sofa. Later I heard a shout of laughter, and when I went in I found they had changed places: the Bishop was the invalid on the sofa, with G.B.S. sitting on a stool by his side, entertaining him.

All these accidents and ailments were trifling enough, and the disabilities of his later years were rarely serious. Until the end, his handwriting, for a nonagenarian, was remarkably clear; if

latterly it did tremble a little, his mind remained alert. Corrections of what he wrote were no more frequent than they had
been. He might avoid work not strictly relevant to his own: just
as he had put off from week to week the reading of Lawrence's
Seven Pillars, so for more than a year he refrained from tackling
the proofs of Hesketh Pearson's book about himself. But there he
was dilatory because of his concentration upon what he was
doing. He did, as I have said, become a little deaf; and,
although he could not follow general conversation too closely,
he was all right when spoken to directly. For a man of his years
his sight was good. In my day he always used glasses for reading, but he was prejudiced against wearing them except for
work, saying that it was a mistake to get into the habit unless
you had to. He would in fact have been wiser to have used distance glasses, yet, although he could never see things a long way
off, he always refused. Once when I tried to point out to him
from the garden at Ayot an aerial clearly visible to me upon the
sky-line, I found it difficult to convince him that it was there.

He had an eye defect which is not uncommon with men—at
least I have never met a woman suffering from it. When I was
at Ayot during the war he asked me how the cuffs of his coat
could be repaired. He was particularly fond of this coat, and
clothes rationing had now come in, so he did not want to give it
up, and he said that leather round the edges would chafe his
wrists. I offered to bind the cuffs with strips of coloured felt
which I happened to be using for my hobby of toy-making. To
this he agreed. The coat was greyish, and unfortunately I had
no grey felt, so I used a bright green which took his fancy. He
was delighted; as was the village by the sight of him stepping
out to the Post Office with the bright green sleeve edging, giving
him a vaguely Tyrolean air. One morning he brought me a tie
which he declared matched the cuffs. "But," said I, "your tie is
blue." He put the colours together and insisted that they were
identical. At this it was plain that, as far as blues and greens
went, he was colour-blind, a disability of which I knew something for when my mother's father went on a painting holiday
from the Bank of England, where he worked, he could use only
blues, browns and sepias: he never knew the colour of a straw-
berry or a redcoat. Confirmation of Shaw's colour-blindness
came with a scarf woven for him by a woman admirer in Scotland. He was very pleased with it, but, he wrote to ask her,
would she do him one with less green in it? It was not green,

I pointed out, but blue; and the weaver herself settled our argument by regretfully informing him that his secretary was right. By chance G.B.S. himself happened to be right, at least as far as the colour was concerned, when he described Charlotte on the back of a photograph as 'The Green-Eyed Millionairess'; but her eyes might have been blue for all he knew.

Trivial although these defects and minor ailments may have been, it is only fair to balance them against his boast that he was "seldom less than ten times as well as an ordinary carcass eater". And it was in fact to one of the lesser products of a carcass, according to Shaw the "gastric juice of a hog", that he probably owed his recovery from the only serious illness before his last he had in my experience of him. "I was suddenly attacked", he told a friend, "by what they call pernicious anæmia; and it seemed that my number was up. To my intense disgust they inoculated me with liver extract, but I cannot deny that it rejuvenated me. . . . The doctors, called in by my distracted wife, had begun by 'ordering' me beef and whisky, a prescription which I received with the thumb to the nose. However they guaranteed a cure if I allowed them to squirt into the muscles of my seat a hormone extracted from the liver of countless unspecified fish or animals by a process which gets rid of the liver tissue and leaves the mysterious hormone which reds the blood. . . . I dropped dead twice after inoculations and frightened my wife. They were afraid to inoculate me again: and now I take a tablespoon twice a day of some liquid preparation of this loathsome stuff of which there are over sixty different sorts. . . ."

After lying on a sofa and doing absolutely nothing for six weeks he got rid of his angina pectoris and other disablements and showed signs of "a new lease of life (of sorts)". It all happened at Whitehall Court just after G.B.S. had attended the ceremony of handing over the site for the National Theatre when he received a symbolic square of turf from the Borough of Kensington; and it shocked the sterner members of the vegetarian flock who with some justice regarded extract of pig's liver as a "serious deviation from their ethics". One of the three doctors who were called in declared after diagnosing Shaw's condition that he would not have been surprised if he had dropped down dead in the midst of the Kensington ceremony.

Shaw was no bigot for the orthodox either in vegetarianism or medicine. He told the vegetarians who were disturbed about his liver extract that it was not their business to bother about what he ate or what he did not eat, and he urged them to "stop lying and bragging about vegetarianism and stick to the facts". Nor was he really prejudiced against doctors: he listened equably to what they had to say and then he used his own judgment. Thus, on the one hand, he would be attracted by the osteopaths, faith healers and any form of yoga, but when, on the other, a doctor succeeded in convincing him that extract of pig's liver would cure his pernicious anæmia, he placed himself in the doctor's hands and was an obedient, immobilised patient for more than six weeks, keeping indoors and doing no work, although not actually confined to his bedroom. He would maintain that doctors often performed operations simply as experiments, or for their own profit, and he regarded their faith in vaccination as an unclean superstition, yet it was never difficult to persuade him to call in his doctor if he was really ill.

He was a good patient because his mind was tranquil. His days lay mapped out ahead, and if illness or accident interrupted their ordered progress he would quietly withdraw from the world, as animals do, and wait unperturbed until he got well again. This tranquillity of spirit was, I think, as responsible for his long life as what he had to eat and drink or what he refrained from eating and drinking. Unlike the vegetarians, he himself never gave that diet credit for his long life. Like my own people, none of the Shaws had been vegetarians, and both his family and mine had lived to a good age. My mother was twenty years younger than my father, and, as he was, a Londoner born and bred. Judging from the stories she told us she must have travelled frequently on the Continent with her father, David Blaiklock, and it was on one of these journeys that she became engaged. My father had pursued her from London to Belgium, and, having obtained permission to take her on a sight-seeing expedition, he proposed to her on, or near, the field where the battle of Waterloo was fought, which rather confused me when I was a child, as I jumped to the conclusion that the proposal had been made while the actual battle was on, and I was puzzled that in these circumstances my parents should look as young as they did. Mama in fact lived until she was over seventy; my father was in his eighties when he died; and one of my grandfathers was ninety-five. Shaw's own mother lived to be eighty-three; a grandmother died at eighty-eight; and even that old reprobate his father lived until he was seventy-one.

"Health," Shaw once told someone who asked him for the key to it, "is a function of wisdom." He in his own wisdom refused to be fussed, even about food. He ate what he wanted, and if what he wanted was not there he just went without. For breakfast he would eat one of the prepared cereals sold in packets, and drank a coffee substitute until it was unobtainable, when he consented to accept very weak ordinary coffee. After Mrs. Shaw's death he would be up most mornings by eight o'clock, rather too soon for the household staff who never got early to bed and were given little chance to straighten his rooms before he appeared. After breakfast during those war years, he would put on his heavy boots and march off down the garden to his shelter where he remained shut up until summoned back to lunch; until that hour approached no one was allowed to disturb him.

In his later years he took a fancy for sandwiches and salads of chopped-up, uncooked vegetables, drinking a glass of apple juice or supping a glass of yoghourt afterwards, but I never saw him drink tea or plain water. Eggs he ate when he could get nothing else, but he finally turned against them because he said that if he were asked to a house where they knew he was a vegetarian they thought almost automatically of eggs and spinach, and he grew thoroughly tired of the dish. I once heard him tell a neighbour that if she dared to give him such a meal again he would get up and leave the house. I never saw him eat ordinary butter, which will explain why, in gallantly defending Dr. Edith Summerskill when she was Parliamentary Secretary to the Ministry of Food, he declared that he could not tell the difference between butter and margarine. Between lunch-time and the evening meal at half-past seven he would more often than otherwise drink nothing at all. If he were alone he would never bother about the glass of milk which he might take should a visitor be staying to tea, preferring, after his afternoon rest, to go off to the garden and chop wood. When this became too much for him, he just strolled round the paths or down the lane which ran alongside his house. Before he passed into his last decade he might settle to work again round about six o'clock. Always before he sat down to dinner he would turn on the wireless and keep it going until it automatically ceased. I have a suspicion that he did this so that no one could talk to him while he was having his meal.

His meals being so light, and eating so frugally, he never

weighed much more than nine stone. "One look at you, Mr. Shaw," the ample Alfred Hitchcock once said to him, "and I know there's famine in the land." "One look at you, Mr. Hitchcock," Shaw riposted, "and I know who caused it." He was neither gourmet nor gourmand. He was fond of fruit, yet often he would leave untouched the gifts of it which came to him from home and overseas. He must have been the sole inhabitant of our island who remained uninterested in what was in the food parcels arriving from Australia, Canada, New Zealand and the United States: he would even tell his admirers not to send him any more because none of us were starving, and he himself got all that he required. Certainly I myself always had enough to eat at Ayot. While, then, as he announced in a postcard broadcast at the age of ninety-two, his objection to carnivorous diet was partly æsthetic and partly hygienic, it was mainly because it involved "an unnecessary waste of the labour of masses of mankind in the nurture and slaughter of cattle, poultry and fish for human food"; or, as he told an earlier disciple, the mischief lay in the waste of human energy in breeding and rearing and slaughtering millions of animals daily, a process which involved an appalling slavery of men to these creatures. Far from showing any sympathy for "these creatures", he almost blamed them for the trouble they gave in being slaughtered. Shaw was not sentimental about animals. His loathing for vivisection was a hygienic loathing. He was more civil about dogs than his fellow-countryman George Moore, but I would not have called him a dog-lover. He did assure one of them, that, while he had no lies to tell about dogs, he was very glad that he had been brought up with a dog in the family as it put him on easy terms with what was in effect a pleasant extension of human society. "If I am at a loss for company I can always talk to a dog; and if, as happens oftener, I want a moment to myself, a dog does not disturb me." In fact, the last, and the only dog I knew in either of the Shaw households, belonged to the housekeeper at Ayot. He barked and snapped at everyone except his mistress, and G.B.S. called him a "horrid little beast", though he would speak to him in a kindly way, but he was certainly not obsessed by its existence as a dog-lover would be. He was friendly towards all animals in a casual fashion; once, after a walk through the woods at Ayot, he told me that he had released a rabbit which he had found with its leg caught in a trap.

Yet he had no objection to the slaughter of animals as such. He argued that, if we did not kill animals, they would kill us. "Squirrels, foxes, rabbits, tigers, cobras, locusts, white ants, rats, mosquitoes, fleas and deer," he reminded his vegetarian friends, "must be continually slain, even to extermination" by them "as ruthlessly as by meat eaters." To him flesh eating was no more than "a mischievous luxury"; he did not regard it as mischievous to those who practised it, for men, he conceded, would thrive on almost any diet "not directly and violently poisonous"; the Laplander, on fish and reindeer, and the gaucho, said to eat nine pounds of horseflesh a day, were not physically inferior to the Turkish porter or the Chilean miner, both living on rice and beans. And, he granted, it would be hard to convince the world that Shelley and he, as vegetarians, "surpassed Shakespeare and Keats and Dickens and the rest of the carnivorous authors". Nevertheless, meat meals for children at school were not only "an absurd extravagance" but made the children callous to butchery and bloodshed and apt to suffer from ordinary feverish ailments more acutely than vegetarian children. He returned to the gaucho with his nine pounds of horseflesh a day when they asked him for recipes during the war. Although, he replied, he knew nothing about food that would qualify him to write about it, he could not agree with proposals to kill and eat any living creature that we could domesticate, or any grain or vegetable that could be grown. The most successful diets, said he, would seem to be potatoes and buttermilk; grass; bread and butter; nine pounds of horseflesh a day with plenty of riding exercise in the open air.

But, as the last of the postcards disclosed, as he lived he learned. He had already realised that "trying to live on cabbage and rice pudding and carrots" had discredited vegetarianism more than anything else and that the convert would starve who tried to live on the ordinary meat diet with the meat left out. He now pointed out that also included in a vegetarian's diet were cheese, butter, honey, eggs, "and, on occasion", a shock to the faithful, "cod-liver oil". On this diet, without tasting fish, flesh, or fowl, he had reached the age of ninety-two, in as good condition, he remarked with pride, as his meat-eating contemporaries, and it was beyond question that persons who had never from their birth been fed otherwise than as vegetarians were at no disadvantage, mentally, physically, or in duration of life, with their "carnivorous fellow-citizens". Nevertheless, he had come to see that his diet had included an excess of protein, a fact which may have been noted in Mrs. Shaw's menu, already quoted, which I typed out for the guidance of ship stewards. The result, G.B.S. owned, was that "until he was seventy he accumulated some poison that exploded every month or six weeks in a headache that blew it off", and left him quite well after disabling him for a day. He tried every available treatment to get rid of the headaches, all quite unsuccessful. He then made uncooked vegetables, chopped or grated, and their juices, with fruit, the staple of his diet, and found it markedly better than the old high-protein diet of beans, lentils and macaroni. There he was fortunate indeed in his house-keeper, Mrs. Laden. Shaw's diet, and G.B.S. himself, were safe with her.

Shaw held that vegetarians were inherently more aggressive than eaters of flesh; nevertheless, the latter always grew much more heated over his diet than he ever did about theirs. Meat and alcohol were not, he held, stimulants but narcotics. Meat, said he, was a sedentary diet: no vegetarian could do with as little exercise and fresh air as a carnivorian, and vegetarians were the "most ferociously pugnacious people in the world"; animals that lived on grass and leaves the most dangerous. The carnivora were aggressive only when hungry. The tiger, if it missed its first terrible spring, "slinks away discouraged; but the bull in the ring fights to the death; and the rhino is im-placable". I do not know whether he was a mythical waiter who is alleged to have remarked, "I see you are wearing new boots, Mr. Shaw", when G.B.S. reproved him for serving meat. One excited individual certainly did ask us why, if he was a veget-arian, he should wear leather, and also woollen clothing. There was nothing in the point, said Shaw brusquely. As long as huge numbers of animals were brought into existence for feeding mankind, their hides and fleeces would be used for clothing, and "no vegetarian who was not also an idiot would refuse to wear woollen clothes and leather boots unless he wanted to demonstrate that clothes and boots could be made if cattle were exterminated".

I myself never had much to do with Shaw's wardrobe. He would ask me to get him a sun umbrella for a cruise; or he would write from Ireland, "no letters, no news, no nothing, except a bundle of most repulsive gaiters"; or during the war he would discourse gaily on utility braces. "Mine," he wrote to me, "are in the last stage of ruin, and Mrs. Laden, who has tried to buy me a pair, tells me that I must get a permit or else be satisfied with utility braces, which she considers unworthy of my dignity. Last time I bought any, I bought three pairs," he added, "so will you look through my wardrobe and see if there are any left. They may be in one of the small drawers on the left side of my big looking glass. If there are none, I am afraid you must buy me a utility pair; for the utility of braces is extreme. Without them my dignity would disappear altogether."

My main contribution to Shaw's wearing apparel were the mittens which I first made for him during the war when I did a lot of knitting for the Services, and for others who seemed to need them: one pair I gave to a porter at Charing Cross, another to a bus conductor whose hands were blue. G.B.S. also felt the cold acutely, and during the winter he was always trying to get his hands warm, so I thought that, as a surprise, I would make him a pair of fingerless mittens with some khaki wool I had over. He was very pleased with them and Charlotte liked the idea too. He asked me for several pairs because he would leave one pair out in his shelter, and he liked to have others lying around the house so that if he wanted them there was always a pair in whichever room he happened to be. I did them in all colours, and Dorothy Walker, daughter of an old friend of Shaw's, and I appointed ourselves unofficial mitten-makers to G.B.S. As his liking for them got known to admirers, quite a number of them, including Gertrude Lawrence who, as I have told, worked a pair for him one Christmas, expressed their homage in mittens. Before he put his mittens on, he would always warm them by laying them on the top of the electric stove, with the result that they were frequently scorched. Among my collection of Shaw relics is a box containing one badly scorched mitten with a compliments card on which G.B.S. had written "Urgent. Can this be repaired?" It was too badly burned to be mended.

I never knitted socks for G.B.S.; he always had plenty of them, specially shaped for his right foot and his left. They were much more comfortable like that, he would, with his passion for detail, declare. If this can be called an oddity, it was one of the few surviving from those earlier eccentricities in dress which time and the chroniclers have probably elaborated. In the first

December of the war he did wear a long white coat to show himself up as he went along the country lanes in the dark. He had a keen road sense and loved to direct motoring visitors, swinging the stick, which he took with him pretty well everywhere, as he hurried out to the gate to see that the road was clear. He was an indomitable old gentleman, rather tottery as he and his staff confronted those pitch-black byways; and he imagined that the white coat would help the motorists. One of them, who did not agree, asked me to suggest that the coat should be left at home because, he explained, it was rather startling, on rounding a bend in the lane, to come upon that tall spectral figure stalking through the night. I said nothing; apart from the fact that the coat did not seem to me to be warm enough. I felt that, if G.B.S. wanted to wear it, that was his own affair. So he kept it on, both in the country and in the London black-out. As a rule he scorned an overcoat, but he did have a cape coat to pull round his shoulders when he was in the car or went out into the garden in winter. On the whole, then, he dressed much better in his later years, than, according to the gossips, he had done as a young man. He was always tidy; he carried an umbrella when it was wet; and his only departure from the normal was a collection of hats as numerous and strange as Winston Churchill's own.

One evening at Ayot during the war he seemed to be more than usually busy in the bathroom. Later, when I came downstairs I found his knickerbockers hanging on a chair in front of the fire. He saw that I was puzzled and explained that one kneeband was loose and kept slipping down. As he felt that it would be tiresome to alter the button, he had been soaking the kneeband in the bath and drying it in front of the fire to shrink it! The idea was not very successful, for, a few days later, the kneeband began slipping down again. He valued time above all things, yet he would rather waste it than give any of us trouble.

He had his hours neatly planned, keeping his own calendar for appointments, working on Sundays as on weekdays. He may have disliked the celebration of anniversaries because they ruffled this tidy procession of the years; or he may have objected to them because they are a conservative institution with their roots in the past, while he was for ever advancing with his Life Force into the future. Whatever the reason, his aversion was shared by Charlotte, and they included in it their own

birthdays and silver wedding. When Mr. and Mrs. Pethick
Lawrence were entertained to dinner to celebrate their silver
wedding, G.B.S., who was in Italy, told me to write and
condole with his friends on having failed to conceal their silver
wedding as successfully as he had concealed his, and to add
that he was "so nearly killed by his seventieth birthday that
nothing will ever induce him to celebrate any personal festivals
except those of his worst enemies". Some of his friends in the
Labour Party gave him a dinner on that occasion in a hotel
which has since disappeared from Northumberland Avenue.
In 1926 the spirit of the Labour crusaders had not yet been
quenched by power, so Shaw and they were still able to
acclaim one another with a kind of hesitant heartiness which
left what they might say in such doubt that a broadcast of the
celebration had to be banned. It was a festive affair. "I have a
vague idea," G.B.S. wrote to me a day or two later, "that I was
given a present at that dinner, and I must have left it behind
because I can find no trace of it." I went off to inquire. The
present turned out to be a silver inkstand engraved with "To
Shaw on his 70th birthday from some of his friends. Will he
ever die? Not bloody likely!" Many years later he gave it to
William Maxwell, his Edinburgh printer. "If," he told a disciple after this experience, "you start any birthday celebration,
I will do my best to defeat you."

Much as we when children would present Papa with little
gifts like ink and stamps, so one year at Malvern G.B.S. went
merry and agreed to accept any present which did not cost more
than sixpence. They all flocked to Woolworth's, and Shaw
vowed that never in his life had he received such a useful collection of pens, pencils, ink, sealing wax, and so forth. He was
delighted, just as he was a year or two later when a vanload
of Ayot landgirls passed Shaw's Corner chanting "Happy
birthday, dear Bernard, happy birthday to you!" Although he
appreciated these impromptu outbursts of affection, he honestly
disliked an annual flurry of presents. Nor did he ever remember
other people's birthdays, whether Charlotte's or my own; in
fact I was one of the few who knew when Charlotte's was. She
on her part never gave him a birthday present; and, if I did, it
would be some little thing, once a tiny thermometer with a
vacuum attachment to make it stick to his writing pad; another
year, a little weather indicator shaped like a goblin. This
was left on the study mantelpiece when the Shaws were going

H

off on a trip, and it was not until they returned three months later that Charlotte asked what it might be. I told her that I had given it to G.B.S. for his birthday. "And he never noticed it!" she exclaimed. "He really is too bad!"

At Christmas she would send a few cards and give one or two presents, but she did not like to get presents from anybody. For both of them the day went by like any other day, with the customary routine and the usual meals. No waits carolled at the Shaws' front door. Once, in the days when a shilling was a shilling, any child who came to the house was given one. None of his own household ever embarrassed him with a present, and, as the years passed, those outside it gradually gave up remembering him at Christmas time, as more and more of them realised that he preferred it that way. In his later days there was a marked falling-off in both presents and cards; the cards would just lie around until someone in desperation threw them away. His own nearest approach to the sentiment of the season was the Christmas after Charlotte died when he sent a photograph of her to those who had known her. The picture of himself gazing like a wild thing through his new gate at Ayot appealed to him, and he would drop a postcard of it to his friends at all seasons.

Nobody could have been more punctual than G.B.S. when he was not in his garden shelter; when he was down there at work he had invariably to be summoned to lunch, and if there were guests he would be warned ten minutes before they were due so that he might be there to greet them. After lunch he would always rest for about an hour and a half, during which interval it was laid down that he must not be disturbed by anyone. When he was a gay young septuagenarian he would protest that he never slept during this afternoon rest, but latterly he admitted that he did doze off. He would begin by picking up a book of a sort which would certainly have induced slumber in most of us, and as I often looked in to see that he was all right I know that the book had the same soporific effect on him.

Before the war, when they spent three or four days every week in London, they would go out to receptions and meetings in the evening; but if they went to a theatre, except for the first night of his own plays, it was usually to a matinée. Out of curiosity G.B.S. did once see *Chu Chin Chow*, but he seldom went to a musical comedy, and Charlotte could not tolerate them at all. They both liked films, but not, as G.B.S. once said, if they were of the Tom Cat order, and in the late afternoon before the war they would often go off to a cinema together. G.B.S. once told Sir Cedric Hardwicke that he was the third greatest actor of our time, adding that Groucho Marx and Lew Lake came first and second. He knew the old music-hall and liked the lilt of its songs. The B.B.C. were quite wrong, he assured one of his correspondents, in thinking that favourites like Marie Lloyd, Bessie Bellwood, and the rest, owed their popularity to their horribly vulgar jocularity and the silliness of their songs. Their real attraction was that they sang absolutely dead in tune, and made you want to dance by the perfection of their rhythm. "Lauder," he added, "who is never vulgar, is a conspicuous example." I have already related how I once heard him sing one of the old music-hall lilts to Charlotte after her accident, and another at Ayot with Gertrude Lawrence.

I don't think that Shaw was ever very fond of the gramophone. He himself listened in a lot, although, in those days before the Third Programme, Mrs. Shaw was less keen. G.B.S. would switch on during lunch to listen to the schools' broadcasts, and I remember one talk, on the difference between real and artificial manures, which, Charlotte remarked, did not seem to be quite apposite as an accompaniment to the repast. The Shaws seldom spoke to one another at meal times: their silence, said G.B.S., showed they were so intimate that they did not need to keep up a conversation. Sometimes the wireless which filled the silence was quite unbearable. Mrs. Shaw was a little deaf, yet even she would occasionally sit with her hands over her ears. One week-end when I was down at Ayot the programme was unbelievably dull, and, "Do you think," Shaw inquired during a pause, "that anyone is interested in this?" "Certainly I'm not," said I. But he left the radio on with, "It will be better presently; it will be The Week in Parliament." He would be down at eight o'clock of a Sunday morning to listen in, perhaps because his *Observer* did not arrive until late, and he was afflicted with the craving for news of some sort or other. Both Charlotte and he invariably switched on for the nine o'clock news, and at six o'clock too during the war. At one time he would be off to bed quite early, at ten or half-past, but as he got older and returned, as he put it, to his bachelor days, he would stay up an hour or so longer, usually keeping the radio going during and after dinner, perhaps not turned full on but always there in the background until the programme closed down. He might even switch on for something special and fall asleep before it came on. His taste was catholic: he liked Wee Georgie Wood and Gracie Fields, and he was, of course, a Third Programme fan.

Although, like many women, I find politics tedious, when it came to music Shaw and I met on common ground. Both our families had been enthusiasts. My mother was a quite brilliant pianist, particularly good at reading music at sight, an accomplishment which was very useful for our Social Evenings held in Winchelsea's old Town Hall. Several of us inherited her love of music, and in addition to two pianos in the house there were also banjos, mandolines, flutes and whistle pipes. At one time these latter goaded my eldest brother, John, to such a pitch of fury when he came home from Cambridge that he stuffed them all up with butter, a somewhat natural reaction to such an irritating noise.

Most of the Shaws either sang or played some instrument; so G.B.S. reproved Sir Stafford Cripps for his "cultural and social ignorance" when he put the Purchase Tax on musical instruments up to 66 per cent., assuring the Chancellor that they were "among the first necessities of civilised life", and that even the brass bands of the Salvation Army, and the factory and colliery bands competing every year at the Crystal Palace, could show "first-rate artistic quality". Shaw's Uncle William played the ophicleide; his father, the trombone; his cousin Emily, the 'cello. His Aunt Charlotte had the piano "at her fingers' ends", and, as Shaw said, "used a tambourine to shew them off (she had pretty hands)". They played "by ear", however, and knew no classical music, whereas G.B.S. knew nothing else. Trifling compositions bored him. In the drawing-room at Adelphi Terrace was a piano which later on was moved to Whitehall Court where also stood the spinet, acquired from the head of the Dolmetsch family at Guildford. There was a similar piano at Ayot St. Lawrence. On these Shaw used to play, not elaborately perhaps, but reasonably well, with never a wrong note: and he was still playing quite a lot until Mrs. Shaw died. He would sing the old Italian operas and accompany himself. He had a good voice, trained by his mother, herself the leading exponent of the "method" invented by George John Vandaleur Lee, to demonstrate which was the

original motive for the flight to London. There are no snobs
like music snobs. Each group of them in a descending scale
looks down its nose at the groups below. Thus G.B.S. was
vividly conscious of the superiority which he believed his good
taste had conferred upon him. He could not too often repeat,
he told someone who appeared to be in doubt about it, that
though he had no academic qualifications he was in fact "more
highly educated than most University scholars" because his
home was a musical one; and the music the sacred "learned"
music that began with Handel, and the dramatic music that
began with Gluck and Mozart, "the two constituting a body of
modern cultural art to which the ancient literature of the dead
languages can make no pretension even in the great translations of Gilbert Murray, which are as English and as modern
as any original works in our tongue".

Until a year or two of the end, taking photographs was
another of his few recreations. I am not sure that I would agree
with Chesterton's comment that Shaw was "even more fond of
being photographed", although he enjoyed that too: Karsh,
who came over from Canada during the war to photograph
the eminent, included G.B.S. among the statesmen, soldiers,
airmen, and sailors. Throughout the year he must have been
taken by every photographer of note, with a final score not
much short of a film star's. In his hale days he would go to the
studio, but latterly the photographer made the journey down to
Ayot. Among the last of them to do so was Mr. Adolf Morath
who was including G.B.S. in a collection of Irish photo studies.
I motored to Shaw's Corner with him, and it was heartening to
see the old man in his nineties as eager to follow what was
afoot as a boy in his teens. For one picture he was posed in a
chair on the garden path; for others, lamps had been fixed up
inside the house to throw the light where it was wanted. "What
are you using now?" Shaw would demand during these operations. At one time or another he must have possessed at least
half-a-dozen cameras; but his zeal vanished when the camera
clicked. He did not do his own developing; nor did he ever
bring home any records of his trips around the world. He
contributed a batch of photographs to the tenth birthday
number of the *Countryman* in 1937, then edited by his friend
J. W. Robertson Scott. There was one of Augustus John at
work on his portrait; three were of Derwentwater; one of Sir
John Squire gazing across a mountainside; one of the Ayot

orchard: another of its cabbages with the house dim in the background; and rather a fine sweep of sea land, and cloud taken between Harlech and Portmadoc. With them went a deprecatory note protesting that he "must not be described as a photographer. An amateur photographer if you like."

For one who wrote so much, reading, which is writing in reverse, should not perhaps be numbered among the recreations. Shaw of course read widely, but always with an eye for raw material to turn into more reading in his writing factory down the garden. Both he and Charlotte followed the news closely from day to day, and when they were out of the country they were hungry for it. Apart from newspapers, both were adherents of the *New Statesman*, and would have no other review, with the exception of the *New English Weekly*. I remember posting on the *Spectator* to them when they were off on the *Empress of Britain*. First from "near Bangkok" Charlotte wrote "We don't want *Spectators* but the *New Statesman*"; then, only two days later, from the China Sea, "It is a mistake to send the *Spectator*. We wanted the *New Statesman*. Thanks for the *New English Weekly*."

I suppose that the rest of us read too much just to amuse ourselves. My mother, for example, would devour everything that came along in the way of books and magazines. On our trips to Hastings for shopping and renewing our school outfits, Mama invariably returned with a supply of periodicals: for herself *Vanity Fair*, then thought a somewhat scandalous journal, and for us children *Ally Sloper's Half-Holiday*, *Scraps*, or *Answers*. Rather a remarkable selection for the family of a country rector. We others read and forget: Shaw read and remembered. His memory was photographic. Once when I could not lay my hands on his copy of Lawrence's *Revolt in the Desert* he sent back a sketch of his bookshelves with a finger pointing to its exact position, and a "Look in the big white bookcase in the tall right hand section—probably the second shelf—next Garnett's *Twilight of the Gods*". The range of the books selected was unexpected. "As I am running short of books to read," he writes to me, for example, from Conway, "send me Belloc's *James II* and the *Diary of a Communist Schoolboy*." From Stresa it is thanking me for *Clissold*, which "came in very aptly. Let us know the names of any books that arrive: we might like to have some of them sent on." But at Cap d'Antibes he has "no use for the Chesterton debate books. You had better send us lists of the books that arrive, and send on only those which we ask for".

As with reading, so with swimming, cycling, motoring, tramping, log-sawing, hedge-trimming and a very occasional set at tennis. Not one of them was undertaken lightly for pleasure; the aim of each was to increase the efficiency of his existence. The car would be used to save time by getting somewhere quickly, never just for a run round the countryside. The morning swim was to rid him of the energy which, he contended, a vegetarian diet had accumulated in his system; and, when he found swimming a bit too much for him, he would instead saw logs for three-quarters of an hour a day when he went down to Ayot during the war. On my own arrival there I found him busy trimming a hedge, wearing gloves and an imitation tin hat with a shield to keep the little bits of twig out of his eyes. He would tackle not only his own hedges but those along a path running through a copse nearby, and I was told that he was as expert as usual at this new craft, which is not nearly so simple as the hiking townsman might imagine. Even at four-score he was a sturdy walker, tramping over the hills during the Malvern Festival. When once, to save time by talking as they walked, he invited an unfortunate interviewer to go with him, the poor fellow was left panting in his wake. He told Malvern Council that they should build a funicular railway from the centre of the town to the top of Malvern Beacon "for the benefit of people too old for the donkeys", but he himself always went up on foot. In his younger days he had done a tremendous amount of walking with Sidney and Beatrice Webb. Sidney Webb had even less use than G.B.S. for doctors. He told me that, until he went to consult one at Presteign, he had not done so for forty years. When he had had a slight ailment, and was waiting for the doctor, who was out, he began scanning the medical books in the waiting-room. In one of these he looked up his own indisposition, decided that the treatment was simple, and went away without waiting for the doctor's diagnosis.

G.B.S. could handle a car with skill, and generally, save for the unfortunate mishap in South Africa, did so. His exploits by bicycle and motor cycle happened long before I knew him. Once he cycled full tilt into a horse and van outside the National Gallery, jumping clear just in time. Not long before his marriage, trying to cycle with one foot (the other being out of action), he fell and sprained his ankle. When an abscess had developed in his instep, a warning that a breakdown threatened through overwork, he had to go to the Registry Office on crutches on his wedding day. Necrosis of the bone was diagnosed. Bone trouble and crutches were to appear again, nearly fifty years later, in a drama at Whitehall Court which filled me with the liveliest alarm.

It was the only occasion on which I saw G.B.S. at the point of fainting. Once before, after he had slipped and fallen in the snow, he sat down to lunch looking very white and shaken; but he roused himself when I asked if there was any brandy in the house. "No, no!" he protested, "certainly not! That's the way drinking begins." As it happened, there was no brandy; there never was at Ayot. On this later occasion he had come up to London, a day or two ahead of the event, to receive the Freedom of the Borough of St. Pancras, where in the old days he had been a vestryman. The day before the ceremony, his Polish translator called at Whitehall Court to see him. G.B.S. was sitting at his desk in a revolving chair, and, as the door opened, spinning round to greet the visitor, he slipped to the floor where the Pole, to his surprise, found him lying flat. I, who had ushered him in, was about to help Shaw to his feet.

"Leave me alone," said he. "I'd rather remain here for a little while."

The Pole took a chair, and sat there to tell Shaw why he had called. It was no easy interview. After about ten minutes of it, the visitor asked G.B.S. if he would like to sit up. Shaw repeated that he preferred to stay where he was; and remain there he did until the caller left. He then agreed to be helped to his feet, so I got him into his chair. I saw that he was rather badly shaken. He had evidently hurt his thigh; and he had now just passed his ninetieth birthday. So I suggested that he should go to his room for a little while and rest on the bed. He agreed, but, as he got up, he turned faint and almost collapsed in my arms. At that I lowered him to the floor and telephoned a doctor who lived at Whitehall Court. He was out. I then rang Shaw's own doctor, who came round to find G.B.S. sitting imperturbably in his chair. Apart from bruising his leg, the doctor did not seem to think that he had hurt himself: my own opinion was that he had fallen on a bunch of keys.

All that afternoon he lay dozing on his bed, and I kept creeping in and out of the room, scared in case he should have passed away. On the contrary, he announced in the evening that he was much better, and calmly began discussing what should be done about next day's presentation of the Freedom. He was all for going off to the Town Hall, insisting that he would be all right. I thought that he ought to do something about his bruises; and then I began to worry, lest, after the shock, he should be ill in the night, but, by good luck, Mrs. Laden, who was in town from Ayot, stayed on at Whitehall Court and she very promptly took charge and relieved my anxiety.

He was still bent on going to St. Pancras next day to receive his Freedom, and he was sure that he would manage it if we could borrow a pair of crutches from somebody, or find those on which he had gone off to the Registry Office to be married almost half a century before. Mrs. Laden knew where these were, so she rang through to the chauffeur at Ayot and asked him to bring them up to London. But G.B.S. was then feeling so stiff that he decided to call in his osteopath, who ordered an X-ray, as he was not convinced that there was no bone injury.

At this I rang up the Mayor of St. Pancras, whom I found worried but resourceful. He suggested that, if he were to come round, Shaw might dictate what he had to say, to which G.B.S. agreed; and soon our flat was full of life. First came two men with their portable X-ray apparatus which they fixed with coils of wire from our window to the street below. On their heels the Mayor arrived with his Town Clerk, closely followed by three young men from the B.B.C. with a recording apparatus. And there was I, supporting the Town Clerk on a pair of steps as he tried to discover what voltage we had for the B.B.C.

The X-ray men left first, telling Shaw straight away that there was no fracture. Next, off went the Mayor to collect a record of the speech Shaw meant to have made, and in the afternoon this was played over to the assembled crowd after the Mayor had announced to them that their new Freeman could not be with them. The news flew round Fleet Street. One paper after another rang me up until I nearly went mad. I stopped all calls. Reporters and photographers swarmed upstairs. I kept most of them at bay until the evening when two young press photographers were so persuasive that I went in to G.B.S. and begged him to see them. I felt so sorry for the young things, and it meant such a lot to them.

"Let them come in!" exclaimed Shaw, who by this time was

thoroughly enjoying the proceedings. They got their picture of G.B.S. in bed, from which he rose and sat up to listen to himself when the recording came through on the six o'clock news. He was quite satisfied with it, and in about a week he left town for Ayot, saying that he hoped he would never come to London again.

But he never used the crutches.

CHAPTER XV

HIMSELF

In the thirty years I was with G.B.S. only twice do I remember him losing his temper.

He seldom swore. He might come away with an occasional "What the devil does he mean by that?" or a "Damn his impertinence!", but only on two occasions can I remember him using "bloody": in *Pygmalion* and when his emotion upon completing *The Intelligent Woman's Guide* was too much for him.

I fear that my own poise did not equal his: often I grew exasperated with him, either because, when he had got an idea into his head, nothing could move him, or because he behaved as if you were not there. Once he annoyed me so much that, if I had been able to afford it, I would have left him on the spot. Our wrangle was not in itself important, but it is worth recording to show how shocked Shaw was by the suggestion that teasing people gave him pleasure. He had passed on certain of my duties to a member of the opposite sex; and no action will arouse greater wrath in any secretary, as Shaw well knew, for, "you hate to have anyone stealing your work," he wrote, "but I do all I can to leave you as free as possible. If this makes you too idle, why not prepare for my death by clearing out all my old rubbish and unwanted books?" He also explained that he proposed to send on to me only those letters which needed typing. I replied that I resented being looked on simply as a shorthand typist, and that I knew it was his love of teasing which had made him write to me as he had done. The spark was in the gunpowder.

"My dear Blanche," he exploded, "you have given me a jolt at last. We have been together all these years, during which you have transcribed almost every word I have written and you have seen nothing in them but a love of teasing: a form of cruelty which I specially abhor and have never practised. To save you from being written off as the stupidest woman on earth I must give you a testimonial.

"You are Shaw-proof; but you are not in the least stupid. That you are sober, honest and industrious and have been for countless years in your present post goes without saying. You are intelligent, sensible, self-reliant, kindly, useful, competent, and almost unbelievably even-tempered and self-controlled. You are the least vain and touchy woman in the world. The trouble you have NOT given me, and the help you HAVE given me are immeasurable. And no man knows your value better than I do.

"It has been a great advantage to us both that you have been completely unaffected by my doctrine and my philosophy, and held your own against it, unswamped by my personality as the Shavians have been. But it has had one drawback. You have mistaken my philosophy for mere fun and malice. I am horrified, and beg you to reconsider the malice."

It was an unusual letter to come from Shaw who in the ordinary way appeared to be wholly indifferent to the feelings of those who worked for him; and, naturally, I prize such a tribute from one who had the tribute of all the world. Even-tempered he always was, and that made working for him easy; but never a word of praise came from him. Now and again he might light upon some small error, but in general he took it for granted that you were just doing your job, and he seldom seemed to notice your existence.

He could be kind when he remembered that you were there. When the war came, he wrote to me from Frinton-on-Sea saying that Charlotte and he were concerned about where I should go to escape the air raids which all of us were expecting, and proposing that I should either join them there or go down to Ayot when the servants returned. He told me that I was always welcome at Ayot, where he knew I could look after myself; but, as I have said, I found the place tedious, for it was cold and isolated, and G.B.S., after inquiring at our first meal whether there was any news from London, would relapse into silence, and, when I had finished dinner ahead of him in the evening, would wave me off with a "Don't wait for me! Don't wait for me!"

Yet, in spite of much that irritated one, Shaw's formal manners were always courteous. Even in his nineties, when he looked as if a gust of wind would whisk him away like an autumn leaf, he would rise if he had a better chair and insist upon my having it. At one time during the war he got it into his head that he needed more exercise, so at Ayot, while the nine o'clock news was on, he took to pacing round and round between the chair where I sat and the dining-room table, which was rather big for the room. He created a considerable draught as he swung past me, and I came to dread this nightly ritual. At last I could put up with it no longer, so one night when Mrs. Shaw, by now an invalid, had gone early to bed, "Do you think," I inquired, "you could take your exercise after I have gone?" He asked why; and, when I told him, he became quite contrite, promising to stay at his own end of the room in future. So there, setting his old shoulders well back, he would take six brisk paces from one wall to the other, to and fro, like a soldier on sentry-go.

There were times when he would be quicker than Charlotte in considering others. One Alexandra Rose Day, when we were living at Whitehall Court, a pretty young girl came to the flat, unaware of the standing instruction to flag day collectors not to call on the Shaws. They were at breakfast, so she said she would come round later, although I assured her it would not be much use.

"Tell her," said Mrs. Shaw, a trifle tartly perhaps, "that we never subscribe to these things."

During the morning G.B.S. went off from his desk into the drawing-room for a few minutes; then Charlotte came into the study and sat down in front of me.

"G.B.S. says I am to apologise to you about the Rose Day," she explained. "He says we are Irish, and don't approve of these English customs, but Blanche, being English, was probably hurt by what you said"; and she added that, if it pleased me, I could buy a basketful of Alexandra roses and decorate the whole flat with them. I assured her I was not hurt in the least and had quite forgotten her earlier remark. Shaw was not always as quick as one might imagine in seeing the next man's point of view, much less the next woman's. It was ridiculous to say, as he did in the letter I have quoted, that I had ever seen malice in anything he wrote. Of malice he was utterly incapable, for, being at peace with himself, he bore malice to no one, answering spite with a tolerant shrug. When he teased people it was for their own good, and few men have ever had as much fun with the eminent: with his friend A. B. Walkley when he put him into *Fanny's First Play* as Trotter; with Balfour, Asquith and Kitchener as Balsquith and Mitchener in *Press Cuttings*; the Kaiser in the *Inca of Perusalem*; Lloyd George as Joyce Burge in

Back to Methuselah; Mussolini and Hitler as Bombardone and Battler in *Geneva*.

One or two who knew Shaw longer, and probably understood him better than I, have said to me that he had a strain of mental cruelty in him. Beatrice Webb may have had that in mind when she called him Puckish, although to compare G.B.S. with Puck does not seem quite fair to Shaw. Puck's mischief was done for devilment; Shaw provoked people to induce them to mend their ways. Yet he was like Puck in his detachment from the world of mortals. Worldliness, as Chesterton said, had no human magic for G.B.S.; he was not "bewitched by rank". I would not myself say that Shaw was altogether unimpressed by rank, although he did possess too sound a sense of values to want a title for himself. After all, he wrote to Mrs. Asquith, as she then was, asking her to be "so kind as to remind the King (either the uncrowned or the crowned will do) that Pinero ought to be knighted". Unaware who had caused him to become Sir Arthur, Pinero continued to subscribe himself "with admiration and detestation" when he wrote to Shaw. For himself, G.B.S. viewed with an Olympian smile the suggestion of the Order of Merit or the peerage which he might have had from Ramsay MacDonald. The only honour he could be induced to accept was the 1925 Nobel Prize of £6,500 for literature, and then he declined the cheque, explaining that, as his readers and audiences had provided him with enough for his needs, the cheque was "a life-belt thrown to a swimmer who has already reached the shore in safety". He invited Sweden to set up with the money a fund for encouraging understanding in literature and art between the two countries. Sweden, he pointed out, invited Britain to buy her paper, but there was nothing printed on it, the function of Swedish paper thus far being, it seemed, "to wrap Australian apples in; and yet Sweden's most valuable export is her literature, of which we in Britain are deplorably ignorant".

Although Shaw knew the value of money, he was never greedy to get it for himself. He preferred rich people to poor people, but he handled both with equal candour; indeed he was rather more candid with kings than with peasants. When George the Sixth was crowned he wanted to set up a Society for the Prevention of Cruelty to Royal Personages. He hailed the Simpson marriage as a diplomatic masterstroke. He accepted George the Fifth quite frankly as a lowbrow, and as

such said he was quite right to go to a Cup Final instead of the
inauguration of the Stratford Memorial Theatre, "one of the
greatest events of his reign". And he had a singular comment
upon the birth of Prince Charles, remarking to me that perhaps
it was a pity that Princess Elizabeth had had an heir. I asked
him why. It would probably be better, said he, if Margaret
were allowed to come to the throne because the second child of
a reigning monarch often made a better sovereign than the
elder: and he indicated both George the Fifth and George the
Sixth to support the theory.

He was equally frank about himself and where he stood
among his contemporaries. Alongside Sidney Webb he saw
himself as "an incorrigible histrionic mountebank" who,
without Sidney, might have been "a mere literary wisecracker
like Carlyle or Ruskin". As a man of action, he swears that he
was not fit to tie Sydney Olivier's shoestrings. William Morris
is "four great men rolled into one". And with curious heat he
denounces, in the vest-pocket booklet about going to church
"all the vulgarity, savagery and bad blood which have marred
my literary work". So Shaw's yardstick was not less exacting
with himself than in measuring up the rest of us. As T. E.
Lawrence told him, the public Shaw wasn't even a caricature,
much less a likeness, of the private one; and Shaw himself has
declared that he had never been taken in by his reputation,
"having manufactured it myself".

A reputation, said he, was a mask which a man had to wear,
just as he has to wear a coat and trousers: "it is a disguise we
insist on as a point of decency". So the real Shaw vanished
among the impersonations which he presented, and posing
became second nature. Thus, when Dame Laura Knight
rescued the original and put him on canvas, "It's not like you!"
Mrs. Shaw herself exclaimed, taking Dame Laura's Shaw as
yet another impersonation. "You're always acting!" And a
capable actor he was, especially proud of his enunciation.
When they were celebrating his ninetieth birthday Sybil
Thorndike told how, at a *Macbeth* rehearsal, he had played every
part "with loving care and humour; and with that lovely voice,
which has four or five octaves, he can make any sort of sound
he wants to". He would take all the parts at the rehearsals of
his own plays, getting up and showing how each ought to be
done. There, as I have said, the ban on outsiders was strict,
and included his secretary. He never even read passages to me;

but at Whitehall Court I would often hear him demonstrate how small bits ought to be done, faithfully imitating the actor's voice. I remember Barry Jones, who played Bluntschli in the film of *Arms and the Man*, telling me how, at a rehearsal, Shaw mimicked Anne Grey so well that, on turning round, he was surprised to be confronted with a white beard instead of the fair Raina. One afternoon, during an innocent country ramble, or so it was reported, Danny Kaye happened to hit Ayot where, by a happy coincidence, a recording unit chanced to be about. When G.B.S. and he had done a trifling impromptu scene to round off a picture, Danny told Shaw he ought to have been an actor, to which G.B.S. retorted that he had trained himself to be one years before, and that he often acted in public when making a speech. Acting became second nature to him: on occasion he would wearily drag one leg after the other, and at other times he would step out briskly to show how well he was carrying his years. It depended upon who was looking on.

His famous flirtations were little more than adventures in play-acting. They seldom got beyond encounters by letter such as he had with Annie Besant, Ellen Terry, and Mrs. Pat Campbell. Sometimes the letters got published; sometimes the thwarted lady packed them back to their author. I found a few at the back of a drawer, and Shaw, completely failing to recollect who Alice might be, told me I could keep them. He did have the knack of defying the conventions in principle, and in practice bowing submissively to them. Of the various stories about how he came to be married, the version which he gave me can be taken as authentic. Charlotte had raced back from Rome to his dustbin of a room in Fitzroy Square where he was laid low with overwork and his damaged foot. She took a house at Hindhead; engaged two nurses, and told him he was to come there to be tended, at which, according to him, he protested "Go out and get a marriage licence! It is impossible for a woman in your position to have a single man living in your house!" Once on my own behalf this father of *The Revolutionist's Handbook* administered a reproof which could not have been more decorous had it come from the president of the Mothers' Union. We had been in correspondence with Ivor Montagu, Lord Swaythling's son, and Shaw must have told me what to write to him. Anyhow, Ivor, who had taken up the Socialist idea of dropping all titles, answered the letter to me direct, addressing me, unintentionally I think, as Blanche Sweet, for at the time there was a film actress of that name. Shaw admonished him.

"Your variations of my secretary's name", he wrote, "betoken the artist rather than the business man, so in future you had better address your letters direct to me."

The correspondence eventually blossomed into a friendship. An austerity which could send up such little shoots of primness was just the soil for yoga and the Life Force. The discipline of yoga had captured him while he was still a boy in Dublin. His mother, he told me, had been taught how to sing by a professor whose method was a yoga of his own invention. She in turn had passed it on to him which, he maintained, was why he could still sing at ninety years old as she could at eighty. He was always eager to know all about the modern yogas by which pianists, organists, violinists and elocutionists had remedied a disablement caused by faulty technique. In the early Dublin days, years before he met that ardent Christian Scientist, Lady Astor, George Vandaleur Lee had already convinced him that a sound mind made the body sound. His mind kept crystal-clear because he had not clogged it with irrelevancies. Shaw never nursed a grievance: a man with a grievance, he told one of them, was a nuisance in direct proportion to its justice and severity, and if he were wise he would take care to drop it the moment he found that redress was impossible. Nor did he ever allow his mind to worry over how he might succeed in this or that. Running through the proofs of his Cousin Charles' book about him, G.B.S. lighted upon a reference to his struggle for fame. He promptly wrote off and told Charles that his incapacity to struggle "amounted to imbecility"; and he once asked me to elaborate the point to somebody else, telling me to say that he had never made a resolution in his life; that he had never struggled nor consulted other people; that his need for expression was not a desire for success but that he strove automatically to bring the world into harmony with his nature. "I tell you this", said he, "because I have observed it, just as I have observed the colour of my hair in a mirror, not because I am always conscious of it." Thus, far from deluding himself, as the scoffers would allege, that he was running the Universe, Shaw rather implied that the Universe was running him; and he would laugh at those who tried to take him as seriously as they thought he took himself. So, when asked at the

age of ninety-two, upon the passing of the Republic of Ireland
Act, whether he had a message for the Irish people, he rapped
back, "Who am I that I should send messages to nations? I
hope I know my place better." Even when he was an ebullient
forty-four-year-old, his greeting to those about to enter the new
century was humility itself. "I warn you," it ran, "that in a
hundred years we shall all be dead. I encourage you with the
reflection that we shall none of us be missed." And, "Nonsense!" he exclaimed when they wanted to set up a Shaw
Memorial Theatre at Malvern. "Even among the playwrights I
was not the only pebble on the beach. I am only one of Ibsen's
Ghosts." He looked at the fame which had overtaken him as if
it were an accident that had happened to somebody else. About
some famous man or other he once remarked to me, "I know
how he feels because I myself am famous"; but he was not boast-
ing. He reminded me then of one of my brothers who could play
the Wedding March when he was six, and when he was nine
sang and played his own accompaniment to The Laughing
Song at a hospital concert. He came on the platform, went over
to the piano, bowed sedately to the audience, and sat down as
calmly as if he were in his own home. I asked him afterwards if
he had not been nervous. "No," said he. "Why should I be?
I knew I could do it." Shaw was like that. He accepted his
gifts and the fame they brought him with rather less pride than
he did his eyebrows, about which, in fact, he tended to be a
little vain. He felt that he was merely one of the battery of
mouthpieces through which a general purpose in human affairs
was being conveyed to man. It is not for me to say whether
some higher power inspired the writings of Bernard Shaw. I
am not a Shavian. I was never, as he perceived and said, swept
away by his personality. I had my own life and my own
interests which might for me be more important than the great
man himself. I remained an outsider, now and again, perhaps,
throwing out some comment which would suggest to him an
outsider's point of view. But I never came under the spell,
and I am now setting down no more than what an outsider
might have observed. These memoirs are just a modest domestic
backcloth for others learnedly debating upon the limelit stage.
Yet in passing one may recall that Shaw is not the only author
who has believed his writing to be inspired. Kipling, for example, thought so too, and Shaw's verdict on Kipling was that
he never grew up. What puzzles me is how messages so diverse

as those delivered by these two could have been inspired from the same source.

My own opinion is that Shaw would not have written one sentence the fewer had it never occurred to him that he was the instrument of some higher purpose. He wrote because he had got to write about something or other, and the range varies from his published comments upon the visit of a couple of evangelists to Dublin in 1875 down to a guide to the village of Ayot St. Lawrence with which he was toying in his last years. When he arrived in London as a youth he had already drilled himself to filling his five quarto pages a day. Out poured the novels; the articles on art, on music, on the drama; the essays, the plays, the prefaces; the pamphlets and the letters to the newspapers about Socialism, a national theatre, a reformed alphabet, the two wars, the Scottish Highlands for the motorist, vaccination, vivisection, vegetarianism. Writing, not the Life Force or the welfare of mankind was his passion, as old as the poet's

> seu me tranquilla senectus
> exspectat, seu Mors atris circumvolat alis,
> dives, inops, Romae, seu fors ita jusserit, exsul,
> quisquis erit vitae scribam color.

His industry was terrific. I have always thought that he wrote too much, perhaps because it was around me that the torrent of words kept swirling. Harold Nicolson relates a conversation in which Edmund Gosse congratulates Browning upon a long life with nothing to regret. Browning replied that he had one regret: not having been a civil servant. "Had I been a civil servant," he explained, "I should have been at my office all day and only written in the evening. I have written too much, my dear Mr. Gosse; I have over-written; I have written myself out. If I had been a civil servant I should have written better and much less."

What was true for Browning is trebly true for Shaw. He would be an uncommonly devoted Shavian who to-day would cheerfully set out again to read through *The Intelligent Woman's Guide*, followed by *Everybody's Political What's What*, not to say explore once more the Sahara of the novels. Nor can anyone have gained a name as prophet on a more slender achievement. He was wrong about the two wars: Kitchener's estimate of three years for the one which lasted four was "soldierly but not very sensible", and he wrote to *The Times* demonstrating how the next had been made impossible by the 1939 pact between Russians and Germans. He assured me too, as I have noted earlier, that the Germans would not bomb London, and in 1942 he was certain that the war must end in a negotiated settlement. He was equally in error with lesser predictions, like the fate of the Jews in Palestine, the chances of the boxer Dempsey and the future of Winston Churchill (who was going to fade away when the Party System came back). But if he did write too much and prophesy too rashly he was incomparable as an apostle of new ideas. Tolstoy railed that the ideas were not Shaw's; nor did he approve of the way G.B.S. jested about the object of man's life on our planet. Perhaps in his later years Tolstoy was growing slightly resentful that the disciples who once flocked to him for guidance at Yasnaya Polyana now seemed to prefer Ayot and G.B.S. In any event the origin of the ideas seems unimportant so long as the ideas themselves were worth making known; and there Shaw was supreme. He may not have been a philosopher or a prophet or an original thinker. Some say this, some that; but the sourest critic agrees that he was usually witty and always a master of prose. His days were dominated by the fascination of finding words for ideas and sentences for the words. Often he was in such a hurry about it that a play would end without a plot, for, as Dr. Johnson once remarked, it is much more easy to form dialogues than to contrive adventures. Writing became an obsession as strong as a craving for opium. "If," he declared in his nineties, "I stop writing, I must die for want of something to do." He doggedly guarded his working day. He had no time for people, and, apart from Charlotte, towards whom he was tenderness itself, he simply snapped down on those who were eager to offer him friendship. He did not want, he once protested, to talk to anyone, alive or dead; for he had no small talk and really little to say unless you were interested in the arts, which will explain why Augustus John and Lady Oxford, as already chronicled, both thought him talkative. Although he would maintain that you should not go to a meal with people if you wanted to talk to them, he might sparkle for the length of a luncheon party; but no longer. In the days when he could be induced to go and stay with anybody, his hosts would find him a disappointing guest. Throughout the first meal he would be quite talkative, and then he would tail off into silence. The same thing happened at Ayot; for the first couple of meals he might make some effort at conversation and then you would sit, conscious that he did not want to utter a word, while he switched on the wireless and kept it on even if he disliked the programme. It made meals a misery. He was a formidable host. This taciturnity may have come to him from his mother who, when asked whether she had any letters from her distinguished son, replied that she could not remember receiving one, explaining that they always got on a postcard all that they had to say to one another.

His very humanitarianism lacked humanity. He did not so much sympathise with the poor as object to poverty because it was wasteful. When he was benevolent it would be in an impersonal fashion. He could be generous to the young, even after they had traded on his good nature, as did one young man, who, upon getting a pair of boots from him, sent them back a second time to be mended; yet, handsome as his benefactions might be, and they could run to thousands of pounds, they were conferred without human warmth. It would be to benefit the children's health that he had the vitaglass put in the windows of the school at Ayot, and he would subscribe to their village party; but, although he talked a lot about them, I never saw any children with him.

Like many who find human beings unattractive, he was friendly towards animals and birds: at the age of ninety-three he joined the Severn Wild Fowl Trust with its sanctuary for more than one hundred species in the river estuary. Each day, both winter and summer, when I was at Ayot, he would soak bits of bread in some of the Marmite vegetable soup with which he began his lunch, walk gravely to the french window, and scatter the bread on the lawn for the birds. Even here he was aloof: he was not interested in the birds themselves and never waited to see them fly down and peck up what he had thrown to them. The cat might have got both it and them for all he knew. There was a much bigger variety of wild birds in Hertfordshire than I ever saw at home in Sussex. G.B.S. and Charlotte used to look out for a woodpecker which would hop around daily, and he would often ask me if the yaffle had come yet, giving it the old name which, says Gilbert White, it gets from its "loud and hearty laugh". Another friendship grew between G.B.S. and Bunch who had belonged to Mrs. Laden since it was a kitten. Bunch would pad behind him when he went round the garden, and it would leave the kitchen to sit in the dining-room with Shaw because he always put the stove on when it was in the least cold. He was kind to Bunch, but he would never allow food to be thrown to it during meals. As the cat was almost orange in hue, G.B.S. decided to have its photograph done in colour by a man who had already taken the old Kaiser and the Dutch Royal Family. To add a splash of red, Shaw chose a background of geraniums, standing beside them with his hand stretched out to the cat in my lap. We made a pretty family group.

Shaw would declare that art and beauty were essential to his life. He had in truth no time for either. His home was built in what Samuel Butler called the Anglican style of architecture, and, save for one or two of the busts of its tenant, the furnishings were not remarkable. The garden was quite an ordinary one; for Shaw, as I have said, was not interested in flowers. He could never remember their names. He disliked cut flowers. One day a caller remarked that there were none in his room.

"I'm very fond of children," said G.B.S., "but I don't cut off their heads and stick them in pots around the house."

He told me that this dislike of his probably arose out of an incident but for which he might never have been born. When his mother was being wooed by his father, there was a rival suitor whom she noticed, as he left the house one day, swishing off the heads of flowers with his cane. Somehow, it made her think of children's heads, so she decided that she could not marry the fellow. We owe George Bernard Shaw and his fifty plays to that woman's fancy of a moment. He used to say that Beatrice Webb tore up flowers, probably because he had seen her plucking off a petal or two; certainly I never saw her do more. If he was indifferent to flowers, he had a real feeling for the landscape which contained them. He never allowed himself time to indulge it, and I doubt whether he would have travelled at all had not Charlotte been there to egg him on. In his last few years, certainly, he refused to budge from Ayot where he rested content amidst its placid meadows, joining as a life member, at the age of ninety-two, the South Beds. Preservation Society.

Shaw's absorption in work and indifference to comfort were blessings in their way. They made him a gift to woman-kind; for so long as he could find his own belongings in their right place he never noticed who did the work or whether the place was untidy or not. All he asked was to be left alone, and, thanks to us others, each of his days remained trim and undisturbed, I taking over the business side; Mrs. Laden coping with the domestic department; Dr. Loewenstein, his biblio-grapher, doing odd jobs. Shaw so shrank from embarking upon needless talk that he would write a note to someone sitting in the next room, whence a note would come back to him, and a correspondence would flourish as if there were an ocean between them instead of one roof over their heads. How to hoard the hours became a mania. "I must cut out lunch," he remarked to me one day, having eaten a reasonably satis-factory one. "Just look at all the time that is wasted in the cooking and the washing up; and I have had quite a good breakfast. It is ridiculous!" Long before I knew him, he was gazing almost with terror at the days flying past, convinced that he had one foot, and, as the years went by, both, in the grave. In his early forties "the younger generation" is already "knocking at the door" as he ushers Max in to the *Saturday Review*. At sixty-three his "sands are running out". At eighty-eight, when asked to go to Malvern Festival, "the only visit I am now young enough to contemplate is to the Golders Green Crematorium". At eighty-nine, "I dare not wait six months", he writes to me: "my days are too narrowly numbered". At ninety-three, death "now knocking at the door" is "no unwelcome guest". The Ancient of Ayot, who sentenced his own Ancients to centuries of time, jibbed at one for himself. He dreaded the idea of reaching his hundredth year. To me the most noticeable sign of his advancing age was the greater ease with which he fell asleep; and when at last he fell into the sleep from which he did not awaken it was as if the light had gone out.

He was very tired, yet determined to keep working while he could. "When my shorthand goes," came a note to me from Ayot, "I shall have to consider a dictaphone." And again, "I am now so senile, like all old men, forgive me if I repeat myself". His writing slowed down. His shorthand grew a little shaky: he would write "job" backwards, making it "bodge"; he would confuse the position of the dot for "a" making it read "the"; and if I had to ask him the meaning of a word he would take much longer than I to read the rest of the sentence to get the sense of it. He was for ever losing something: letters, his pencil, or the insurance and income tax forms with which he quite needlessly bothered himself. He would write to me, bewailing a kind of mass disappearance of things which had "vanished magically", "I am distracted; I cant find anything: and it is abominably cold". He would bemoan his shaky memory with "I forget everything in ten minutes or less", which indeed he often did, although now and again he would forget because he did not wish to remember. Then he would lament his failing eyesight, his poorer hearing, his weakening sense of taste. It was not quite the self-pity to which many old people are prone. He was being sorry not so much for George Bernard Shaw, the human being, who was bored with us all and eager to be gone. He was sad because time was catching up on the pen that had not yet said all that needed saying. For, if I know him, in those last days his thoughts would be going back not to the boy spellbound by Dublin bay lying in the sunshine beyond the cottage on Torca Hill; nor to the young man in the scrap on Bloody Sunday around Trafalgar Square, bewitched by William Morris's lovely daughter; nor to the elderly gentleman, now sailing the seven seas with Charlotte, now dancing with delight upon the stage as Birmingham roared its welcome to *Methuselah;* but to the patriarch toiling down there at the end of the garden in the hut from which so many shams went up in laughter.

INDEX